The Visitor's Guide
to
DENMARK

THE VISITOR'S GUIDE TO DENMARK

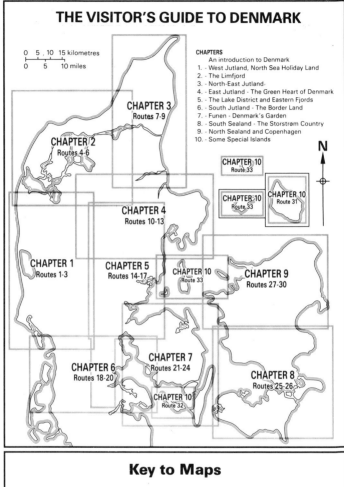

0 5 10 15 kilometres

0 5 10 miles

CHAPTERS
An introduction to Denmark
1. - West Jutland, North Sea Holiday Land
2. - The Limfjord
3. - North-East Jutland
4. - East Jutland - The Green Heart of Denmark
5. - The Lake District and Eastern Fjords
6. - South Jutland - The Border Land
7. - Funen - Denmark's Garden
8. - South Sealand - The Storstrøm Country
9. - North Sealand and Copenhagen
10. - Some Special Islands

N

CHAPTER 3
Routes 7-9

CHAPTER 2
Routes 4-6

CHAPTER 10
Route 33

CHAPTER 10
Route 33

CHAPTER 10
Route 31

CHAPTER 4
Routes 10-13

CHAPTER 1
Routes 1-3

CHAPTER 5
Routes 14-17

CHAPTER 10
Route 33

CHAPTER 9
Routes 27-30

CHAPTER 7
Routes 21-24

CHAPTER 6
Routes 18-20

CHAPTER 8
Routes 25-26

CHAPTER 10
Route 32

Key to Maps

☐ **Routes in Major Towns/Cities**   ○ ○ **Towns/Villages**

═══ **Roads**   ▬ **Direction of Route**

═══ **Optional Extension or Excursion**   - - - **Route for Cyclists only**

〜 **Coastline**   ▪ ▪ **International Borders**

THE
VISITOR'S GUIDE TO
DENMARK

Pat and Hazel Constance

MPC

Published by:
Moorland Publishing Co Ltd,
Moor Farm Road,
Airfield Estate,
Ashbourne,
Derbyshire DE6 1HD
England

British Library Cataloguing in
Publication Data:

Constance, Pat
    The visitor's guide to Denmark
    1. Denmark - Visitor's guides
    I. Title II. Constance, Hazel
    914.89′0458

ISBN 0 86190 295 5 (paperback)

1st Edition 1989
Reprinted 1991

Colour and black & white
origination by:
Scantrans, Singapore

Printed in the UK by:
Clays Ltd, St Ives plc

Cover photograph: *The Little
Mermaid Statue, Copenhagen*
(International Photobank).

Illustrations have been supplied as
follows:
P. H. Constance: pp. 13, 22, 30, 31,
34, 43, 54-5, 58, 66-7, 70, 71, 74, 75,
79, 87, 105, 118, 121, 123, 135, 138,
139, 142, 143, 146-7, 150, 151, 153,
154-5 (and inset), 159, 170, 171,
174-5, 178, 179, 182, 183, 194, 198,
202-3, 206, 207, 210, 211, 215, 219,
220, 222, 223, 226, 227, 231; The
Danish Tourist Board,
Copenhagen: pp. 23, 42, 47, 95,
131, 186, 187; Hoseasons Holidays
Abroad Ltd: pp 46, 59, 78.

Acknowledgements
The authors would like to thank all
those who helped them with the
research for this book, especially
Poul Christensen (Director), Sussi
Loades (Press Officer) and staff of
the Danish Tourist Board in
London; Kurt Nielsen from the
Danish Tourist Board in
Copenhagen, many local tourist
managers, DFDS Seaways and
staff of the Danish Youth Hostels
Association. Without their help the
book would not have been
possible.

All maps drawn by Malcolm
Barnes.

CONTENTS

Key to Symbols Used in Text Margin

 Recommended walk

 Parkland

 Archaeological site

 Nature reserve/Animal interest

 Birdlife

 Garden

 Golfing facilities

 Church/ecclesiastical site

 Building of interest

 Castle/Fortification

 Museum/Art gallery

 Beautiful view/Scenery, Natural phenomenon

 Other place of interest

Note on the maps
The maps drawn for each chapter, while comprehensive, are not designed to be used as route maps, but rather to locate the main towns, villages and places of interest. For general use, the maps published by the Danish Geodætisk Institut are recommended. These maps, at a scale of 1:200,000 cover the whole of the country on four sheets and may be obtained from specialist map shops.

Note on the routes
The routes described in this book are intended to point the way to interesting places off the beaten track. Some form circular routes, and in some the links to other routes have been indicated, but it is not essential to follow them in their entirety, neither should they necessarily be completed in one day, they are simply a visitor's guide.

Note on place names and abbreviations
Some Danish place names have become well known in their anglicised versions. In this book, these versions have been used where applicable, but when the word first appears, the English name will be given, followed by the Danish name in parenthesis. Berlitz *Danish for Travellers* includes more than 1,200 phrases and 2,000 useful words, including common abbreviations and notes on currency.

INTRODUCTION

D enmark is a country with something for everyone. Considered to be the oldest kingdom in the world, it offers an immense variety of landsacpe, a magnificent coastline, and much evidence of prehistoric civilisation. It is a small country, about two thirds of which consists of the Jutland (Jylland) peninsula linked to the rest of Europe by the border with West Germany, the remainder consisting of nearly 500 islands, ninety of which are inhabited.

Its large cities offer many attractions, but the real appeal of Denmark lies in its small provincial towns and villages. A good network of roads, bridges and ferries will help the visitor to see attractive 'out of the way' places in addition to the popular tourist centres. Driving here is very relaxing, as the roads are not busy. For touring cyclists, the country must surely be one of the most pleasant in Europe and there are countless paths and tracks in forests and by lakes for walkers to enjoy.

The green mainland of Jutland lies between the North Sea and the Kattegat, 400km (248 miles) from the northern tip at Skagen to the German border with great contrasts in the landscape. Around the peninsula are the islands of Rømø and Fanø on the west coast, Læsø and Samsø to the east, and Als in the far south which is connected to Jutland by bridges. The country's largest island is Sealand (Sjælland), where the capital Copenhagen (København) will be found and south of Sealand are the islands of Lolland, Falster and Møn. Funen (Fyn), is known as Denmark's Garden and around the coast are many more islands, including Ærø. The other major island, Bornholm, lies in the Baltic Sea 150km (90 miles) east of the rest of Denmark, midway between Sweden and Poland. It is a granite island, and the only place in Denmark with a rocky coastline.

Denmark is generally regarded as an agricultural country, but there have been dramatic changes in recent years and today only some 6 per cent of the population is employed in agriculture. There are no natural mineral resources, and there is therefore very little

DIRECT FERRY SERVICES

Harwich — Esbjerg
Scandinavian Seaways. 6 days weekly most of year. Daily service from mid-June to mid-August. Winter, less frequent. Crossing, 17-21hrs.

Harwich — Hirtshals
Fred Olsen Lines. Saturdays most of year. Wednesdays from third week in June to second week in August. No service in weeks either side of changeover. Crossing, 27hrs.

Newcastle — Esbjerg
Scandinavian Seaways. Summer only. Crossing, 20hrs.

Services via Germany and Holland include:

Harwich — Hamburg
Scandinavian Seaways. Ever other day from March to September, less frequently in winter. Crossing 21$\frac{1}{2}$ hours.

Harwich — Hoek van Holland
Sealink British Ferries and Zealand Steamship Company. Two sailings daily in each direction. Crossing 6-8hrs.

Sheerness — Vlissingen
Olau Line. Two sailings daily in each direction. Crossing 8hrs.

Hull — Rotterdam (Europort)
North Sea Ferries. Nightly service. Crossing 13hrs.

heavy industry. Denmark has a large fishing and merchant fleet and there are strong international trading links. Because of the high cost of importing coal and oil, the Danes are developing their own exploration of North Sea oil and gas. In addition, they are pioneers in non-polluting energy sources, notably the huge wind generators which are found in 'windmill parks' set up throughout the country.

About Denmark is almost entirely surrounded by sea it has a mild maritime climate which can be very changeable. April to July are normally considered to be the driest months but this is not always the case. February is usually the coldest month and July the warmest, with August almost invariably the wettest month.

About 10 per cent of the country is covered by woodland, including commercial forests. All state forests and publicly owned woodlands are open at all times; private woodlands larger than 12$\frac{1}{2}$ acres and to which there is access by a public road are also open during daylight hours, with the proviso that access is on foot and only

DANISH ROAD SIGNS

Road signs follow the international system in Denmark. Other written signs which may be encountered include the following:

Datoparkering — Parking prohibited on even/odd days, as indicated
Ensrettet — One-way street
Farligt sving — Dangerous bend
Fodgængere — Pedestrians
Gennemkørsel forbudt — No through road
Hold til Højre (Venstre) — Keep to the Right (Left)
Indkørsel forbudt — No entry
Jernbaneoverskæring — Level Crossing
Knallert forbudt — No mopeds (or engines)
Korsvej — Crossroads
Omkørsel — Diversion
Overhaling forbudt — No overtaking
Parkering forbudt — No parking
Pas På — Take Care, Attention
Rabatten er Blød — Soft Verge
Rundkørsel — Roundabout
Skole — School
Udkørsel (Ud) — Exit
Ujævn vej — Rough or Broken surface
Vejarbejde — Road works
Vejen er spærret — Road closed

A 'silhouette' of buildings indicates a built-up area with a speed restriction of 50kmh (30mph).

established paths are used.

There are eight major nature reserves, including, in Jutland, the central heathlands, the shifting sand dunes near Skagen known as the Råbjerg Mile, and the Mols Bjerge on the east coast. Part of the Hærvej, or old military road, is also a protected area. Other reserves will be found on the islands of Fur, Møn, Ærø and Bornholm.

The State Forest Service publishes a series of over seventy leaflets under the title V*andreture I Statsskovene* or 'Walks in the State Forests'. These are free and usually available locally in the tourist information offices, libraries and elsewhere, and are well produced, with clear maps. The public also have access, as of right, to all the beaches of the country, including right of passage along privately owned foreshore.

Hire of both sailing and power boats as well as canoes is possible. Sea and lake fishing are popular with visitors and local tourist offices will have information, often selling the necessary fishing permits and giving advice on local rules.

Danish is a Nordic language, very similar to Norwegian. Many Danes speak excellent English, so there should be few communication problems except when referring to place names. German is widely spoken and in South Jutland and Bornholm it is more widely understood than English.

The Danish alphabet has three extra letters, namely Æ, Ø, and Å, in both upper and lower case forms. They are always printed in that order at the end of dictionaries, telephone directories, etc. Sometimes the letter Å is replaced by Aa, and you can find names such as 'Torsminde' also spelt as 'Thorsminde'. The pronunciation of the latter is, however, unchanged, 'th' being spoken as 't'. The Danish letter 'y' is said in a similar way to 'ew' in English. A good example of the two latter sounds occurs in the place-name 'Thy', which sounds rather like 'two' in English but rather shorter. The Danish letter 'J' takes the place of the English 'Y' at the beginning of a word. The letter 'V' may sometimes be replaced by the letter 'W' as in Nørre Vosborg (Wosborg). One or two simple points regarding Danish grammar may help. In general, the indefinite article 'a' or 'an' precedes the noun in Danish, being either *en* or *et* depending upon the gender. The definite article 'the' is added to the end of the noun, as in *bilen* (the car) or *toget* (the train), an exception to the rule being when an adjective precedes the noun. Plural nouns end in 'ne' or 'ene', and 'not' is *ikke* in Danish. A few simple phrases — such as *tak for hjælpen* — (thanks for your help) are worth learning. When a Dane gives you something, for example a waitress placing your cup of coffee before you, the word *værsågod* or *værsgo* will be used, meaning 'this is for you' or 'if you please'.

Music of all kinds has an important place in Danish life with concerts and festivals performed in many different locations every year. The many Danish contributors to the arts and sciences are well represented in the hundreds of museums open to the public throughout the country. Of particular interest are the numerous 'open-air' and farm museums, with historical buildings preserved and furnished with much original furniture, where many traditional crafts can be seen.

WEST JUTLAND
NORTH SEA HOLIDAY LAND

W est Jutland has some of the finest coastline in Denmark with miles of sandy beaches and plenty of space for holiday-makers, backed by high sand dunes amongst which are some of the holiday villages so popular with summer visitors. Behind the dunes are areas of forest and heathland and wide shallow fjords formed in ancient times when the sea broke through the dunes, and behind them areas of fertile farmland are crossed by streams and rivers. Jutland was originally desolate heathland where nothing would grow and much of this was reclaimed during the nineteenth century. Consequently there are few very old towns and the development of new ones has been linked to specific industries. Nevertheless, apart from the fine coastline there is still a surprising number of places of interest for the visitor to see, including one of the country's most famous attractions, Legoland.

ROUTE 1 • IN AND AROUND ESBJERG
The West Jutland coast with its shifting sandbanks provided few natural harbours between the German border in the south and the Skaw in the far north. Esbjerg was little more than a coastal fishing village when the rapid growth of agriculture necessitated the building of a modern North Sea port in the mid-nineteenth century. Esbjerg, founded in 1868, now has more than 80,000 inhabitants and is the largest town in West Jutland.

Prior to 1868 there were just two farms in the area where the town is now situated. The construction of the first 'export' harbour was followed by the foundation of the original town, built on a chessboard pattern along the classical lines of the times. The first houses were built by dockers, tradesmen and fishermen, and a few may still be seen in Vesterbyen, the old fishing quarter. From the 1890s, Esbjerg rapidly developed into an important industrial and mercantile town

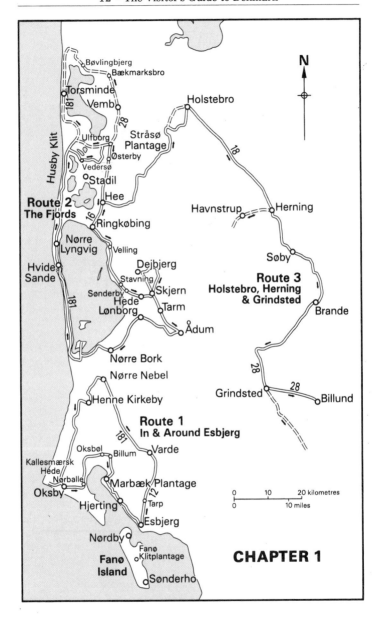

N

Bøvlingbjerg
Bækmarksbro
Torsminde
Vemb
Holstebro
181
28
Stråsø
Plantage
Ulfborg
Østerby
Husby Klit
Vedersø
Stadil
Hee
Route 2
The Fjords
Ringkøbing
Havnstrup
Herning
18
Nørre
Lyngvig
Velling
Søby
Hvide
Sande
Dejbjerg
Route 3
Holstebro, Herning
& Grindsted
Stavning
181
Sønderby
Hede
Lønborg
Skjern
Tarm
Ådum
Brande
Nørre Bork
Nørre Nebel
28
Henne Kirkeby
Grindsted
28
Billund
Route 1
In & Around Esbjerg
181
Oksbøl
Billum
Varde
Kallesmærsk
Hede
Nørballe
Oksby
Marbæk Plantage
11
Hjerting
Tarp
Esbjerg
Nørdby
Fanø
Klitplantage
Fanø
Island
Sønderho

0   10   20 kilometres
0   10 miles

CHAPTER 1

Gallery and restaurant in an old warehouse, Esbjerg

with a consequent rapid increase both in population and building projects. Large Victorian style buildings began to dominate the centre of the town, many examples of which can still be seen, particularly in Kongensgade, Esbjerg's famous pedestrian shopping street, more than 1km (½ mile) long.

A walk through the old streets gives an insight into the town's development and a descriptive leaflet in English is available from the tourist office in Torvet (The Square). The town's most famous landmark is *vandtårnet* (the watertower) which can be seen from the ferry on approaching the harbour. It stands in the town park, near the Kunstpavillonen, a museum of modern Danish art with over 400 paintings and sculptures from 1920 to the present day, and more than 1,000 graphic works by Danish and foreign artists.

Exhibits in the Esbjerg Museum in Nørregade include set pieces from the period 1890-1940 giving an impression of the town's development and an insight into life and work in the late nineteenth century, plus a collection of costumes from the nearby island of Fanø.

The Fisheries and Maritime Museum, Salt-water Aquarium and Sealarium (Søfartsmuseet) tells the story of the area's fishermen, their tackle and their catch. Visitors may board a fishing cutter and there are many large scale models illustrating the different vessels used on the west coast, plus Arctic whaling. The Salt-water Aquarium shows a broad section of Danish marine life, including fish and the creatures they eat. The Sealarium contains about ten seals and in the summer months orphaned and injured seal calves are nursed in special tanks. Breeding and research is an important aspect of the museum. Special paths alongside the tanks enable the visitor to watch the seals under water.

Near the ferry terminal for Fanø Island is an old fish-packing warehouse converted into a gallery, Galleri Slugen, and a restaurant, Café Pakhuset (the Warehouse Café) offering excellent fish dishes in a pleasant atmosphere.

South of the town, near Tjæreborg, is one of the world's largest wind turbines, developed as part of a European research programme. The visitor will see many such turbines and 'windmill parks', which play a large part in providing energy for the nation. A special visitors centre is open during the summer months as announced in the local press.

A short tour from Esbjerg to the nearby town of **Varde**, returning through the dunes and along the coast road is worth while, and is suitable for cyclists as well as motorists. Details of other cycle tours in the vicinity may be obtained from the tourist office.

Leave the town by Road 12 towards Varde. A cycle path runs alongside the road for much of the way. Go into the little town which received its first charter in 1442. The medieval church of Skt Jacobi is worth seeing and there are some attractive old merchants houses in the centre of the town. Varde is particularly well known for its 'Miniby' a miniature town set in the grounds of the Arnbjerg Park and a reconstruction of Varde as it looked around 1800. Traditional materials have been used; even the bricks are traditionally made and to scale. The town museum displays items of local and regional interest, furniture, silver and porcelain, a collection of locally-made pots known as *Jydepotter*, and a collection of Danish paintings and local art. Fårup Sommerland in Varde is a large amusement park for the whole family. Once the entrance fee has been paid all activities are free.

Those who prefer more peaceful pleasures will enjoy the nearby Tambours Have situated on the road to Nordenskov to the east of the town. These gardens were established by a plant collector who wanted to see plants from all over the world growing in his own garden. Starting in 1940, he looked after the project for 40 years until the local authority took over the management and maintenance of the gardens, which now extend to cover an area of $7\frac{1}{2}$ acres.

From Varde, take the secondary Road 181 to Nørre Nebel from where Route 2 can be joined at Nymindegab. Otherwise continue the present route south on a minor road along the edge of the Blåbjerg

PLACES TO VISIT IN AND AROUND ESBJERG AND FANØ

Esbjerg Museum
Cultural/historical museum.

Søfartsmuseet
History of local fishing industry,
Salt-water Aquarium and Sealarium with nursery.

Galleri Slugen
Art gallery and restaurant.

Esbjerg Wind Turbine
Tjæreborg
Visitor's centre explaining development of wind energy.

Varde
Miniby

Miniature town, Varde Museum,
Fårup Sommerland, Tambours Have.

Marbæk Plantage
Remains of Iron Age villages,
visitor centre and small museum.

Sædden Kirke
Beautiful modern church.

Fanø Island
Fanø Søfarts- og Dragtsamling and Fanø Museum.

Nordby
Maritime and cultural historical museums.

Plantage (Blåbjerg Forest). Here is one of Denmark's highest shifting dunes, the Blåbjerg, which is 64m (210ft) high. A walk leaflet is available. Continue to **Henne Kirkeby** whose church has a beautifully decorated altar, then on towards Henne Strand and south again towards Kærgård Klitplantage, another fine area for walking among the oak woods. The forest road leads to Vejers and the large holiday village of **Oksby**. Nearby is the windiest point in Denmark, Blåvands Huk, and the high lighthouse whose beam can be seen as far as 50km (31 miles) out to sea. Return towards Ho and the Skallingen Nature Reserve then north towards Oksbøl and Varde. At Billum turn south towards Esbjerg, crossing the Varde Å (Varde stream) at Tarphage Bro. After crossing the river, turn right and follow the road to **Marbæk Plantage**, an extensive heathland with clumps of heather and wild roses in the midst of which are two preserved villages from the early Iron Age. A map of the area is available showing waymarked walks which are also suitable for disabled visitors. Beautiful scenery with fine views over Ho Bugt and a rich bird life make this a popular destination for nature lovers. There is a visitor centre and a small agricultural museum and restaurant, and the nearby golf-course is considered to be the best in northern Europe.

Continue south again to the old fishing port of **Hjerting**, now the local centre for sailing and wind surfing. There are still many attractive houses in the old part of the village dating back to the time when this was the main port for Varde.

Continue along the coast road to Sædden Kirke, built as an integral part of Sædding Centret, a large modern shopping centre. The church interior is quite beautiful, being lit by thousands of ordinary electric light bulbs. Follow the coast road past the Søfartsmuseet to the ferry terminal for Fanø.

FANØ ISLAND

The island of Fanø lies in the North Sea immediately opposite Esbjerg harbour. Ferry services leave Esbjerg every half hour during the summer months, but less frequently in winter. This is one ferry service on which no reservations are accepted. It is necessary to queue and wait until space is available. Since the boats are small, this has the effect of controlling the numbers of vehicles and persons on the island at any one time; even so, the population is almost trebled in the season.

Fanø is the most northerly of the Wadden Islands, that chain of small islands off the coasts of Holland, Germany and Denmark which are characterised by their landscape of sand dunes and wide, clean beaches on the North Sea coast. Fanø was crown property until 1741 but because funds were at an all-time low King Christian VI put the island up for sale by public auction. The inhabitants heard of this and managed to buy the island for themselves, at the same time receiving ship-building rights. Fanø's prosperity was thus assured and up until 1900 more than 1,000 ships had been built in the island's four yards. The captains of these vessels were often natives of Fanø and while the men were away at sea the women took over the full burden of home and family. With the end of the age of sail and the silting-up of the harbours tourism began to develop as an industry.

The island is some 18km (12 miles) long, and has one major road. For this reason the best way to explore is by cycle or on foot. The tourist office in Nordby has a number of leaflets available. In **Nordby** itself, there are two museums. Fanø Søfarts- og Dragtsamling, which is a maritime museum and costume collection, and Fanø Museum, in an old Fanø house, illustrating the life on the island some 300 years ago. It contains many curiosities brought home by the sailors from their travels. The church dates from 1786 and has a number of model ships inside. Between Nordby and the west coast are hundreds of holiday homes, camp sites, etc, sited among the dunes. South from Nordby the road goes across heathland and dunes and through forests to the small village of **Sønderho** with picturesque streets containing old thatched and gabled houses and a windmill. The oak-beamed Sønderho Kro is 300 years old and has both accommoda- tion and an excellent restaurant. The little seamen's church has no tower but has a fine collection of models of Fanø-built ships hanging from the ceiling and an impressive monument to the 500 Fanø

seamen who lost their lives at sea. Hannes Hus is a well preserved
Sønderho home dating back to the days when the village was home
port of a large fleet of sailing ships. Traditional festivities include the
'Fanø Fair' and 'Sønderho Fair' which both take place in July.
Dancing, folk music and traditional costumes are much in evidence
at these times.

The West Coast Fjords

Ringkøbing is the county town for a large area of Jutland stretching
from the southern end of the Ringkøbing Fjord to the Nissum Broad
in the north, and including the large towns of Holstebro and Herning.
An old medieval trading town, Ringkøbing has a history dating back
to around AD1250, when it was known to be a port. Unfortunately the
channel into the town became silted up at Nymindegab, otherwise
the town may well have developed as the main North Sea port,
instead of Esbjerg. Today Ringkøbing is still a busy trading centre,
but has succeeded in preserving much of the atmosphere of the old
town. The tourist office publishes a guide illustrating the different
types of buildings, making it easy for the visitor to explore on foot. In
the square is the town's oldest house, built around 1600 and now a
hotel. The church with its interesting sundial (dated 1728) once used
to set the clock on the tower is the only building to have survived from
the town's earliest times. The old town hall (rådhus) dates from 1849
and forms the background for the folk dancing which takes place on
Friday evenings in the summer months, with women wearing the
distinctive local costumes with their tall black hats over lace caps and
the men wearing red stocking caps.

There is an excellent museum, with prehistoric collections, and
exhibits relating to the town's history. In addition there are many
exhibits related to the exploration of Greenland by Mylius-Erichsen,
the Greenland explorer.

With the construction of the sea locks at Hvide Sande in 1931,
Ringkøbing Fjord is again open to small craft. Today there is a well
appointed harbour with a marina for pleasure craft, and there are
always plenty of sails to see on the fjord.

Interesting churches in the immediate neighbourhood include
Gammel Sogn Church, on the edge of the fjord. Before Nørre Lyngvig
Church was built, people used to sail across the fjord to attend church
services. **Stadil** Church has a very old altarpiece dating from 1200
and covered in gold leaf and quartz. There are some particularly fine
pews, including late Gothic parish clerk's and priest's chairs. At **Hee**
in the seventeenth century the district courts were held on a slope to
the south-west of the interesting church. Here also is Sommerland

West, a large amusement park within an area of lakes and woodland. Once the entrance fee has been paid the amusements are free.

ROUTE 2 • A TOUR AROUND THE FJORDS

Starting from Ringkøbing, take the road alongside the fjord towards **Velling** where, in the south porch of the church, is an old tombstone dated 1557. Follow the signs to Stauning airfield, home of the Danish veteran aircraft collection, passing the Tændpipe windmill park on the left. Continue into **Skjern** whose oldest building is the 800-year-old parish church. The local museum by the water tower contains exhibits showing the town's development, with examples of old crafts and trades. Skjern windmill, a listed building, is open during the summer. A diversion to the north of the town along the main Ringkøbing road leads to a preserved stretch of moorland at **Dejbjerg Hede**, enabling the visitor to see what the land was like before the advent of farming in the late nineteenth century. A monument to the pioneer of this cultivation stands on a hill commanding a view of the fjord. The Iron Age wagons which are now in the National Museum in Copenhagen were excavated here at Dejbjerg. The local rural museum is at nearby Bundsbæk Mølle where the watermill is still used to grind flour to make bread which is baked in an old-fashioned oven and served in the tea-room.

Return to Skjern and continue south for 2km (a mile), crossing the Skjern Å, Denmark's widest river, before reaching the small nineteenth-century town of **Tarm**, only 6km (4 miles) south of Skjern. The finest building in town is the *apotek* in the main street and a stork's nest on the roof has been in use for many years. South-east of Tarm, on a minor road, is the village of **Ådum** whose church has a fine interior with a beautiful painted altarpiece and carved pulpit. To the south of the church is an old rune stone. Take the road signed to Gråhede, continue to the crossroads and turn left along Kirkevej past Egvad Church to the main road, following signs to Tarm, then cross over and continue to the Romanesque church of **Lønborg** with its magnificent altarpiece, carved and gilded pulpit and canopy and vaulted ceiling with fine frescoes.

From here follow the flat road via Vostrup and Hemmet to **Nørre Bork**, following the sign 'Bork Havn' at the bend in the road. A huge burial stone stands at the eastern end of the nearby church; inside there are old altar panels and some box pews dated 1652. Follow signs for Nymindegab, passing Fahl Kro, now a museum depicting the land use of the area. Nature films are shown, and there is also an interesting fjord aquarium. Turn right to Tipperne Nature Reserve where there is a small nature information centre, offering fine views across the marshes and the fjord. There is restricted access to the reserve itself.

PLACES TO VISIT IN THE WESTERN FJORDS

Ringkøbing
District Museum
Prehistoric and local history collections; also Greenland collection.

Stadil Church
Magnificent interior furnishings, including gold leaf altarpiece.

Skjern
Bundsbæk Mølle
Local history museum in old watermill.

Ådum Church
Beautiful painted altarpiece and carved pulpit. Old rune stone.

Bork
Fahl Kro and Tipperne Nature Reserve with information centre.

Madum
Tvind Wind Generator
One of the world's tallest.

Torsminde Memorials
Monuments to sailors and fishermen lost at sea. Also Nissum Broad Bird Reserve.

The route now swings north and follows the dune road along Holmsland Klit. The long, low thatched buildings of the old dune farms can still be seen, set at intervals among the dunes, interspersed by holiday houses which have done nothing to improve the landscape. One dune farm known as Abeline's Gård, built in 1871, has been preserved as a monument to the farmers of the west coast. **Hvide Sande**, a large fishing harbour, grew up when the sea locks were completed in 1931. The gates were constructed to secure a stable water level in Ringkøbing Fjord, and to improve the fishing from Holmsland Klit. Prior to 1931 the fishing boats were based at several small hamlets along the dunes, and at Nymindegab. Sea fishing is now centred at Hvide Sande which has become one of Denmark's largest fishing ports. About 5km (3 miles) to the north is **Nørre Lyngvig**, whose tall lighthouse forms a distinctive landmark in the area. There is a fine view from the top, and the area around it is a conservation area. Near the lighthouse is a mini-museum describing the flora and fauna of the neighbourhood.

Along the coast road an area full of holiday homes extends past Søndervig to Husby Klit and Vest Stadil Fjord. At **Husby Klit** another old dune farm, Strandgården, contains a collection of typical farm implements and machinery from dune farms. Continue to Vedersø Klit then turn south to **Vedersø** with its Romanesque granite-built church, burial place of Kaj Munk, a Danish priest and poet who was killed by the Nazis in World War II.

From Vedersø, follow signs for Madum, Madum Kirke and the

blue 'Tvind Skolerne' sign. By the school is an enormous wind generator, at 54m (177ft) tall one of the highest in the world. Follow the road into **Ulfborg**, a small town in the centre of beautiful woods and moorlands, then return to Ringkøbing via the main road south. The tour may be extended further by going north along the main road towards **Vemb**, passing, Nørre Vosborg, the oldest preserved manor house in Denmark dating from 1299, on the left of the road. Continue through Vemb to Bækmarksbro, then left to Bøvlingbjerg. About 2km (1 mile) after passing Bøvling Kirke turn left to Nørby, then turn south again taking the coast road along the narrow strip of dunes at Bøvling Klit to **Torsminde**. This stretch of coastline was notorious for shipwrecks and by the old lifeboat house, now a seamen's church, is a memorial to fishermen lost at sea. Further along the coast is a memorial stone to the 1391 English sailors who lost their lives when the warships *St George* and *Defence* were wrecked off the coast in 1811. Nissum Fjord on the left of the road is a bird sanctuary for thousands of web-footed and wading birds. Continue south to Husby, then left to Ulfborg and the main road back to Ringkøbing.

ROUTE 3 • MODERN JUTLAND — HOLSTEBRO, HERNING AND GRINDSTED

One of the most attractive routes to Holstebro from the south is the cycle route from Ringkøbing which is clearly signed (with a white cycle on a blue background on a square board, with the legend 'Holstebro' and the distance beneath it) and can be followed by motor vehicles.

From Ringkøbing take Road 16 north towards Lemvig, turning right at Hee to Hover then turn left towards Torsted through Hoverdal Forest. Cross the Tim-Grønbjerg road and at the T-junction turn right. In about 2km (a mile) turn left through Torsted Woods. Where the metalled road turns to the left go straight ahead on the forestry road leading through **Stråsø Plantage**. This is an area of inland dunes which have been planted with conifer forests sheltering beech and birch trees. Among the plantations are patches of moorland. The road can be quite steep and rough in places and cyclists need to be wary of loose gravel. On the approach to the Fuglkær Å the forest thins out and the landscape changes to open moorland.

By Fuglsang Bro (Birdsong Bridge) is a picnic area. The gravel road continues across Vind Heath where you may be lucky and see some black grouse. At Vind Church the road becomes metalled again and the route follows quiet country lanes into Holstebro. Motorists should leave the cycle route at the crossroads near Hestbjerg, turning right towards Nørre Felding and from there follow Road 11 into Holstebro.

Holstebro is not a new town. It was founded in 1552, but there

PLACES TO VISIT IN MODERN JUTLAND

Holstebro
Det Gamle Postkontor (Old Post Office), Holstebro Museum, Kunstmuseum, Jens Nielsen and Olivia Holm-Møller Museum, Dragon- og Frihedsmuseet, Nørrelandskirken (modern church building).

Herning
Cultural and historical museum, Carl-Henning Pedersen and Else Alfelt's Museum, Herningsholm, mansion and museum.

Jutland Mini-Zoo
Havnstrup

Gøgler Museum
Vorbasse
Devoted to travelling fairground folk.

Legoland Park
Billund
Theme park.

has been a settlement here since 1274; this was the place where all the roads converged to cross the Stor Å (river). The town grew to prominence as a trading centre, but fell into decline in the seventeenth century and began to revive again with the coming of the railway in 1866. It is now regarded as the cultural centre of West Jutland with many museums and art galleries and an amazing number of sculptures in the streets. One which the visitor cannot fail to miss is *Vandkunsten* (water art), known locally as the Weeping Wall consisting of two high glazed brick walls with water cascading down into the trough below. Concerts and theatrical events take place in the town all year round. Of the three historic buildings which are now under a preservation order Nyboes Gård, built in 1796, houses Det Gamle Postkontor (The Old Post Office) with a collection of old post office effects, stamps, etc. The other two are the Toll House and the old town hall. The railway station is a fine example of neo-Gothic architecture and is worth seeing. Modern buildings worth noting include Nørrelandskirken (a church) to the north of the town centre and the nearby Jens Nielsen and Olivia Holm-Møller Museum. The town is recognised for its modern town planning and has twice been voted Denmark's 'Town of the Year'. It has an excellent shopping centre and some attractive parks and open spaces in the surroundings.

The Holstebro Museum contains important Stone Age and Viking discoveries, together with finds from Tvis Monastery and furnishings from the old parish church. There is also a large collection of local silver, a fine collection of dolls, and articles related to the local tobacco industry. Holstebro Kunstmuseum contains collections of

Abelines Gård, on the west coast near Ringkøbing Fjord

Danish contemporary art, European graphic art, and some good examples of ethnic art from South America, Africa and the East. The Jens Nielsen and Olivia Holm-Møller Museum contains works by other artists besides these two, and a collection of religious art. The Dragon-og Frihedsmuseet shows the development of the local regiment from 1679 to the present day and the resistance operations in West Jutland during World War II.

From Holstebro the main Road 11 running north will link into Route 4 at Struer. Otherwise continue this route by Road 18 to **Herning**, an important town developed on the site of nine farms with only twenty-one inhabitants in 1840. The town cannot boast important historical monuments but it has established itself, with the nearby town of Ikast, as the centre of the Danish textile industry and is the home of one of the largest trade fair complexes in Europe. Herning

Museum has collections from prehistoric times to the present day with old heathland farmhouses in the grounds. A beautiful collection of miniature interiors known as Jens Nielsen's Farm illustrates days in the life of the country people around 1920. Part of the museum is the old knitwear factory containing a comprehensive exhibition relating to the history of the textile industry in the area, and next door is the Danish Photographic Museum.

The art museums to the east of the town contain important works

The Statue of Liberty *in Legoland*

of modern artists, including Asger Jorn and Richard Mortensen. The
Carl-Henning Pedersen and Else Alfelt's Museum building has a fine
ceramic frieze by Pedersen decorating the external circular wall.
There is a collection of more than 4,000 works by the two artists and
exhibits are changed at periodic intervals. To the north of the town is
Herningsholm, a sixteenth-century manor house with a fine banqueting hall containing eighteenth-century murals, now restored and
housing a museum commemorating the Danish author and poet
Steen Steensen Blicher. Nearby attractions include the Jutland Mini-
Zoo at **Havnstrup** and the old lignite quarries at Søby, on the road
to Brande.

   Leave Herning in a southerly direction on Road 18 towards

Brande. Turn left at Høgild in the direction of **Søby** where a small museum sited in one of the miner's wooden huts gives some insight into the appalling conditions under which the miners lived and worked. Originally, peat cutting was the major industry of the area but during the two world wars the lignite mines were established and men flocked to the area to try and get their share of 'brown gold'. Along the road, through the now desolate area, are police warning signs emphasising the dangerous nature of the ground.

The road leads to Søbylund and then turns south beside an industrial development by the railway to join the main road at Fasterholt. Along this road to the left is Harrild Hede, an area of moorland with waymarked paths. To get to **Brande** from Fasterholt, turn left at the main road and then right in about 1km (half a mile) and follow this quiet road into the centre of the town. The church (1175) once belonged to the lords of the manor. The town itself was established in the nineteenth century and is known for the gaily painted end gables which have transformed dull buildings into an open-air art exhibition. One notable piece of modern architecture is the brick-built Baptist church which is worth seeing.

It is possible to connect with Route 17 (Hærvej) from Brande along Road 18 south to Give. To continue this route leave the town by the secondary road to Sønder Omme and there join Road 28 going south to **Grindsted**, another town which developed in the nineteenth century as a result of the cultivation of the moorlands. Grindsted specialises in the manufacture of agricultural machinery, and there is also a large canned meat plant in the town. A number of small museums tell and preserve the history of the area, including the Gøgler Museum at Vorbasse which tells the story of the local fair ground folk.

The nearby town of **Billund** is most famous for Legoland park built entirely from the world famous Lego bricks. It also includes a toy museum and 'Titania's Palace', a magnificent miniature palace made in 1922 by Sir Neville Wilkinson, the English painter, for his daughter, who thought she had seen fairies in the garden and asked for a house for them to live in. This magnificent model contains some 3,000 priceless miniatures, a selection which have been mounted in special cases around the exhibition room so they can be studied under magnifying lenses. Outside the exhibition building the park contains many items of interest to all, ranging from model towns and buildings from many lands, with working railways, canals and docks to a reproduction of the Mount Rushmore monument in the USA. There are many activities for children, including a traffic school. From Billund the main Road 28 links into the Hærvej (Route 17) at Randbøl.

2
THE LIMFJORD COUNTRY

I n the north of Jutland is a large area of shallow fjords and broads which are known collectively as the Limfjord. The major islands are now connected by bridges, and there are plenty of small ferries enabling the visitor to make shorter tours around the lakes. It is an area of varied landscapes, including fascinating geological phenomena and large stretches of dunes and heathland ideal for those wishing to find peace and quiet and fine beaches with plenty of opportunities for sailing and fishing. Many fascinating prehistoric remains can be seen, for this was once one of the most densely populated areas of Denmark.

ROUTE 4 • WEST OF THE LIMFJORD

The tour begins at **Struer**, at the southern end of Venø Bay, a small town established in 1917 because of its position with regard to rail, road and water communications. It has the largest marina on the western Limfjord and a museum with prehistoric and local history collections, established in an old farmhouse which was once the home of the local priest. Next door is the home of Johannes Buchholz, one of Denmark's well known poets, now a small museum to his memory. The inlet to the north of the town, Kilen, is a nature reserve, and from nearby Kleppen there is a small ferry to the island of Venø, which has the smallest church in Denmark.

From Struer, take the road to **Vinderup** and turn right in the town centre following signs to Hjerl Hede and then in about 2km (1 mile) turn left to **Sahl**. The church here has one of the finest golden altars in Denmark, dating from around 1200. From Sahl continue to Hjerl Hede open-air museum 'Den Gamle Landsby' (The Old Village). This has been established in an area of outstanding natural beauty, and shows the development of the Danish village from the sixteenth century until 1900. Included in the complex is an interesting forestry section and a small prehistoric settlement. The visitor may also walk along the beautiful lakeside paths by the Flyndersø.

From the museum, take the road south to Sevel, then turn left and drive along the quiet wooded lane to the main road near Mogenstrup. Turn left here and continue towards Skive. **Estvad** Church has a beautiful interior, with a fine carved altarpiece and pulpit, and a seventeenth-century chandelier. The wall paintings are even earlier, from around AD1220.

Because of its position at the southern end of the Salling peninsula, **Skive** has always been the focal point of the district. There is an interesting museum in the town with a local history collection, a section on Greenland, a fine collection of amber and an art department. In the town centre is Frøken Michelsens Mindestuer (Miss Michelsen's Memorial Rooms), a display of items collected by an eccentric local confectioner on her travels, displayed exactly as she left them. The old church in Skive, Vor Frue Kirke (Church of Our Lady) has a beautiful vaulted and frescoed ceiling.

From Skive, take the Holstebro road out of the town, then continue ahead to Lem and Lihme on Road 189. From here it is possible to drive to the shore by the public road which passes through the courtyard at Kås Manor House. To the left can be seen a number of

Bronze Age barrows and more will be seen from the small road between Lihme, Ålbæk and Rødding. At the crossroads about 5km (3 miles) beyond Ålbæk, turn right to Spøttrup Castle. This magnificent fifteenth-century medieval fortress has a double moat, with 9m (29ft) high intermediate ramparts which must have made the place virtually impregnable. Inside it conveys the impressions of life as it was in the Middle Ages, with old dungeons and kitchens, and medieval toilet facilities. The Great Hall is often used for concerts, and, since there is no electricity in the castle, it is quite an experience to be there by candle light. Within the grounds a small Renaissance

garden contains medieval herbs and medicinal plants.

From Spøttrup, take the road to Sønder Balling, then turn left through Nørre Balling and Oddense to the main Skive-Nykøbing road. Turn right, then left, and at Roslev turn right again to Kirkeby.

By turning right along Road 591 through Thise and taking the ferry to Hvalpsund, Route 6 may be joined. Otherwise go straight ahead at Kirkeby and continue to the major Road 551 then turn left for the

ferry to **Fur**. A good starting point for visiting the island is the museum at **Nederby**, which has a good cultural and historical collection and an exceptional collection of fossils. The island is very flat in the south, but in the north there are hidden valleys in the hills and deep ravines

leading down to the sea. From Bette Jens Høj there are fine views. Nearby is Rødsten, a large rock formed from sand, ice melt-water and iron compounds. A similar one is to be found on the beach. Fur is one of the places in Denmark where deposits of 'moler' or white clay are found. The cliffs clearly show how the 50 million-year-old clay, with more than 170 layers of volcanic ash, has been compressed and

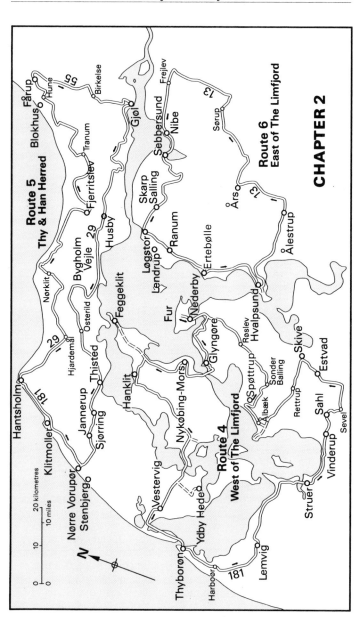

folded by the glaciers during the last Ice Age. Fossils may be found on the beaches nearby. The clay is quarried on the island, and is used to make high-insulation lightweight bricks for furnaces and chimneys.

Leave Fur and return to Salling. Take the narrow winding coast road through Risum, then in about 500m (457yd) turn sharp left. There is no sign at this point. After about 2km (1 mile) turn right again following the narrow coast road, and at the next junction follow signs to **Glyngøre**, a little village with a fishing harbour, marina and sandy bathing beaches. From here follow signs for Skive, along the coast road towards the high Sallingsund Bridge which connects the islands of Salling and Mors. Continue over the bridge towards Nykøbing. A road to the right leads to Jesperhus Blomsterpark, Scandinavia's largest flower park covering more than 12½ acres. In addition to the gardens there are greenhouses, a fresh-water aquarium and a bird house. An amusement park for children, and a camp site with tropical swimming pool are within the complex. Nykøbing is not the only town with this name in Denmark, and is usually referred to as **Nykøbing-Mors**, or simply Nykøbing-M to avoid confusion. It is best known for its fine yachting marina, but there is a good historical museum in the town's only remaining medieval building, Dueholm Kloster. The collections cover the development of the island from the early Stone Age to the turn of the century, regional costumes and a permanent exhibition of work by local artists. A foundry museum in the former office buildings of the Morsø Iron Foundry contains a fine collection of old stoves, including many produced by the foundry in its heyday. Old photographs and tools illustrate the processes involved. Also in the town is the Museum of Archaeology and Geology and a Museum of Bottles. Leave by the Thisted road and at Vodstrup turn right following signs for Feggesund as far as Sønder Dråby. From the road beside the bay there is a good view of the cliffs of Fur.

If you wish to visit **Feggeklit**, said to be the place where Hamlet murdered his stepfather, continue along the main road for another 11km (7 miles). Route 5 at Vesløs may be joined by taking the ferry across the Feggesund. Otherwise, from Sønder Dråby turn left onto the Thisted road, then right into Flade. In the village turn left, then right following signs to Salgjerhøj. Follow the road marked Bjørneborg to the parking area, from where there is a superb view over the Thisted Bredning (Broad). Return to the village and turn right, following Hanklit signs. The road down to the cliffs at **Hanklit** is steep, winding and rather narrow, but it is worth the effort, for the cliffs are quite magnificent examples of moler clay and volcanic ash compressed together. Here too can be found examples of the red sand and ironstone boulders seen on Fur. A path runs along the top of the cliffs, but the best view is on the beach, although visitors are warned to beware of high tides and rock falls. Return up Hanklitvej and, at the

PLACES TO VISIT
WEST OF THE LIMFJORD

Struer Museum of Local History
In old farmhouse.

Sahl Church
Thirteenth-century golden altarpiece.

Vinderup
Hjerl Hede Frilandsmuseum Development of village life.

Skive
Frøken Michelsen's Mindestuer Local museum.

Spøttrup Castle
Preserved medieval moated and fortified castle.

Fur
Island with geological features, museum at Nederby.

Mors
Jesperhus Blomsterpark.

Nykøbing-Mors
Dueholm Kloster, Foundry Museum, Museum of Archaeology and Geology, Bottle Museum.

Feggeklit
Site where Hamlet murdered his stepfather.

Glomstrup Manor House
Open-air museum.

Vestervig Church
Largest village church in Denmark.

Harboøre
Lifeboat House Museum.

give way sign, take the road to the right signed Sundby, then left towards Bjergby. At the next give way sign turn left into the village, and at the T-junction turn right towards Solbjerg. Cross the main road and continue to Øster Jølby, and at the T-junction turn left and first right towards Redsted. To the south of **Hvidbjerg** village lies Glomstrup Manor House, containing a rich collection of furniture, tools and interiors from the seventeenth and eighteenth centuries, in a total of fourteen buildings in an open-air setting. Return to the village and turn left in the direction of Karby and the ferry at Nees Sund.

Continue towards Hurup and Vestervig, but at the main road a diversion may be made to the south to **Ydby Hede** where more than fifty Bronze Age burial mounds command a fine view over the fjords. **Vestervig** Church can be seen from far off, and is the largest village church in Scandinavia. Built as the abbey church of a large Augustinian monastery in the twelfth century, it has a high vaulted roof and an altarpiece originally painted for Viborg Cathedral in 1740. The font is unique, being carved from soft soapstone and believed to be older than the church itself. Most of the frescoes have disappeared, but in the northern aisle there is a star-decorated vault in the original colours. Most of the furnishings are seventeenth century.

The marina at Nykøbing-Mors

Take the road leading to Agger at the crossroads by the church, bearing left at Tåbel to follow the main road to the ferry to Thyborøn. It takes about 15 minutes to cross this busy stretch of water, and cuts out a very long drive round the Nissum Bredning. The road to the ferry is built on a 6km (4 mile) long dyke running parallel to Agger Tange, a narrow spit of low dunes through which it is possible to walk and cycle. On the quay at **Thyborøn** is an anchor from the Russian ship *Alexander Nevsky*, wrecked off the coast in 1868. On the North Sea coast at Thyborøn it is possible to find amber, especially after a storm, and the shell house in the town is rather attractive. At the other end of the peninsula, in Harboøre cemetery, is a memorial wall to the many fishermen who have lost their lives in this part of the North Sea, and the old lifeboat house on the nearby coast, one of the first to be built in Denmark, is now a museum containing the last rowing lifeboat used here. The road leading out of town to **Lemvig** offers fine views over the surrounding countryside, especially on the approach to Lemvig, which is quite steep. Lemvig is a busy fishing harbour with an interesting old church in the centre of the town having a distinctive 'onion' tower. Take the Struer road out of Lemvig, up the steep hill and turn left on Road 565 towards Nissum and Humlum. There are some magnificent views of the Toftum Hills and the windmill park north of Humlum, from where the main road leads back into Struer.

Denmark is a paradise for geologists. These cliffs are at Hanklit, Mors

ROUTE 5 • THY AND HAN HERRED

Thy is the area in the north-west of Jutland separated from the south by stretches of water and linked to Han Herred in the east by the cliffs at Bulbjerg and the marshes of Bygholm Vejle. Han Herred is a narrow strip of land between sea and fjord, lying to the west of Ålborg and the Ry Å. The whole area has a maximum width of about 20km (12 miles) and a length of some 120km (74 miles) and is bounded on the north by the North Sea and on the south by the Limfjord. There is a superb coastal path from Agger Tange to Hantsholm and Bulbjerg, a distance of about 65km (40 miles) with convenient camp sites along the route. A good map with a description in Danish is produced by the State Forestry Service and is obtainable locally.

The route starts at **Thisted**, the main town of Thy, a busy modern town surrounding an older centre in which is the Gothic church dating from about 1500. The town has the regional museum which includes memorial rooms to the poet J.P.Jacobsen and the scholar Kristen Kold, both local men, and a considerable collection of antiquities relating to the Bronze Age occupation of the area.

Leave the town on the Sjørring road and in about 5km (3 miles) a sign for **Sjørring Volde** will be seen. This is a large medieval earthwork, site of a Viking castle which was burned down in the Middle Ages. Turn right just past the earthworks to **Jannerup**, passing an attractive slated windmill on a mound, and continue to Nørre Vorupør. Throughout the area many tumuli can be seen, some of them very high. At **Nørre Vorupør** the fishing boats are drawn up on the beach and at the beginning of the twentieth century it was one of the leading fishing hamlets on the North Sea coast. The villagers were pioneers of boat building and fishing tackle development, as well as establishing co-operatives for the sale of their fish. It is one of the very few places where inshore fishing is still practised in the old way, and the new North Sea Aquarium displays all the different species of fish caught in the North Sea. At **Stenbjerg**, a tiny fishing hamlet to the south, the landing place of the fishing vessels has become a museum with a collection of winch-house tackle and rescue equipment.

Leave the village and take Road 181 to the north through forest and dunes towards **Klitmøller**, another fishing village which has developed into a holiday resort. The road continues northwards with the State Wildlife Reserve — 10,000 acres of magnificent scenery — on the right and the North Sea on the left. The reserve is open to the public outside the breeding season but access is on foot only. Ahead is **Hantsholm**, one of the largest of Denmark's fishing ports with a fleet of modern North Sea cutters. The harbour includes fish auction facilities and frequent ferry services leave here for Norway, the Faroe Islands, Iceland and the Shetland Islands during summer. During World War II, the town was converted into an enormous fortification with one of the largest gun emplacements in northern Europe, and one of the gun positions is now a museum. The lighthouse in Hantsholm, erected in 1842, has one of the most powerful lights in the world. A museum has been established showing the history of the lifeboat service as well as a local history collection.

Leave Hantsholm by Road 29 towards Thisted and Fjerritslev, and at Hjardemål turn left through dunes and forest towards **Frøstrup**, a place noted for the storks which winter there. Turn left at the T-junction on the main road and follow the signs to Bulbjerg, a 40m (131ft) high hill with fine views along the coast and inland to the Limfjord. Drive back along the road for about 300m (330yd) then turn left and follow a concrete track as far as the asphalted road. Turn right and then almost immediately left again through Torup plantation. At the next T-junction turn left towards Torup Strand, then right again through the heathland and woods and into **Fjerritslev**. The old brewery is the best preserved in northern Europe, and now houses a collection of brewing equipment and objects of local historical interest.

From Fjerritslev go north again, following the road to Tranum, then turn left towards Tranum Strand. Drive through the forest and at the cross roads turn right and continue through the dunes to the next

T-junction. Turn right and in about 4km (2½ miles) turn left again through Tranum Klitplantage. At the next junction turn left towards Rødhus Klit then in a short distance right and continue to Hune. The road to the left leads to **Blokhus**, a large and popular holiday area but turn right and in about 1½km (nearly a mile) turn left towards Fårup and Saltum. At **Fårup** is the large 'Sommerland' or summer recreation centre with plenty of activities for everyone. Continue northwards from here towards Saltum Kirke avoiding the road into Saltum village. Visit this lovely church whose beautiful sixteenth-century frescoes, fine carved fifteenth-century altarpiece and elaborately carved and painted pulpit dating from around 1600, make an interesting study. The granite font is from about 1100, and the carved and painted font cover was added around 1600, at the same time as the carved pews.

From the church, Road 55 north will link with Route 7 at Løkken. To continue the present route, follow Road 55 south as far as Åbybro, then take the road to Ryå and Birkelse in the direction of Brovst. At the main road cross over onto the minor road and take the third turning on the left which leads to **Gjøl**. In the porch of the church is a twelfth century self-portrait depicting a mason hewing a piece of stone. The altarpiece and frescoes date from 1525. Take the road out of the village leading west towards Gjøl Bjerge and follow the unmade road across the causeway between the Limfjord and Ulvedybet Bird Sanctuary until the asphalt road is reached at Østerby. Turn left and follow the road through Hammershøj.

Continue towards Oksholm Manor House, founded as a Benedictine monastery in the twelfth century, and turn left following signs to Vesterby and Torslev. To the left of the road is agricultural land which has been reclaimed from the fjord. In Torslev, turn left along Kokkedalsvej, passing the moated manor house of Kokkedal currently used as a boys' home, on the left. Follow Erik Bannersvej to Attrup, then turn right along Kokkedalsvej. In about 1km (half a mile) turn left again, and in a further kilometre turn right along Alsbjergvej, a narrow unmade road leading to Hvissehøj, a unique passage grave more than 4,500 years old having three interconnected chambers. Continue ahead to Aggersundvej and turn left towards Lørsted, through Bonderup towards Skræm and then to **Husby**. A small sign on the right directs the visitor to Husby Hole, the site of a battle in the fifteenth century between the peasants of North Jutland and the Bavarians. A stone monument recalls the event and the area is now a peaceful picnic site with waymarked nature walks. Return to the road and turn right towards Korsholm.

By turning left along the main Road 29 to cross the Aggersund Bridge, Route 6 may be joined in Løgstør. To continue the present route, cross main Road 29, and continue through Korsholm and Gøttrup to the main road and then turn left towards Thisted. The road

Lemvig Church

crosses the dam enclosing the **Bygholm Vejle**. This is now the largest wild fowl sanctuary in northern Europe, and information charts have been set up in lay-bys along the road. Continue to Vesløs, then turn right towards Tømmerby. If you are lucky you may see a stork nesting on top of a pole in Vesløs village. Further along the road is a group of Viking burial mounds known as Skårup Høje. Turn left in Tømmerby to Langvad then left at the main road through Østerild Klitplantage to Østerild, then by the main road back to Thisted.

This route may be split into three shorter tours by using short road links from Hjardermål to Østerild, from Frøstrup through Tømmerby to Vesløs, or through Fjerritslev to Skerping, near Husby Hole.

ROUTE 6 • EAST OF THE LIMFJORD

This route takes the visitor through West Himmerland, an area offering some of the most varied scenery in Jutland. Towns and villages are small with some interesting and unusual museums and beautiful old churches set in quiet and peaceful surroundings.

The tour begins at **Løgstør**, a small fishing port situated where the Limfjord narrows into Aggersund. The town owes its existence to the great Viking fortress of Aggersborg situated across the shallows to the north of the town. This is the largest known Viking fortress in

PLACES TO VISIT
IN THY AND HAN HERRED

Thisted
Regional Museum
Collection of Bronze Age finds.

Nørre Vorupør
North Sea Aquarium.

Hantsholm
State Wildlife Reserve.
Gun emplacement museum
Lighthouse Museum - history of
the lifeboat service and local
historical collection.

Fjerritslev
Local history and brewing
museum in old brewery.

Fårup Sommerland
Fårup

Leisure park in natural setting.

Saltum
Church with sixteenth-century
altarpiece and frescoes.

Gjøl Church
Twelfth-century 'self-portrait' in
church porch. Sixteenth-century
altarpiece and frescoes.

Husby Hole
Monument to fifteenth-century
battle.

Bygholm Vejle
Largest wild fowl reserve in
northern Europe.

Scandinavia but there are few remains to be seen here. Løgstør has been a fishing and trading port but because it was regarded as a threat by the city of Ålborg it did not receive its charter until 1900.

The streets give an impression of past times. The canal warden's house now houses the Local History Museum with well arranged exhibits illustrating the significance of the fjord as a fishing ground and as a means of communication. Two traditional Limfjord boats are kept in the old boat house and other exhibits illustrate the life and work of the people of the area right up to the twentieth century.

From the museum the towpaths on both sides of the canal may be followed for about 5km (3 miles) to **Lendrup** at the southern end of the canal, where a smaller exhibition devoted to the history of the canal and the biology of the Limfjord has been established in the canal keepers' houses.

Take the road south to **Ranum**, with history dating back to the foundation of the nearby monastery in the twelfth century, but now noted for its college of education. Between the town and the coast are many wind generators and at Rønbjerg Huse there is a small ferry which takes pedestrians to the nearby island of Livø, a conservation area. The huge twin towers of Ranum Church look old, but only date from 1907. To the south is Vitskøl Kloster, given to the Cistercian Order in 1157 by Valdemar the Great as a thank-offering for his escape from the massacre of Roskilde. In the seventeenth century it became a manor house and in 1942 the state took over the property and established a community home for young offenders in the main buildings. It is noted for its fine herb garden.

The road continues along the coast through Trend Forest. Turn right to **Ertebølle**, the site of the 'Kitchen Middens' or rubbish tips which give their name to a period of Danish prehistory. Only traces of the middens remain but there is an interesting exhibition in the small building near the promontory. Many of the finds from the area together with a collection of Stone Age flint tools are on display in the museum at **Strandby**, the next point on the route. In the church are two model ships, one of which is Christian IV's naval vessel the *Justinia* and the other the training ship *København* given by King Frederik IX.

Continue along the coast road towards Hvalpsund taking the minor road into the village through Dollerup. **Hvalpsund** is the departure point for ferries to Salling, but turn left in the centre of the town following signs to Hessel, the last surviving thatched manor house in Denmark. It is now used as a museum. The building dates from the early eighteenth century when it was built to replace one destroyed by fire. Only the barn, believed to be constructed from ships timbers in 1650, survived the fire. The curved timbers can be seen above the threshing floor. About 1km (half a mile) further along the road is a car park which is the starting point for four waymarked walks around the Lovns peninsula. A leaflet and map is available locally.

Leave Hessel and return towards Hvalpsund, but turn right at the next junction towards Lovns. Continue along the road keeping the church on the right, then turn left and continue to the T-junction at the main Hvalpsund-Farsø road. Turn right and in about 1km (half a mile) turn right again through Gedsted to **Ålestrup**. Here the Danish Bicycle Museum is housed in the former home of the director of the local cycle factory. Not far from the museum is Den Jydske Rosenpark, the Jutland Rose Garden set in parkland. The town is also the centre for trout fishing in the Simested Å and Lerkenfeld Å and permits are available locally.

Leave the town in the direction of Hobro and immediately after crossing the bridge over the main road turn left onto the main Road 13 running north towards Store Binderup. At the major cross roads just beyond the village turn left on Road 29 towards Års and almost immediately on the right is the parking place for Borremose. This is an important Iron Age fortification, situated in the middle of the marsh land and dating back to 200BC, making it the oldest fortress in Denmark. A plan at the car park indicates the size of the settlement, and a further plan inside the remains of the ramparts indicates the position of the houses, etc. The stone road into the settlement is clearly visible. Just north from here is another boggy area known as **Rævemose**, or Fox Moor. During peat digging in 1891 a huge silver bowl weighing 17lb (8kg) known as the Gundestrup Cauldron, was found. There is a good copy of the bowl in the West Himmerland Museum in **Års**, about 3km (2 miles) north of Borremose and the original can be seen in the National Museum in Copenhagen. Also on display in Års is the largest collection of Stone Age amber in the country, a local historical collection and an art collection. Outside the church, rebuilt in 1921, is a large rune stone erected to commemorate a son of Gorm the Old. Inside is a granite font made by the local cycle repairer, Christian Andersen, from an old road roller! It is now considered to be one of the treasures of the church.

Leave Års on the road going east towards Gundestrup, continue to the main road and turn left in the direction of Ålborg. Turn left again in about 1km (half a mile) and continue through Sønderup and Suldrup to Sørup. Turn right at the crossroads and keep ahead to join the main E3 road, then turn left towards Støvring and Ålborg. At this point the route coincides with Route 9.

Follow the main road for about 5km (3 miles) and then turn off for Svenstrup. Through Svenstrup continue on the old main road towards Ålborg for a further 3km (2 miles), then turn left for Frejlev. Follow this road to just beyond Store Restrup where there is a lay-by and a sign 'Gangsti til Troldkirken' (Footpath to the Troll Church). This is one of the best preserved long-barrows in Denmark in a most beautiful situation. It is well worth the walk for the magnificent view from the barrow. The road continues through Sønderholm to the town of **Nibe**. Walk around the narrow streets of the old town situated near the fjord, which is now a conservation area. Nibe was once a famous herring port and a reminder of this can be seen in the church where the model ship is a simple herring fishing boat from 1703.

Continue towards **Sebbersund**, cross the bridge and go into the town. Turn left in the direction of Store Ajstrup, passing the old abbey church of Sebber Kloster on the left. Continue to Store Astrup and in the centre of the village turn left in the direction of Borup. This road traverses **Kyødale**, an area of outstanding beauty. At the T-junction in Borup turn right and follow the road to Lundby, then follow signs to the left to Brårup and Vindblæs. In Brårup go right to **Salling**, also known as Skarp Salling. At the main road turn right towards Løgstør, then immediately right again to the unusual church built of granite in AD1150. It is a basilica with three aisles and a large square choir with a large semi-circular sanctuary. There are many similarities to Viborg Cathedral and it is believed that many of the same craftsmen built the church here. After visiting the church return to the major road, cross over to Kornumvej and on to Kornum and left to return to Løgstør.

PLACES TO VISIT
EAST OF THE LIMFJORD

Løgstør
Local History Museum.
Canal Warden's House concerned with fishing and communications in the fjord, and life and work in the area.

Lendrup
Canal Keepers' Houses
Exhibits on history of the canal and the biology of the fjord.

Ranum
Vitskøl Kloster
Ruins and herb garden.

Ertebølle
Kitchen Midden
A Stone Age site.

Strandby Museum
Stone Age tools and church with interesting model ships.

Hvalpsund
Hessel Agricultural Museum in thatched manor house.

Ålestrup
Danish Bicycle Museum

Jutland Rose Garden
200 species in lovely park.

Års
Church and Borremose
Iron Age fortress from 200BC.

West Himmerland Museum
Copy of Gundestrup Cauldron, collection of Stone Age amber, local history and art collection.

Sønderholm
Troldkirken
Preserved long barrow.

Nibe
Old fishing village with picturesque streets.

Salling Church
Large Romanesque church with three aisles and square choir.

For cyclists and backpackers who wish to take their time in exploring the fine countryside in this area there is a long-distance path (Natursti) from Nibe to Hvalpsund, a distance of some 55km (34 miles). Part of it follows an old railway track and the rest is on minor roads. There are camp sites at Nibe, Års (halfway) and Hvalpsund. A map produced by the State Forestry Service is available locally.

3

NORTH-EAST JUTLAND

T he north-east of Jutland covers the area known as the Vendsyssel, the city of Ålborg, and East Himmerland as far south as the
Mariager Fjord. It is an area of old and new towns, small fishing
harbours, busy commercial ports and Viking remains. Denmark's
'wilderness' is in the far north, a place where the visitor can walk for
hours on end among the dunes without seeing another soul, and
south of Ålborg is the Rebild National Park, a beautiful area of steep
valleys and heather moors of special significance to American
visitors.

ROUTE 7 • AROUND THE FAR NORTH
The route starts in **Frederikshavn**, the largest town in the Vendsyssel. Originally a small fishing hamlet known as Fladstrand, it was
fortified during the Thirty Years War and was particularly important
because of its excellent natural harbour which has developed into a
busy modern ferry port. Outside the town are some attractive areas
for walkers including Bangsbo Deer Park and the Åsted river valley
offering a number of waymarked routes. In addition, the local tourist
office has details of short cycle rides in the area written in English and
accompanied by sketch maps.

The oldest part of Frederikshavn is Fiskerlyngen, the fishing
quarter, with narrow streets and eighteenth-century half-timbered
cottages with yellow-washed walls and red tiled roofs. Traditionally,
the mortar along the gables and ridges is whitewashed. On the coast
a little to the north of Fiskerlyngen is Nordre Skanse, the first
fortifications built here in 1627, and inland is the old half-timbered
Fladstrand Church. In the churchyard is a memorial to fishermen and
sailors lost at sea, and some British and German war graves from
World War II.

The central feature of the Fladstrand fortifications was
Krudttårnet (the Gunpowder Tower), built in 1686 in support of the
Danish fleet. It was moved in 1974 from its original site, 270m (294yd)
east of its present location, because of the enlargement of the

shipyard. A scheduled monument, the building now houses a museum with graphic material describing the history of the town and an exhibition of weapons and uniforms of the seventeenth century.

Frederikshavn Church is almost opposite Krudttårnet and was built in the late nineteenth century in Romanesque style. The light spacious interior is noted for the fine altarpiece painted by Michael Ancher depicting Jesus and His disciples by the Sea of Galilee. One of the model ships is a modern roll-on, roll-off ferry as built in the local shipyard. The new Kunstmuseum (Art Museum) is situated in Parallelvej behind the pedestrian street, near the new town hall and library.

A link to Route 9 can be made by going south along the coast Road E3 to Sæby, otherwise continue the present route by leaving the town via Søndergade, a continuation of the pedestrian street which then becomes Møllehus Alle where signs for Bangsbomuseet will be seen. This is the Local History Museum, in an attractive old manor house with collections of various items and pictures from Frederikshavn (1600-1900) and a special collection of ornaments made from human hair. There is a large World War II collection and an excellent nautical department. Next to the museum in Boolsen's Stenhave or Stone Garden is a collection of stone objects.

Leave the museum and drive along Bangsbovej to the cross roads at Gærumvej and turn left along Road 585 through Kilden to Cloostårnet, a 60m (197ft) high observation tower the top of which stands 160m (525ft) above sea level. A lift takes the visitor to the top, from where there is a view of virtually the whole of the Vendsyssel. About 5km (3 miles) further along the same road opposite the turning to Understed, turn right to the neolithic passage grave known as Blakshøj. One of the most impressive of its kind dating from about 3500BC. It is unusual in that a man can stand upright inside.

Return to the road and about 2½km (1½ miles) after passing Blakshøj turn right to Lendum. Turn left and continue through Tårs towards Vrå, passing Vrejlev Kloster and church en route. The monastery is now a private residence and the church is used as the parish church. Continue to the main road and turn left to **Brønderslev**, a modern town with a church dating back to 1150. The Store Vildmose, or Great Wild Bog, which was impenetrable until the beginning of the nineteenth century, and not fully accessible until the early 1920s, lies to the south-west of the town. Its history is illustrated in the Vildmosemuseet in Brønderslev. Store Vildmose is now one of the largest natural habitats in the country with a rich variety of bird and animal life.

Leave the town by the road which leads to Manna, noting the beautiful gardens in Banegårdspladsen (Station Square). In Manna, turn right towards **Tise** then take the next road on the right leading to Tise Church with a most unusual Renaissance pulpit situated in a

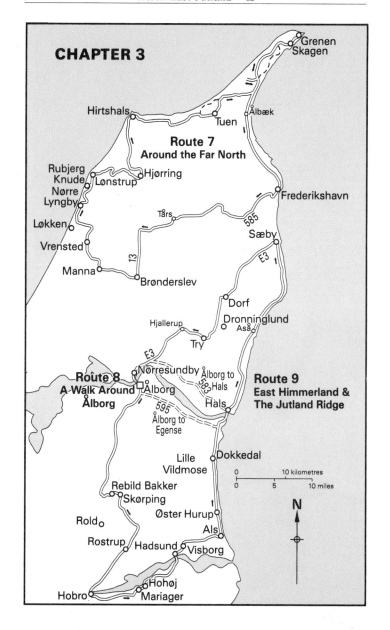

CHAPTER 3

Grenen
Skagen

Hirtshals

Tuen

Ålbæk

Route 7
Around the Far North

Rubjerg
Knude
Nørre
Lyngby

Lønstrup

Hjørring

Frederikshavn

Løkken

Tårs

585

Sæby

Vrensted

Manna

13

Brønderslev

E3

Dorf

Hjallerup

Dronninglund

Aså

Try

E3

Nørresundby

Ålborg to
Hals

585

Route 9
East Himmerland &
The Jutland Ridge

Route 8
A Walk Around
Ålborg

Ålborg

595

Hals

Ålborg to
Egense

Dokkedal

Lille
Vildmose

Rebild Bakker

Skørping

Rold

Øster Hurup

Als

Rostrup

Hadsund

Visborg

Hohøj

Hobro

Mariager

0   10 kilometres
0   5   10 miles

N

Rubjerg Lighthouse and the Drifting Sand Museum

Hjørring Museum and herb garden

gallery spanning the chancel arch. Continue to **Vrensted** where the church contains a rare crucifix from 1250 and a modern altarpiece painted by Niels Larsen-Stevns. The road continues north to Børglum Kloster, one of Denmark's oldest historic buildings which dominates the area and can be seen for miles. Continue towards **Løkken**, where the small local history museum is in one of the oldest houses, built by a small boat skipper using materials obtained in Norway and brought back by him in his boat. Continue to **Nørre Lyngby**, formerly a fishing hamlet and now a holiday resort. The church here replaces the old baroque church which had to be demolished because of coastal erosion. Some of the granite blocks from the old church have been used in the choir and the granite font was also in the old church.

Continue towards Lønstrup and detour to the old lighthouse at **Rubjerg Knude**. In 1968 it was converted into a museum containing displays relating to the shifting sands which have dominated the area. Return to the Lønstrup road and continue to turn left at Mårup

Kirkevej and follow the road to the church, abandoned because of the drifting sands and now in the care of the National Museum. The sixteenth-century Gothic altarpiece remains in the church, but most of the furnishings are now in the church at Lønstrup. The large anchor outside the west end is from the British frigate *Crescent* which sank off the coast in 1808. The anchor was only found in 1940, when it was placed here. **Lønstrup** is an old fishing hamlet which has managed to retain its character despite modern holiday developments. It nestles in a ravine formed in 1877 when torrential rains turned the local stream into a raging torrent causing trees and houses to be swept out to sea. A stone commemorating the event is situated in the town centre. Leave the town along Møllebakvej towards Skallerup Church and at the T-junction turn right towards Sønderlev where there is an amber and silver workshop and small amber museum.

From here, follow the road into **Hjørring**, the ancient capital of the Vendsyssel which has had a municipal charter since 1243. It has three medieval churches and a number of other old buildings. Four of the town's old school buildings together with the former deanery built in 1770 are now used to house the Vendsyssel Historical Museum. There is a unique collection of Iron Age pottery and a display of ecclesiastical art including some fine examples of medieval wood-carving. In the old deanery mews is a collection of nineteenth-century agricultural implements, an exhibition of country life being housed in the deanery itself. Hjørring Kunstmuseum has a collection of works connected with northern Jutland since 1945 and a comprehensive collection of works by Niels Larsen-Stevns. The main church in the town near the museum is dedicated to St Catherine, patron saint of the town. It was rebuilt in 1924 and the original Romanesque brick building now forms the transept of the present church. The pulpit, despite its appearance, was made in 1926. The oldest church is Skt Olai Kirke, also a Romanesque building but with no tower. Inside there is a Renaissance pulpit, a thirteenth-century crucifix and a sixteenth-century altarpiece. Skt Hans Kirke contains a wall painting from about 1350 representing St Christopher carrying the Christ child across the river. The altarpiece and pulpit were made by the same joiner who made the pulpit in Skt Olai Kirke.

Leave Hjørring and continue northwards to **Hirtshals** via Tornby, with the dunes to the left. Just before entering the town turn left, signed 'Fyret' (the Lighthouse), and continue towards the town with good views over the sea and the harbour. After more than a century of effort the inhabitants of Hirtshals were given the right to build a harbour in 1917 and the port came into operation in 1930. There are two important museums in the town. The Nordsø Museum is a salt water aquarium and museum of Danish sea fishing and Hirtshals Museum is housed in a nineteenth-century fisherman's home.

Leave the town past Nordsømuseet in the direction of Skagen but take the road on the left leading through Lilleheden Klitplantage and Uggerby Klitplantage to a T-junction and turn right for Uggerby. Turn left on reaching the Skagen road, and in about 5km (3 miles) turn left into Tversted. Pass Gammel Skagensvej and turn right by the tourist information sign, along Østervej. Go straight ahead (do not follow Skagen signs) through an area of scattered holiday homes and farms. Turn left at the give way sign and follow the road through the beautiful Tversted Plantage to the large car park at the end of the road. Cyclists will be able to continue their journey through the plantation, but motorists may not continue along the gravel roads. There are waymarked walks in the forest and some attractive small lakes which have been created by damming a stream.

Return to the main Skagen road and turn left towards Skagen again. At **Tuen** there is an eagle sanctuary (Ørnereservatet), which is internationally known for its sensational success in breeding the larger eagles and falcons. From here, take the road north towards Skiveren then turn right to the tiny Råbjerg Kirke built in the fourteenth century and having a rather special atmosphere due to its low interior height and beautifully carved baroque figures. The bell which hangs in a separate bell-frame is dated 1150 and is one of the oldest in Denmark. Continue along the road to cross the railway at Bunken, then turn left and follow the main road towards Skagen. After crossing the railway bridge at Hulsig, turn left again towards Råbjerg Mile, an area of 2sq km (about $\frac{3}{4}$sq mile) of unplanted natural dunes up to 40m (131ft) high, protected in their natural state as a reminder of the great sand drifts of the seventeenth and eighteenth century. The dunes are often called the 'Desert of Denmark' and move about 8m (26ft) every year in an easterly direction aided by the prevailing west winds. Visitors may walk through the dunes, and can link up with waymarked paths in the adjoining Bunken Klitplantage.

Back on the main road, continue north to Skagen. This very busy but exposed road is the only one for motor traffic. Cyclists should go into Hulsig and use the old road which is now the official cycle route into Skagen. On the way into the town, detour to visit Den Tilsandede Kirke (The Sand Filled Church) in the dunes north of Hulsig. Once the parish church of Skagen, with one of the longest naves in Denmark, it had to be abandoned in the eighteenth century because the sand had accumulated in such large quantities that the local people had to dig their way to church. Most of the building was demolished but the tower remains as a lasting monument to the time when the whole area was ravaged by sandstorms.

Skagen is the most northerly town in Denmark, situated at the base of the narrow spit of land known as Grenen separating the Skagerrak from the Kattegat, which has often been the victim of fierce

Having fun on one of Denmark's many beaches

storms and sand drifting. It received its charter in 1413. The major event which was to re-shape its history was the coming of the railway in 1890, followed by the building of the harbour in 1907. It is now internationally known for its artists' colony, tourism and industry, as well as for fishing.

On entering the town turn right along Drachmannsvej past Svallerbakken where the fishermen's wives used to stand and wait for their menfolk to come home. Nearby is Skagen Fortidsminder, a small open-air museum with old fishermen's houses, a windmill and a fishery museum. Follow Østre Strandvej beside the fishing harbour to the reconstruction of the old *vippefyr* or bascule light at the end of the road. Climb the steps to the top of the mound and the other light-

Råbjerg Mile

houses in the area can be seen: the nearby white lighthouse of 1747, the grey lighthouse further north towards Grenen, built in 1858 and the new Skagen West lighthouse, standing tall and slim and erected in 1956. Visitors may climb the tower of the grey lighthouse, which has 210 steps and is the tallest in the country. From the old bascule light, return to the town centre along Østerbyvej, passing typical Skagen houses. Some buildings still have the original half-timber work and tarred gables.

Owing to the special quality of the light reflected from the surrounding seas and dunes, Skagen became the centre of a school of painting in 1910, attracting a number of artists including Michael and Anna Ancher, P.S.Krøyer and Holger Drachmann. Michael and Anna Ancher's house in the town has been restored to preserve the special atmosphere of their home. Many of the works of the Skagen School of Painting can be seen here, and in the Skagens Museum which contains 1,000 drawings, paintings, sculpfures and handwork by artists working in Skagen between 1830 and 1930. It also contains the dining room from the Brøndums Hotel where the artists used to meet. More paintings are to be seen in Drachmann's House, a memorial to the painter and poet who lived here.

Oddevej leads north past the memorial for eight fishermen who lost their lives in a rescue attempt in 1862, to Grenen car park. From

PLACES TO VISIT
AROUND THE FAR NORTH

Frederikshavn
Krudttårnet Gunpowder Tower,
Bangsbomuseet Museum of
Local History.
Boolsens Stenhave
'Stone Garden' collection.

Brønderslev
Vildmosemuseet
Peat cutting tools, machinery.

Tise Church
Renaissance gallery pulpit.

Vrensted Church
Modern altarpiece painted by
Niels Larsen-Stevns.

Rubjerg Knude
Lighthouse Museum.

Hjørring
Vendsyssel Historical Museum,
three medieval churches,
museum of modern art.

Hirtshals
Nordsø Museum, Hirtshals
Museum.

Skagen
Fortidsminder (open-air
museum), Drachmann's House.

Grenen Art Museum
Museum on the tip of Denmark.

here it is a short step to Holger Drachmann's grave at the foot of the high sand dune nearby. It is also possible to walk out to the very tip of Denmark, **Grenen** otherwise known as the Skaw, but it is a long hard walk through the sands. The best way is to go by 'tractor bus' from the car park, a ride which takes about 15 minutes across the sands. The bus waits while passengers disembark to stand with one foot in the Baltic and one in the North Sea. This is one place where it is strictly forbidden to bathe, as the currents are extremely dangerous. There are plenty of safe bathing beaches in the nearby area, both on the North Sea coast and on the Baltic. On returning to the car park there is a small museum of modern art and a cafeteria with a good view of the Skaw. One more word of warning: do not be tempted to drive your car onto the beach, even though this is allowed. The sand is very soft in places and if you get stuck it is very expensive to be rescued by Falck, and travel insurance does not cover this eventuality.

Return to Skagen and continue along the main street, passing the very modern town hall and back to the main road. The hamlet of Højen, also known as Gammel Skagen, lies on the North Sea coast, and is now primarily the holiday resort area of the town. Return to Frederikshavn along the main road.

In And Around Ålborg

Ålborg is situated at the narrowest point of the Limfjord and its origins go back to Viking times. The largest city in North Jutland with a population of over 121,000, it is a busy modern commercial, industrial and cultural centre and makes an ideal base for exploring North Jutland's varied scenery; the city well deserves at least a day to itself.

ROUTE 8 • A WALK AROUND ÅLBORG

A good starting place is the city tourist information office in Østerågade in the heart of the city, where brochures describing cycle rides in the neighbourhood and walks around the city can be obtained. Across the street is Jens Bang's House, one of Europe's finest examples of Renaissance domestic architecture. Built in 1624 by a wealthy merchant and ship owner, this ostentatious house on the site of the former harbour has housed Ålborg's oldest pharmacy for over 300 years and its historic wine cellar is the meeting place of the guild of Christian IV. The carvings on the façade are worth studying before turning right along Østerågade to the late baroque rådhus which lies to the right in Gammel Torv. Built between 1759 and 1762, it carries the national coat of arms and the motto of King Frederik V over the main entrance, which is flanked by the only remaining gas lamps in Ålborg and overlooks the oldest square in the city. Cross this square along Strandstien to Algade, then right past Grotums Gaard, a school from 1738 to 1911, to Budolfi Domkirke (St Botolph's Cathedral), named after the English patron saint of seamen.

The building dates mainly from the fifteenth century with older parts from the eleventh century, although the baroque spire housing a carillon is later (1779). The interior is of interest with a seventeenth-century altarpiece and pulpit and a variety of carvings and paintings. To the west of the cathedral, still in Algade, is the Ålborg Historical Museum with fine collections of local history, antiquities, glassware and silver, also an outstanding furnished Renaissance room from 1602. Turn back through an alley between the post office and Den Danske Provinsbank, then right along Adelgade to C.W. Obels Plads on the left, the site of a tobacco factory until 1896. The red and white half-timbered building on the right is part of Brix's Gaard, dating from 1580 but with remains of a medieval stone building. On the opposite side of the square is the entrance to the former monastery of the Holy Ghost, an important foundation from the fifteenth century with sections for both monks and nuns who cared for the sick and aged; this work still continues.

Return to Adelgade and through the narrow stepped alley known as Latinergyden, originally a watercourse, then into Gravensgade, a pedestrian area. Turn left then right into Algade again. At the far end is Vesterbro in which are two well known sculptures, the *Goose Girl* (Gerhard Henning 1937) and the *Cimbrian Bull* (A.J.Bundgård 1937). Turn right towards the *Bull* then right again, along Bispensgade to a small fountain, left into Vesterå for a short distance, then to the right between small houses along Nymøllestræde, another old watercourse, to Jomfru Ane Gade, a short street lined with restaurants and with a special atmosphere.

On the other side of the street is a large building which formerly housed Ålborg Cathedral School. A gate leads through the old school yard to a warehouse converted into the Jomfru Ane Theatre. Continue past a multi-storey car park into Ved Stranden, turning right then right again into Maren Turis Gade, an area of the city which contains a number of beautifully restored sixteenth- and seventeenth-century houses and warehouses, including one of the best preserved Renaissance merchant's houses in Denmark, Jørgen Olufsen's House. Go through the yard of this house to Østerågade from which the starting point of the walk can be reached.

Further exploration of the city can include the large white gable-ended building of Aalborghus Castle in Slotspladsen. This dates from the mid-sixteenth century, with a large courtyard, dungeon, underground passages and ramparts. It was never used as a fortress, becoming instead the residence of the king's representative. It now houses administrative offices. Not far from Aalborghus, along Nytorv and Nørregade, is the new civic centre, and in the same area are a number of well restored houses of varying ages, particularly in Nørregade where a group of reconstructed buildings form an especially attractive feature. Much effort by the city of Ålborg is being put into preserving the old houses to form model residential areas, in collaboration with the Society for the Preservation of Old Houses. Before leaving the city itself, mention must be made of the Limfjord railway which operates steam trains from Ålborg station along a stretch of former private railway to Grønlandshavnen, a 40 minute journey. The line is operated one day a week in summer by the North Jutland branch of the Danish Railway Club.

Not far from the city centre is Tivoliland, an amusement park set in beautiful gardens with entertainments, restaurants, sideshows and much more, for the whole family. By way of contrast on Kong Christians Alle, part of the city ring road is the Nordjyllands Kunstmuseum (North Jutland Art Museum) with permanent and changing exhibitions of modern and contemporary art, both Danish and foreign. A sculpture garden and a special section for children are included. Near the museum, on Skovbakken, is the Ålborg Tower, 105m (344ft) high, from which outstanding views over the city and fjord can be seen. Running south from the ring road along Hobrovej a turning on the right, Mølleparkvej, leads to Ålborg Zoo, Scandinavia's second largest zoo, set in beautiful surroundings in a park. Many of the 1,500 animals from all over the world wander freely, and a new sealion and penguin pool has underwater observation windows.

About 2km (a mile) south, by the Mariendals windmill is the Danmarks Tekniske Museum, a department of the Danish Science Museum with exhibitions relating to science and technology with special emphasis on communications. Continue south along Hobrovej for about another 2km (a mile) and a right fork leads into Nibevej along which will be found Vandland (Waterland). Opened in 1988, this is described as a covered water paradise, with an enormous indoor wave pool, outdoor heated pool, sauna and exercise rooms and much more to provide activities for the whole family.

North of the Limfjord is the neighbouring town of **Nørresundby**, reached either by a road bridge from the city or by a new motorway tunnel to the east. On leaving the tunnel, take the road through Nørresundby and along Thistedvej, then right at traffic lights into Viaduktvej, over the railway, then left along Voerbjergvej to Frederik Raschsvej. A right turn here leads to the Sundby-Hvorup Parish Historical Museum in a former tied farmhouse. Exhibits include farm implements and textiles, and there is a herb garden containing over 250 species of spice and medicinal herbs from all over the world.

From the museum follow the road to Lindholmsvej and turn left, later right, along Højens Alle to Lindholm Høje. This is the site of the largest known cemetery and settlement in Denmark dating from the late Iron Age and Viking Age. There are nearly 700 graves covering a period from about AD500 to AD1000, and some 150 of these are surrounded by stone enclosures in the shape of a ship. Remains of a Viking settlement and Viking fields can be seen, and the whole site lies on a sloping hillside with views over the fjord and surrounding countryside.

ROUTE 9 • EAST HIMMERLAND AND THE JUTLAND RIDGE

Starting in Ålborg, go south on the Hobro road to Støvring, using either the E3 motorway or the road through Svenstrup, which joins the E3 at the end of the motorway section. About 6km (4 miles) beyond Støvring turn left onto the road to Skørping. The lovely winding road goes through **Rebild Bakker**, a hilly area with steep-sided valleys providing superb walking country. Ample car parking is available and a leaflet in English describes a number of waymarked walks through the neighbouring hills and woods whose particular scenery results from the melting of the Ice Age glacier which terminated at this point. In 1912 a group of Danish-Americans purchased some 247 acres of moorland hills to the north of Rold Skov

PLACES TO VISIT IN AND AROUND ÅLBORG

Jens Bang's House
Renaissance town house (1624) with historic wine cellar.

Rådhus
Late baroque town hall.

Budolfi Domkirke
(St Botolph's Cathedral)
Mainly fifteenth century with baroque spire and carillon (1779).

Historical Museum
Fine collections of local history, glass and silver ware.

Monastery of the Holy Ghost
Fifteenth-century foundation which still cares for the sick and aged. May be visited.

Jørgen Olufsen's House
Renaissance merchant's home and warehouse.

Aalborghus Castle
Mid-sixteenth century, planned as fortress but never used as such.

Tivoliland
Family amusement park.

Nordjyske Kunstmuseum
Exhibitions of modern and contemporary art, sculpture garden and childrens' section.

Ålborg Tower
Viewing platform. Outlook from Skovbakken over city and fjord.

Danmarks Tekniske Museum
Department of Danish Science Museum specialising in communications.

Vandland
New aquatic recreation complex.

Sundby-Hvorup Parish Historical Museum
Nørresundby
A collection arranged as furnished rooms in former farmhouse.

Lindholm Høje
Nørresundby
Largest known late Iron Age and Viking settlement and burial ground.

(Rold Forest) and presented them to the Danish nation as a National Park. Since that time, American Independence Day has been celebrated by immigrants to the USA and their descendants at a festival held here. There are many features in the park to mark this link between the two countries, including the Lincoln Log Cabin and the Local History and Folk Music Museum.

Continue to **Skørping** and turn right. In about 2km (a mile) is the entrance to Den Jyske Skovhave (Jutland Arboretum), a collection of all Danish tree species and many from abroad. The road passes through part of the Rold Skov, the largest forest in Denmark which although covering some 16,000 acres is only part of the enormous trackless forest which once covered most of Himmerland. The area contains very varied scenery including woodland, meadows, bogs, heaths and lakes, and traces of ancient man show that it had been inhabited over 4,000 years ago. A number of springs exist, whose water emerges at a constant temperature of about 8°C (46°F). This gives rise to a rich variety of unusual plant and insect life. One such spring is Store Blåkilde, found by following a signpost on the right of the road about 3km (2 miles) beyond the arboretum. In some parts of the forest trees up to 300 years old can be found, and many legends abound.

Leaving the forest area, follow the road towards Astrup, but turn right past Villestrup Manor, the main wing of which was built in 1538 on an island in an artificial lake. The manor is private but the public may visit the very fine baroque gardens known as 'Willestrup Barokhave' which date from 1750.

At the next road junction the main route goes right and immediately left towards Rostrup. However, a detour may be made by omitting the left turn and going through Arden to **Rold**, to visit the Circus Museum, located in the former winter training quarters of the Circus Miehe. Exhibits illustrate circus costumes and life.

Either go direct from Rold to Hobro along Road E3, or if omitting the detour, continue along the road through **Rostrup**, with its church containing a unique carved pulpit dated 1544. About 4 to 5km (2 to 3miles) beyond the village, a tall radio mast can be seen on the right of the road, on top of a hill called Tinghøj, a name which indicates that it was the meeting place for the local 'elders' or council in former days. At Valsgård, turn right and follow the major road into Hobro.

Hobro is a small town in a superb situation at the head of Mariager Fjord, and is the commercial and industrial centre of the region with a number of department stores and shops in attractive pedestrian streets. The imposing and rather unusual nineteenth-century church was designed by M.G.B. Bindesbøll, who also designed the Thorvaldsen Museum in Copenhagen. Externally, the alternate bands of red and yellow bricks are very distinctive and the tower, with a steeple, is positioned at the east end of the building. In 1931 the artist Joakim Skovgaard was commissioned to design a new altar and ornamentation, but it was not until 1952 that his son Johan actually completed a superb mosaic and altar. The site was probably occupied by a church as long ago as about 1100, and a number of pieces of furniture from earlier churches have been incorporated into the present building, notably the seventeenth-century pulpit and altar candle sticks and a bell dating from about 1400.

Although the town was founded in AD980, there are few listed buildings. One such is the old brewery in Adelgade which now accommodates the tourist information office. The oldest preserved building in the town was built in 1827 as a grocer's shop in Adelgade, but was moved to its present position in Vestergade where it houses

Mariager Museum, in the courtyard

the Hobro Museum with fine collections of glass, porcelain and china, together with a splendid collection of local silver. In addition, many finds from the Viking settlement at Fyrkat have been deposited here. From Hobro a link may be made to Route 11 at Sjørring via Roads E3 and 517 through Sønder Onsild.

Just outside Hobro, signed along the road past the museum, is Fyrkat Viking Fort discovered as a result of aerial photography. In the form of a ring, it was probably built around AD1000, in a strategic

position at the head of the fjord to the south-west of the present town of Hobro. During the 1950s the site was excavated by the National Museum and re-created to show the circular rampart and other details. During 1982-5 a full size reproduction of a Viking house was constructed using contemporary materials and methods, and the whole site forms a fascinating insight into the Viking period and way of life. Demonstrations of weaving and carving are often staged on the site. Nearby is Fyrkat Møllegård (Mill Farm), now a restaurant. The watermill alongside the car park is still in operation.

The local scenery on either side of the fjord near Hobro is quite special. On the north side, the Bramslev Bakker (hills) stand high above the water, offering many fine waymarked walks through juniper covered hills, including one to Hjerritsdal watermill. The views over the fjord are superb. With care it is possible to drive from Valsgård through the forest road past Kielstrup Sø (lake) to the tiny fishing hamlet of Stinesminde. The road is narrow and steep in places, but makes a lovely trip on a summer evening with the light reflected on the water. The route may be used by cyclists, but an easier way for cars would be along minor roads from Ove.

Lying on the south of the fjord is Østerskoven, one of Denmark's beautiful self-sown beech forests. From the town, follow Mariagervej then turn left along Amerikavej, passing Hobro Sports Centre and the new Youth Hostel on the right. Traffic lights mark a narrow road uphill, then past a nursing home to park in a space on the left in the woods. Walk down through the woods to the shore of the fjord. Leaflets with maps to show the footpaths are available from the tourist information office in Hobro. A restaurant (*traktørstedet*) is situated near the car park. From the car park return past the nursing home but instead of going to the right down the narrow hill, keep straight ahead along Kirketoften to the main road, and turn left towards **Mariager**, 'Town of the Roses', characterised by its cobbled streets and timber framed houses, a beautiful abbey church and a fine museum, with the added attractions of a busy and interesting harbour and a vintage steam railway running 17km (10½ miles) to Handest.

The abbey church was built in the fifteenth century as part of a nunnery, and was given to the town as a parish church at the Reformation. Although it has been largely rebuilt it is a fine lofty building with a superb carved altarpiece depicting the Last Supper and Crucifixion, surrounded by the eleven apostles. A memorial tablet to the last abbess is in the south transept and the tower contains a small museum with some of the original wood sculptures from the abbey church. The abbey building is now used as a court house and is not open to the public.

Mariager Museum is in an eighteenth-century merchant's house and has a good collection of domestic utensils and tools, also prehistoric artefacts, all from the immediate neighbourhood. A model shows the reconstruction of the abbey church, and the building also serves as an art gallery and community centre. From the courtyard may be seen the beautifully preserved long gallery. The Hotel Postgaarden was originally the eighteenth-century vicarage, becoming an inn in the nineteenth century. Other buildings of note include Apothekergaarden built over a fifteenth-century basement, Bugges Gårde (1735), Bryggergaarden, an old brewery, and the sixteenth-century grammar school in Kirkebakken, with lime trees trimmed in two 'storeys'. The little nineteenth-century town hall has its gable topped by the town's symbol, a crane.

Just outside the town is **Hohøj** topped by one of the biggest burial mounds in the country from which superb views can be obtained over the fjord, and all around this area is evidence of prehistoric occupation in the form of burial mounds, passage graves, barrows and stone circles.

Leave the town by the road alongside the fjord to Assens and Sønder Hadsund, where a bridge crosses the fjord into **Hadsund** itself. The local museum in the town has a varied collection of oriental items, textiles, toys and hand tools, also old cameras. After crossing the bridge, turn right towards Als, and at **Visborg** take a minor road left, signed to Korup, turning right past Visborggård, a fine Renaissance building from 1575 rising directly out of a moat, now in use as an institution. Continue along the same road towards **Als**, where a mid-nineteenth-century thatched half-timbered building just south of the church is the setting for the local museum giving a splendid impression of a late nineteenth-century country home in south-east Himmerland.

Continue along the coast road north to **Øster Hurup**, a small fishing harbour which is also a resort with Sommerland, a pleasure park with entertainment and activities for the whole family, and holiday houses and a camp site. North of here the fenced road follows the coast, passing an extensive area of heath and woodland, with salt flats on the seaward side. The whole area, known as **Lille Vildmose**, was a peat bog and in 1936 the northern part was bought by the state, drained, the peat layer removed and the land brought under cultivation. During World War II this was extended to include the growing of potatoes after peat digging. A high single sand dune marks the approach to the town of **Dokkedal**, the high point known as Mulbjerge 48m (157ft) high giving good views out to sea. Keep straight on to Egense, to reach a ferry which crosses the Langerak, the stretch of water which leads to Ålborg and the Limfjord. This ferry can be quite busy and is small but carries caravans. The crossing time is only 5 minutes but delays are possible.

The Langerak ferry connects with **Hals** on the north of the waterway. It is a pleasant town first mentioned in the tenth century as the scene of battles, owing to its strategic importance at the fjord entrance. There are few signs of the fortifications which once existed, but a local museum is located in the old arsenal dating from 1812. In the square two huge whale jawbones form an arch, and beyond the square is the church which contains a fourteenth-century incense vessel. At the road junction, take the right turning towards Hou, passing more plantations and heath, with holiday homes and picnic places. A good cycle path runs through the area, with more sand dunes and salt marsh, much of it protected. At Voerså turn right along

The old bascule light at Skagen

Nordøstvejen with views over the water towards the island of Læsø, and follow the coast road to the town of **Sæby**.

On reaching the ring road (Søndre Ringvej) turn right towards the harbour and left into Strandgade, and there is a car park near the church. The town dates back to Viking times, and has kept its very pleasant atmosphere ever since. This is what probably attracted many artists and writers to the town, including Henrik Ibsen at the end of the nineteenth century. The church was originally the monastery church of the Carmelite foundation set up in 1462, which explains the large size of the present church. At the Reformation the monastery was dissolved and subsequently the buildings were demolished, only the church remaining. The magnificent altarpiece dates from the early sixteenth century, but of greater interest are the rare late medieval murals, painted over at the Reformation but uncovered during restoration in 1905-6. The impressive Renaissance pulpit has a canopy with the date 1577. Other interesting features include a ship model so common to Danish churches. The one in Sæby Church bears the name *Trekroner* and the date 1694. The museum occupies what is known as Konsul Ørums Gård, a fine half-timbered house dating from the eighteenth century, and contains interesting exhibits showing the development and everyday life of the market town from the fifteenth century to the present day. The house stands at the

Fishermen unloading their catch in one of Denmark's many harbours

junction of Algade and Søndergade, the centre of the old town in which are many of the well preserved houses from the eighteenth and nineteenth centuries. Just along Søndergade is the bridge over the river, the Sæby Å, from which may be seen the attractive seventeenth-century watermill.

Leave the town along Ålborgvej and turn right along Sæbygårdvej, passing under the main E3 road to Sæbygård. This beautifully preserved and furnished Renaissance manor, the oldest wing of which dates from about 1570, was once the country house of the Bishop of Børglum. It now contains one of the most important collections of textiles from 1700, and has been owned by the same family since 1682. In the nearby woods a mineral spring was discovered in 1883, but the spa sanatorium eventually went bankrupt.

Return to the main road and continue to Dybvad, then turn left to Idskov and Voer. To the left Voer Church has a splendid memorial to a noble family from about 1600 and an altarpiece and family pews dating from about 1621. Nearby is Voergård, one of the finest and most opulent Renaissance mansions in Denmark, much of it unchanged since its building in 1591. It is not a museum but houses a unique and valuable collection of Louis XV and Louis XVI furniture, works by El Greco, Rubens, Rafael, Goya, Hals and Watteau, and porcelain and china which belonged to Napoleon I, Louis XVI and Marie Antoinette, mainly items brought from France by the last owner, Count Oberbeck-Clausen.

From Voergård turn right along the minor road towards Dorf, through the village to the major road. Turn left, and in a short distance right to **Dorf**. The windmill appears on the hill ahead, but take the first left down a narrow lane past the old watermill in the valley. This lane leads back to the major road, where the route turns right and continues for 2 to 3km (1$\frac{1}{2}$ to 2 miles). Then after a bend in the road turn right along Kirkevej towards Dronninglund Kirke. This is a gravel road through the lovely beech forest of **Dronninglund** Storskov which lies at the southern end of the Jutland Ridge. Continue to where the road becomes asphalted, passing on the right a very old cottage, and at the T-junction near Dronninglund Kunstcentrum (Art Centre) turn right towards Dronninglund Castle and church where the car park is across the moat. The castle was formerly the convent of Hundslund whose origins go back to 1268, but after the Reformation it was bought in 1690 by Queen Charlotte Amalie and renamed Dronninglund. It was rebuilt in neo-classic style in 1786 and is now an exclusive conference centre and hotel. The convent church which became the parish church in the Middle Ages is part of the main building, and contains some beautiful and interesting frescoes from about 1520 and pulpit and altarpiece from the end of the sixteenth

PLACES TO VISIT IN EAST HIMMERLAND AND THE JUTLAND RIDGE

Rebild Bakker National Park
Lincoln Log Cabin and Museum.

Skørping
Den Jyske Skovhave (arboretum), Rold Skov.

Villestrup Manor
Baroque gardens.

Rold
Circus Museum.

Hobro
Church with mosaic altarpiece.
Museum with local cultural and
historical collections.
Fyrkat Viking Fort and recon-
structed Viking house.

Mariager
Abbey church with beautiful
altarpiece and old wood carvings.
Museum of local history and
culture. Steam Vintage Railway.

Hadsund
Museum of local history.

Als
Thatched house with museum.

Hals
Local museum in old arsenal.

Sæby
Watermill, old monastery church,
local history museum. Sæbygård
Manor.

Voer
Interesting church, Voergård
Mansion.

Dronninglund
Castle and church. Church and
grounds open.

Try
Nineteenth-century farmhouse
museum.

century. The grounds and church are open to the public.

On leaving the castle turn left towards Hjallerup then left again
before turning right at the main crossroads into **Try**. By the village
pond is Try Museum with a smithy, farmhouse and old handicrafts
school. The excellent farmhouse interior shows the lifestyle of a local
farming family in about 1800. Follow the road towards Hjallerup, and
turn left along the main road back to Nørresundby and Ålborg.

NOTE: This route may conveniently be divided into two shorter
routes by using Road 583 from Ålborg to Hals and Road 595 from
Ålborg to Egense, so by-passing the ferry link from Egense to Hals.

4
EAST JUTLAND
THE GREEN HEART OF
DENMARK

In and Around Viborg

Viborg is officially in North Jutland but much of the surrounding country is in East Jutland and it makes a good base for touring the area. There are good major and minor roads linking the lakes and woodlands, hills and moors, including the 1,000-year-old Hærvej running south to the German border.

The town itself has a beautiful setting beside two lakes and is dominated by the magnificent twin towers of the *domkirke*. Its history goes back as far as the eighth century when Viborg was a trading centre and pagan place of sacrifice. It later became the coronation place of the Danish kings, a bishop's residence and market town. Modern Viborg has attractive pedestrian streets, and a stroll through old Viborg makes a good start to a tour of the area. The tourist information office in Nytorv has an attractive booklet in English describing a walk and the buildings to be seen, together with details of their history.

ROUTE 10 • VIBORG TOWN WALK

This walk begins at the tourist office in Nytorv. The houses on this side of the square are owned by the municipality and are being restored in order to preserve the old town atmosphere. Notable buildings in the square are Stillingsgaard, a large early nineteenth-century house in classical style now used by the local authority for offices. The Svaneapotek is Viborg's oldest 'business' established in 1573, while the building next to the tourist office known as the Amtsgården was built in 1757 in Danish baroque style. Go through Nytorvgyde, passing an old warehouse. Look up at the old sign above the archway

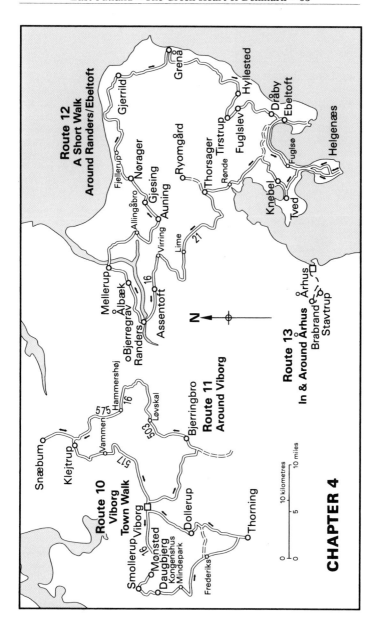

and look into the courtyard.

Cross the bottom of Nytorvgyde to the cathedral whose entrance is on the south side. This church, after being subjected to numerous restorations was re-opened in 1876 having been restored to the Romanesque style of the original building. The frescoes on the walls were painted by Joakim Skovgaard in 1901-6, and he also did the paintings on the ceilings in 1912-13. Of the original cathedral furnishings there is a fine late Gothic crucifix opposite the pulpit and a large fifteenth-century seven-branched candlestick. The light fittings in the nave were created by Skovgaard in antique style and the altar was modelled in the style of the altar at Sahl, typical of the Valdemar period. The medieval altarpiece was donated by Karup Church.

Opposite the south door of the cathedral, across Gammel Torv (Old Square) is the old town hall. It now houses the Skovgaard Museum. Joakim Skovgaard came from an artistic family and the museum contains a great variety of work from this family, including paintings, sculpture, furniture and silver, the most prized exhibit being a collection of Joakim's sketch books and the original drawings for many of the cathedral frescoes.

Facing the west door of the cathedral is the eighteenth-century Cathedral School or Latin School. Beside it is the Latin Garden, a peaceful spot in the middle of the town. The headmaster's summer house, a small brick house from 1780, can still be seen in one corner. There are also memorials to the ornithologist H.C. Mortensen who introduced the system of bird ringing, and to Steen Steensen Blicher, the Jutland poet, preacher and author.

Walk down Store Skt Mikkels Gade to Søndre Sogns Kirke, a lovely brick building from about 1250 with a most beautiful gilded altarpiece with painted side wings which close over the gilded centre panel. This is probably Viborg's greatest treasure, dating from 1520, and was originally in Copenhagen Palace chapel, being given to the church together with the pulpit in 1728 by Frederik IV. Also in the church are some 200 pew ends, all painted with biblical scenes.

Return up Store Skt Mikkels Gade and into Skt Mathias Gade, then to Hjultorvet where the District Museum is located in a nineteenth-century building formerly headquarters of the Heath Society. The museum contains workshops and products from the town's craftsmen, and an interesting exhibit on 'The Town and its Citizens'.

Viborg Tourist Office has a number of suggested routes suitable for cyclists. The tour suggested here is a figure of eight route which can be easily split into two sections. The first part is suitable for cyclists but the second section may be rather long. Also, Route 17 starts at Viborg.

ROUTE 11 • AROUND VIBORG

Leave Viborg by Road 16 towards Holstebro, and about 4km (2 miles) beyond the village of Ravnstrup is a large stone on the left beside the road opposite a lay-by. The stone marks the exact geographical centre of Jutland. Continue to **Mønsted** and follow tourist signs for Mønsted Kalkgruber. These underground galleries are believed to have a total length of some 35km (22 miles) and all have been excavated by hand to extract the chalk which was brought to the surface to make lime. Work began in about AD1000 and there are three galleries, the lowest being about 35m (115ft) below ground level. A museum explains the history of the mining operations and the bats which inhabit the caves.

Continue in the direction of Stoholm, to **Smollerup** Church which has an interesting beehive shaped bell, the oldest in Denmark. 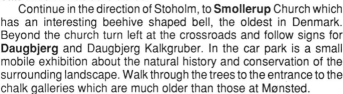 Beyond the church turn left at the crossroads and follow signs for **Daugbjerg** and Daugbjerg Kalkgruber. In the car park is a small mobile exhibition about the natural history and conservation of the surrounding landscape. Walk through the trees to the entrance to the chalk galleries which are much older than those at Mønsted.

After leaving the mines continue to Daugbjerg, cross the main road and carry straight on passing Daugbjerg Dås over to the left. It is said that the chalk mines extend under that hill. Turn left in the direction of Thorning, and in a short distance Kongenshus (The King's House) will be seen. Here is a small museum dealing with the struggles to reclaim and cultivate the extensive areas of heath and moorland in this part of Jutland during the last 200 years. Past the house is a gravel road leading to a car park. Walk from here down a path through a moorland valley lined with memorial stones carved with inscriptions denoting the various parishes involved in the efforts to reclaim the land. There are about 10km (6 miles) of roads through the park area.

After driving through the park to the exit on the other side, turn left then left again onto the road to Grønhøj. Turn right along the main road to Frederiks and continue to **Thorning** to visit the District Museum illustrating the history of civilisation, with many relics of Steen Steensen Blicher. The museum is in the former vicarage which was Blicher's home and where he wrote many of his works. From Thorning follow Road 13 north through Neder Hvam and turn left into Lysgård. Alternatively, at Frederiks take the first turning on the left past the church, which was built in 1766 by Frederik VII for the 'potato Germans'. Continue to Sjørup and turn left to Lysgård.

At Lysgård is the old schoolroom known as 'E Bindstouw', signed from the road. On his walking tours, Blicher often called on the schoolmaster and some of his experiences here are recalled in his collection of poems and short stories called '*E Bindstouw*' (The

Viborg Cathedral and the Latin School Garden

Knitting Room).

Opposite the museum follow the road to Katballe, turn left and in 1km (half a mile) right to **Dollerup**. The Dollerup Bakker (hills) and Hald Sø (lake) can be seen ahead. The hills mark the edge of the moraine where the advancing ice stopped before the glacier melted. In fact the whole of the landscape in this part of Jutland results from the action of the glaciers during and following the Ice Age. Continue down the road, turn right in Dollerup and continue towards **Hald**. The *kro* on the lake shore (Niels Bugges Kro) noted for its superb food is named after Niels Bugge, leader of the Jutland rebellion in 1351, who built a fortification known as Hald on the lake shore opposite the site of the inn. The manor is now owned by the State Forestry Service and part of it is leased as a cultural centre. A large barn has been restored and houses an excellent exhibition about the geology, history and biology of the area. A guided walk leaflet on the area with an English translation is available from the Viborg Tourist Office. An interesting line of high stone blocks leads from the manor house to the road, marking the boundary of the original royal game reserve. At the main road turn right then first left through Hald Ege and back to Viborg.

The second part of the tour begins at the bridge separating Nørresø and Søndersø. On the north side lies a park surrounding the old castle mounds of Borgvold. Cross the bridge away from the town and take the second turning on the right, towards the Youth Hostel, then turn right to Asmild Church, once an abbey church built in the twelfth century. The superb pulpit and altar are dated 1625, the pews are from the sixteenth century and the screen and font cover are eighteenth century. Elaborately carved doors lead into the tower room which was once a chapel of rest. From a well in the grounds some gold objects were recovered which had been hidden by the nuns at the time of the Reformation.

Along the road past the Youth Hostel a number of grave mounds will be seen on the left. Continue through Bruunshåb towards Rindsholm, go under the main road and turn left, then left again back over the main road, following signs to Sønder Rind then left again towards Vindum, passing through Vindum Skov. Shortly after turning right beyond the woods notice the church on the left with its unusual onion spire and a delightful manor house beside it. Continue down the road to Tange, going straight ahead at the next two crossroads, then turn left in Tange itself towards Bjerringbro. Follow signs from Tange to Elmuseet, passing under the railway bridge near the electricity sub-station.

Elmuseet is a most interesting museum located in Gudenåcentralen, Denmark's largest hydro-electric power station built in 1920 when the Guden river was dammed to create the Tange lake. The turbine hall which is still in operation can be seen and there is a

PLACES TO VISIT IN AND AROUND VIBORG

Nytorv
Fine preserved old buildings.

Viborg Cathedral
Restored building with twentieth-century paintings and frescoes by J. Skovgaard.

Skovgaard Museum
Collection of works by family, housed in old town hall.

Søndre Sogns Kirke
Thirteenth-century parish church with outstanding altarpiece and painted pews.

Viborg District Museum
Craft workshops, products and exhibitions of antiquities, etc.

Mønsted Kalkgruber
Old limestone caverns used for quarrying with museum.

Smollerup Church
Oldest bell in Denmark.

Daugbjerg Kalkgruber
1,100-year-old tunnels with guided tour (in Danish only).

Thorning Museum
In Blicher's former vicarage.

Lysgård
'E Bindstouw'
Old schoolroom museum with Blicher relics.

Dollerup Bakker
National Trust area.

Hald
Ruins, walks and exhibition of natural history. Niels Bugges Kro.

Asmild Church
Twelfth-century former abbey church with fine interior.

Bjerringbro
Gudenådalens Museum
Viking artefacts.

Fussingø
Lake, manor, ruins, old baroque garden, eighteenth-century manor house, watermill and forest trails.

Snæbum
Jættestuerne
Stone Age passage graves.

Klejtrup
Klejtrup Sø World Map.

Bjerregrav
Hvolris archaeological site.

Tjele
Denmark's oldest manor house.

pleasant path around part of the lake which is a conservation area. A short detour may be made by driving along the lake shore towards Ans where there is a good picnic area. From this point it is possible to link up with Route 14 via Grønbæk to Grauballe.

From the museum take the road to **Bjerringbro** where the Gudenådalens Museum contains replicas of the silver-coated axe and gilded bronze harness mount with superb Viking ornamentation which were found nearby at Mammen. The Gudenå which flows through the town is the longest river in Denmark. Leave the town along Road 575 north through Lee and at the junction with Road 503

'E Bindstouw' (The Knitting Room)

turn right through Løvskal to Skjern Church and right again to **Ålum**. By continuing straight ahead through Tånum to Randers, Route 12 may be joined.

Turn left at Ålum Church then take the second turning to the left near the thatched forester's cottage, continuing down hill through the forest to Fussing Sø. At the bottom of the hill on the right, just where the road bends left, is a car park. From here it is a short walk to the ruins of the original Fussingø Manor and the remains of an old baroque garden. There are waymarked paths from the car park to the gardens of the 'new' late eighteenth-century Fussingø Hovedgaard (manor house) and to waymarked forest trails. A forest service leaflet with details of the walks (in Danish) is available. Turn left by the manor house and in about 1km (half a mile) another car park near the watermill gives access to more walks. Continue to the main Road 16 and turn left through Hammershøj then right along Road 575 through Vorning in the direction of Sønder Onsild. At the T-junction with Road 517, turn left then right to Lindum and on through Lindum Skov, bearing right through Hvornum to the main Hobro-Skive road. On the right just before the crossroads is Lillemølle Fuglepark, a bird park. Cross straight over the main road and continue to **Snæbum**. Keep right, passing a small lake on the left, and follow signs for 'Jættes-tuerne' to the left along Tværvej. At the T-junction turn right along

Dollerup Bakker, overlooking Hald Sø

Hvilsomvej and park at the farm on the right. Up a track from the farm is a group of late Stone Age passage graves dating from around 3000BC.

Return through Snæbum to Hvornum and turn right towards **Klejtrup** and visit Verdenskortet, the world map by the shore of Klejtrup Sø. This was created in 1944-69 by a Danish-American Søren Poulsen, using only a shovel and a wheelbarrow, and takes the form of a map of the world, each country being laid out in shallow water at the edge of the lake.

From the village take a left fork to Troestrup and **Bjerregrav**. On approaching Bjerregrav, the Hvolris archaeological site will be seen on the right. Finds include Stone Age pit houses right through to remains of farm communities from the Middle Ages. From Hvolris, turn towards Troestrup again but take the right fork towards Hersom and Vammen, and follow signs to Tjele, claimed to be the oldest manor house in Denmark — the oldest surviving part dates from 1380. The remainder was restored in 1585 following the civil war of 1534. Tjele Langsø is accessible from the camp site about 1km (half a mile) north-east of the manor or from the camp site at Vammen.

From Tjele go via Foulum to the main Road 16 and turn right, returning to Viborg.

Randers And The Djursland Peninsula

The Djursland peninsula is a particularly attractive part of Denmark with varied scenery and a long history. Randers is one of Denmark's oldest towns, founded where the Gudenå could be forded between North Jutland and South Jutland. First mentioned in 1080 when the mint was established, it became the capital of the old crown lands of Jutland, since when it has flourished as a trading centre with a very important position at the mouth of Denmark's major river.

There are several notable monuments including the superb statue of the *Jutland Horse*, symbol of the town's historical connection with horse fairs. The tourist office produces an excellent leaflet in English describing some of the attractions.

ROUTE 12 • A SHORT WALK AROUND RANDERS

The walk starts at the tourist office, Helligåndshuset, built in 1500 and a monastic hospital for the sick and aged until the Reformation. It became a grammar school in 1784, and Steen Steensen Blicher was a student and later a teacher here. The granite blocks in the walls may have come from churches left derelict after the Black Death. The nearby square takes its name from King Erik Menved who gave the town its first charter in 1302.

Turn into Houmeden and through to the town hall square, on the west side of which is the oldest stone house in the town. Walk behind the town hall opposite, built in 1778, down Rosengade and Nygade, where numbers 2 and 4, the oldest half-timbered houses in the town, have been carefully restored. Turn right into Østervold on the site of the old town moat, noticing the fine statue of the *Jutland Horse*. Turn right and walk down this wide busy street to Kulturhuset, a modern building housing the library, local archives and two important museums—the Cultural History Museum and the Randers Museum of Art.

Cross Østervold into Dytmærsken and continue into Brødregade, where a beautiful half-timbered house, number 24 and 26, built in 1592 contains a small doll and toy museum. Walk to the left down the street towards Storegade, where number 25 Brødregade is a scheduled building. This merchant's house has a fine gateway and had stabling for 100 horses. Turn right into Middelgade, in an area containing many fine scheduled houses in the care of the National Trust. At the bottom of Torvegade is the Svaneapotek or chemist, built in 1802 as the county sheriff's residence. Continue ahead up Kirkegade to Skt Mortens Kirke, built as the monastery church in 1500. It is notable for the elaborately carved main doors and the beautifully carved pulpit and font cover. The fine organ and chandeliers were gifts from merchants of the town in the seventeenth and eighteenth centuries.

Cross Kirkegade from the church into Store Kirkestræde where a beautiful half-timbered house has a carved beam over the gateway   bearing the date 1626. Back in Kirkegade, continue to the junction with Hospitalsgade where Randers Kloster is situated. This was never a monastery but is and always has been a hospital for old people and is one of the best half-timbered properties in the town.

Kirkegade leads into Vestergade where, in Favergården, the Scouting Museum is found containing material covering the history of the Scout Movement, together with an extensive library. The starting point of this walk can be reached by walking along Store Voldgade and Houmeden back to the tourist office.

Leave Randers by the road along the northern side of the fjord through Tjærby and Vestrup, an area with big farms and attractive old buildings. Continue to **Ålbæk**, turn left by the church then right by some red thatched houses. Good views of the fjord can be obtained from this road, also of the long narrow farms below in the valley. Ignoring the sign for Støvring continue through Østrup to Støvringgård. This manor house on the right was erected in 1622 on a large artificial castle mound and was extended to its present size in 1747. Continue to **Mellerup** and follow the sign 'Færgestedet' (Ferry Pier). There are some old thatched stables in Mellerup and a thatched cottage by the ferry pier. Once across the fjord continue ahead through Voer, turning right past the large farm and attractive mansion in a park at Stenalt to Allingåbro.

From Allingåbro take the road signed Drammelstrup, continue to the main road and turn left. About 1km (half a mile) further on to the left is Gammel Estrup, an imposing sixteenth-century castle in which is the Jutland Manor House Museum with a fine collection of furniture, porcelain and paintings from the sixteenth century onwards. Some of the best can be found in the Renaissance hall (seventeenth-century paintings and furniture) and some superb Flemish tapestries are in the Great Hall. In a separate museum within the grounds is the Danish Agricultural Museum. Displays of interiors from different periods tell the history of the past 200 years of the Danish farmer and his life and work. The manor house gardens are also worth visiting.

From Gammel Estrup continue to **Auning** where the Scheel family, former owners of Gammel Estrup, are buried. By continuing ahead for about 10km (6 miles) along Road 16, the family pleasure ground of Djurs Sommerland may be visited. Return to Auning along the same road, then take the road signed to Gjesing. In **Gjesing** turn right to Løvenholm, a late sixteenth-century moated manor house standing on the edge of woods. At the T-junction turn left through Nielstrup to **Nørager**. In the village, turn left past the church and follow this road, passing a prehistoric burial site on the heath on the right of the road, with dolmens and a passage grave.

Gammel Estrup Manor House

Turn right at the crossroads and continue on the road towards **Fjellerup**, with fine views to the left over the Baltic Sea and a small thatched farm in the hollow at Hegedal. Fjellerup Strand is a big holiday resort. Continue through the attractive village of Fjellerup to the main road, turn right, and in about 3km (2 miles) turn left towards Mejlgård Slot, a lovely white moated manor house which was completely renovated in the nineteenth century. Travel on to Bønnerup Strand, and then take the road signed Glesborg. After about 2km (1½ miles) turn left along a winding road through woods towards **Gjerrild**, a pretty little village with a hotel and Youth Hostel. Here is Sostrup Slot, a moated manor house built in the sixteenth century and owned by the Scheel family of Gammel Estrup for more than 200 years. Today Cistercian nuns own and manage the castle. From Sostrup continue through Veggerslev and Thorsø to **Grenå**.

This busy town has a history going back to 1300 when the church was built. A small market town grew up on the sound 3km (2 miles) from the sea. In the nineteenth century the harbour was constructed and a large land reclamation project began, then the largest in

The garden and orangery, Gammel Estrup

Denmark. The sound was drained, new road and rail connections established, and modern Grenå emerged. The old streets of the town, notably Lillegade and Nederstræde, contain some particularly attractive half-timbered buildings, and in Den Gamle Smedje (The Old Forge) in Smedestræde visitors can see the blacksmith at work on certain days. The tourist office can be found in a fine old building in the church square, while in the town hall square, folk dancing takes place during the summer. Not far from the church the Regional Museum occupies an eighteenth-century merchant's house. The archaeological section covers the history of Djursland and a pottery collection from the seventeenth century to the present day shows the development of the industry through the ages. Finally the museum houses an excellent fishery section of model fishing vessels. Craft demonstrations take place during the summer months. From the busy fishing and ferry harbours, which seem almost a different town, it is possible to take a day trip to Sweden or visit the island of Anholt. Ferries also connect with Hundested in Sealand.

From Grenå take the new main road inland past the sports centre and modern Youth Hostel, and continue in the direction of Århus for about 4km (2 miles). Turn left along Høbjergvej to Katholm and continue through Ålsrode and Hoed to Balle, then turn left along Rugårdsvej to the picturesque sixteenth-century brick manor house of Rugård Slot on the edge of a lake. Take the road from here to **Hyllested**, an attractive village of narrow streets and half-timbered houses. The church has a profusion of frescoes making it a medieval picture book with devils and animal-like figures on the white walls and arches. The murals were uncovered in 1965 and are believed to date from around 1500. About 5km (3 miles) north-west of here is another interesting village church at **Tirstrup**, where there is a priceless altarpiece, carved, painted and gilded, dated 1522. The Norwegian soapstone pulpit is thirteenth century and reputed to be the oldest in Denmark. Opposite the church, take the road to **Fuglslev**, burial place of the former owners of Rugård Slot, and on to Gravlev, then turn right along the narrow winding road to Stubbe Sø and Dråby, crossing on the way the route of the old railway from Ebeltoft to Grenå which is now a *natursti* (nature path). In **Dråby** village take a sharp left turn towards Dråby Strand and the church known as the Cathedral of Mols because of its size. It dates from the thirteenth century and was restored in 1970. The interior is notable for an ornate early eighteenth-century carved altarpiece and font cover, some very old candelabra in the sanctuary and delicately painted frescoes and elaborately carved doors to a family memorial chapel. Return to the main road in the village, turn left and continue into Ebeltoft.

IN AND AROUND EBELTOFT

Ebeltoft is a lovely old market town with cobbled streets and half-timbered houses. The town is a major holiday centre due to its long shore line and sheltered bays and to its proximity to the superb scenery of the Mols Bjerge. Ebeltoft regards itself with good reason as 'Denmark in a nutshell'.

Shipping and trade are the roots of the town's prosperity but after the boom in the nineteenth century, shipping slumped somewhat during the early twentieth century. With the opening of the ferry service to Sjællands Odde in 1966, Ebeltoft has regained its importance as a major shipping centre.

Start the walk from the car park by the frigate Jylland, the largest wooden naval vessel ever built and the last full-rigged ship of the Danish navy. Cross from *Jylland* over Strandvejen and bear left then turn right up Jernbanegade and right again into Adelgade, one of the town's many attractive old streets and the main shopping centre. On the right is Den Gamle Farvergård (Old Dye Yard) which was first used as such in 1772. Now the property has been preserved and contains dwellings, an old shop and the dyehouse, all furnished and equipped in their original condition as a museum. Other old buildings along this street include Jørgen Fåborgs Gård, over 225 years old, and opposite is Sigvald Rasmussens Gård, once used as a granary, with an interesting inscription above the gate into the courtyard. On

PLACES TO VISIT IN AND BETWEEN RANDERS AND EBELTOFT

Randers
Helligåndshuset
Old monastic hospital, now tourist office.
Kulturhuset
Library, Cultural History Museum and Randers Museum of Art.
Skt Mortens Kirke
Built as monastery church.
Scouting Museum
History of the Scout Movement.

Gammel Estrup
Sixteenth-century castle with Jutland Manor House Museum, Danish Agricultural Museum and manor gardens.

Djurs Sommerland
Family pleasure ground and amusement park.

Nørager
Prehistoric burial site described as the 'Stonehenge of Denmark'.

Gjerrild
Sostrup Slot
Moated sixteenth-century manor.

Grenå
Regional Museum
Old craft exhibits and demonstrations, archaeology of Djursland, development of pottery industry and fishing.

Hyllested
Church with outstanding murals.

Tirstrup
Priceless altarpiece and Denmark's oldest font in church.

**Dråby Church
(Cathedral of Mols)**
Fine carvings and frescoes, also copy of notable old print (wood cut).

Fregatten Jylland
Last wooden full-rigged warship being restored in special dock.

**Det Gamle Rådhus
(Old Town Hall)**
Part of museum.

Ebeltoft
District Museum
Local crafts, archaeological and Siamese collections.
Ebeltoft Church
Recently discovered frescoes.
Missers Dukkemuseum
Collection of old toys, dolls, etc.
Glass Museum
Collection of modern glass items.
Vindmøllepark
Experimental windmill farm for electricity generation.
Øer Ferieby
Modern holiday complex on islands in old gravel workings.

the same side of the street is the old *apotek*.

At the top of the street is Torvet across which, on the corner of Juulsbakke, is the old town hall built in 1789. With its distinctive spire it is thought to be the smallest town hall in Denmark. In the former council chamber is an exhibit showing how a well-to-do Mols family used to live. Today the room to the right of the entrance is used for weddings. The remaining departments of the Ebeltoft District Mu-

Ebeltoft

seum are accommodated in adjoining buildings in Juulsbakke and include local craft, archaeological and Siamese collections.

An interesting custom dating from about 1721 is the 'watchmen's round'. Today the Ebeltoft watchmen patrol in pairs starting from the steps of the old town hall, across the square from which is the tourist information office in yet another of the attractive old buildings.

 Beside the old town hall runs Overgade, a most attractive narrow street which leads to Kirkegade and the church. A church has stood on this site since before 1301 when the town received its first charter. Next to the church, in the old vicarage, is Missers Dukkemuseum (Misser's Doll Museum). Across from the bottom of Kirkegade, Havnevej runs down to the fishing and commercial harbours where something interesting can always be seen. Return the same way and turn left along Nedergade between more old houses. Another left turn down Toldbodvej leads out to Strandvejen, across which is the old custom house, now the home of Ebeltoft Glass Museum, actually a changing exhibition of modern international glass items. The car park near the frigate *Jylland* adjoins the museum. Before leaving the area, an interesting diversion can be made from Strandvejen south along Færgevejen to the Mols Linien ferry terminal, where the Ebeltoft Vindmøllepark is situated. A total of seventeen wind generators are located along a breakwater projecting into the water of Ebeltoft Bay.

The frigate Jylland *being restored in dry dock*

Not far from here is the Øer Ferieby or Island Holiday Village, a modern complex of bungalows built on small islands. The whole area is accessible by water and each bungalow has its own mooring.

From Ebeltoft take Road 21 north towards Grenå and look for signs to Femmøller on the left after passing the camp site on the shore. Keep on the road along the shore to the left, following signs for Helgenæs-Fuglsø. The Mols Bjerge (Mols Mountains) can be seen to the right and fine views over Ebeltoft Bay to the left. Continue to Fuglsø Kro then left near a small lake towards Helgenæs, keeping left at the major road by a café and driving over the narrow neck of land connecting Mols with the **Helgenæs** peninsula. The sea is visible on both sides, with Ebeltoft Bay to the left and Århus Bay on the right. At the next junction keep right following the coast road signed Sletterhage. The winding road through hilly country ends at the lighthouse and from here there is a coastal waymarked path to a former radar observation tower (Tysktårnet) from World War II which has been converted into an observation platform with wonderful views over Århus Bay towards the island of Samsø. On fine days it is possible to see as far as Funen and Sealand, and it is well worth the 1km (half a mile) walk. Return along the road as far as the sign 'Galleri Helgenæs' then turn right through Esby and Borup where there is a beautiful thatched farmhouse.

Follow signs for Knebel, turning right at the major road then left at the next junction (signed Knebel). In Begtrup turn left opposite the general store to Strands then left again to Torup. Turn right then left at the next give way sign and left again to **Tved** where signs to Tved Kirke should be followed. The little church which contains beautiful frescoes stands in the woods by the shore near a lovely old farm. Return along the coast road to **Knebel**, an interesting village by the water with an old obelisk sign post at the junction with the road to Agri, to the right. Follow this to Poskær Stenhus, a superb example of an encircled dolmen from 3000BC. Continue up the road to Agri then follow signs for Mols Bjerge. In about 500m (457yd) fork left and park near Agri Bavnehøj. Climb the path for a superb view of the surroundings from the top of the 137m (449ft) high hill. A state forest *vandreture* (walking tour) leaflet entitled *Mols Bjerge* is available which gives forest roads open to motorists as well as waymarked walks in the area. From the parking place continue along the gravel road to the first crossroads and turn left to Basballe where the tarmac road begins again. Bear right to meet the major road at Femmøller.

At this point, to return to Ebeltoft turn right, then sharp left immediately after passing the hotel, signed to Lyngsbæk where there are some fine half-timbered thatched barns on the right in front of a beautiful manor house. Turn right at the T-junction following signs for Lyngsbæk Strand, then left towards Handrup and the main road, where a right turn leads through Egsmark and back to Ebeltoft.

To continue to Randers from Femmøller turn left at the major road, continuing through Egens towards Rønde and Kalø Slot. The ruins of this large castle built by Erik Menved in 1313 lie on a tiny peninsula and are reached by walking along an ancient stone causeway. A drawbridge leads over the moat to the curtain wall and the large square courtyard. Some of the cellars of the womens quarters have been preserved. The massive keep was used as a prison for the Swedish king, Gustav Vasa in 1519 and has defied destruction and the decay of centuries. It is still about 10m (33ft) high and the holes for the joists of the three floors can clearly be seen. Continue into Rønde, turn left then right in the direction of **Thorsager** and the very impressive structure of Jutlands only round church, built of brick in 1200.

A 5km (3 mile) diversion may be made to visit the Djursland Railway Museum at **Ryomgård** (not open every day). Otherwise turn left in Thorsager along the main road to Fårup then right to Ommestrup. Cross the main road and at Bale turn right to Rosenholm Castle, built in 1559 and owned by the Rosenkrantz family for over four centuries. Paintings and 300-year-old Flemish tapestries, a manor chapel and an extensive park and gardens make this a place to visit when open during the summer.

PLACES TO VISIT IN MOLS BJERGE AND SOUTH OF RANDERS

Helgenæs
Sletterhage Lighthouse
Observation tower and way-
marked walks.

Mols Bjerge
Spectacular scenery, viewpoints,
walks and forest drives.

Kalø Slot
Impressive fourteenth-century
castle ruins on peninsula.

Rosenholm Castle
Paintings, tapestry, manor chapel
and gardens open summer.

Clausholm Slot
Most complete baroque mansion
and estate virtually unchanged
since eighteenth century.
Concerts during summer months.

Ammelhede
Hamlet's grave with memorial
stone and fine views.

From the castle drive north to Termestrup and turn left along the main Road 21 for about 5km (3 miles) turning left through Lime and Mygind, then through Mygind Skov to Clausholm Slot. This beautiful mansion house with its stables and park represents one of the earliest and most complete baroque establishments in Denmark and was built between 1699 and 1723 for Count Conrad Reventlow. The organ in the chapel is Denmark's oldest and has recently been restored.

Continue northwards along the Randers road for 1km (half a mile) then turn sharp right to Tustrup and in 2km (a mile) left to Hørning. Turn right near the church and continue across the main road through Mosekær to **Virring** where the church has a fine stained glass window, the oldest in Scandinavia. There is a lovely view from the churchyard over the Alling Å valley. Opposite the church take the road to Ammelhede (Hamlet's Heath) where Hamlet's grave may be found. Although it has never been proven that he was buried here, it has never been disproved and a stone was erected in 1933. The spot commands a fine view typical of sites chosen for ancient burial places of kings and chieftains.

On reaching the main road, turn towards **Assentoft** where the church has a very old entrance arch in the wall of the churchyard from which a fine view of Randers Fjord is obtained. The way into Randers is along the main road.

Århus — Ancient and Modern City

The Vikings first built a settlement at Århus about AD900 in the area where the cathedral now stands which has grown into the second largest city in Denmark with a thriving harbour, one of the busiest in Scandinavia.

The attractions of the city are widely scattered and the local tourist office has done much to help the visitor find the way around. Special bus tickets are available with instructions as to their use and bus route numbers are indicated with information on specific attractions. In the summer months the tourist office publishes details of special events and activities in the area together with transport information.

ROUTE 13 • IN AND AROUND ÅRHUS

The tourist office is situated in the city hall, an impressive modern building completed in 1941 and faced with Greenland marble. It is set in an attractive park and there is a good view over the city and Århus Bay from the top of the 60m (197ft) high tower. In the square outside is a large sculpture of a sow and piglets appropriately called the *Pig Fountain*. Walk through the park at the rear of the city hall to reach Frederiks Alle and cross over to Thomas Jensens Alle which leads to Musikhuset (The Concert Hall).

Walk from the tourist office in the opposite direction along Park Alle going north then right into Sønder Alle and left into Søndergade which is the main shopping centre in attractively laid out pedestrian precincts. At the end of Søndergade is Skt Clemens Torv and in the basement of the Andelsbank building is a superb Viking Museum.

From here it is a short walk to the cathedral dedicated to St Clement, patron saint of seafarers and the largest cathedral in Denmark. With a nave 93m (300ft) long and an impressive spire, this Gothic brick-built structure was actually built as a Romanesque church in 1201 but was altered considerably in the fifteenth century to the style seen today. The Romanesque chapels on the eastern side of the transept give an idea of how the original church looked.

Next to the cathedral is Kvindemuseet (The Women's Museum) housed in the old police station, with exhibits on womens life and work through the ages including the present century. A short walk across Store Torv to Lille Torv and into Vestergade comes to Vor Frue Kirke beneath the choir of which archaeologists discovered the first stone church in Århus, built about AD1060. The chapter house, used as a hospital after the Reformation, has been re-consecrated and is known as the Cloister Church, so there are three churches within the one building.

The most notable attraction in the city is Den Gamle By (The Old Town), reached from the tourist office via Vester Alle and Thor-

PLACES TO VISIT
IN AND AROUND ÅRHUS

Viking Museum
In basement of Andelsbank.

St Clement Cathedral
Impressive brick building with fine interior.

Vor Frue Kirke
Three churches in one.

Den Gamle By (The Old Town)
Museum of old buildings in town setting.

Tivoli Friheden
Amusement park with entertainments, concerts and gardens.

University Park
Art Museum, Natural History Museum, Medical History Museum and Antiquities Museum.

Marselisborg Palace
Royal park, arboretum and rose gardens open when royal family not in residence.

Moesgård Manor Prehistory Museum
Collections including Grauballe Man and Prehistoric Trail.

Storskoven and Fløstrup Skov
Walks and cycle routes.

valdsensgade, or by one of the city buses and situated in the Botanical Gardens. The 'Old Town' is a unique cultural and historical museum with an international reputation comprising of reconstructed buildings to give an impression of an old Danish market town. The museum's history goes back to 1909 and it is administered by a private foundation. More than 60 buildings are arranged along typical cobbled streets with a mill stream, and many of them are fully furnished and equipped as shops. Illustrated guides in English are available.

In the University Park are several other museums, notably the Kunstmuseum with an exceptional collection of Danish paintings and sculpture from the eighteenth century to the present day (supplemented by frequent temporary exhibitions) the Natural History Museum dealing with zoology and geology, both Danish and foreign, and the Medical History Museum. Within the main university build- ings is the Antiquities Museum with Greek, Roman and Egyptian collections, while further north in the School of Journalism is the Danish Press Museum and Archives with a permanent exhibition on the history of the printing press.

In the southern part of the city, in Strandvejen at the junction with Dalgas Avenue, is the Danish Fire Brigade Museum located in the old tram depot, with over eighty fire engines of all kinds together with uniforms and equipment. Just up the road in Skovbrynet is Tivoli

Friheden, the popular amusement park on the edge of the Marselisborg Skov. A map of the area with descriptions of the walks in English is available from the tourist office.

The nineteenth-century Marselisborg Palace was built as a wedding present for Crown Prince Christian (later Christian X) and his bride and it is still used as a royal residence. When the royal family is not in residence, the park is open to the public. Nearby is the Mindepark and memorial to 4,000 Danes from North Slesvig, then under German rule, who lost their lives during World War I. From here it is a short drive along Oddervej through Højbjerg to Moesgård Alle leading to Moesgård Manor House. The house is not open to the public but the Prehistory Museum is housed in the adjoining farm buildings. Associated with the museum is the Prehistoric Trail running for several kilometres past reconstructed dolmens, cists and Stone Age and Iron Age houses. The woods to the north of Moesgård (Storskoven) contain many footpaths and cycle paths which link with those in the Marselisborg Skov, also to Fløjstrup Skov to the south. Brochures and maps are available in English.

For cyclists a map of cycle paths in and around the city can be obtained from the tourist office with captions in English, and a particularly attractive route leads from the city around Brabrand Sø. Starting from Musikhuset, cycle along Skovgårdsgade to Carl Blochs Gade, cross over to Brabrandstien and follow the path to Vestre Ringgade. Cross this road and follow the path into Søren Frichs Vej. Just after passing the end of Frejasvej on the right, the Brabrandstien begins again on the left. Follow this alongside the river and immediately after crossing under the railway turn right and follow the path between the railway and the river, keeping near the river until Viby Ringvej is reached. Pass under this road and continue along the path around the north of the Brabrand Sø. In **Brabrand** carry on along the path left, crossing the river valley alongside the main road and turning left again along the southern side of the lake. In about 2km (a mile) at **Stavtrup**, is an observation tower and picnic area with toilets and information board at the old railway station. There is also a mini-museum with a small exhibition about the Brabrand Sø. Plenty of opportunities for bird watching and good views over the lake can be obtained from along the path which continues to rejoin the outward route by the railway bridge. Alternatively, turn left at Høskov and take the path across the eastern end of the lake to rejoin the outward route just to the west of the Viby Ringvej. This path along the south of the lake also forms part of a waymarked route for walkers which runs for 23km (14 miles) from Århus to Skanderborg. A leaflet is available although in Danish. Much of the route is also permitted for cyclists.

5

THE LAKE DISTRICT AND EASTERN FJORDS

The Lake District of central Jutland is a magnificent stretch of natural scenery forming a recreational area offering all kinds of activities together with a number of historical sites and other attractions. The Hærvej or so-called old military road runs through the western part from north to south, continuing beyond Vejle on its way to the German border. It is superb walking and cycling country, with plenty of opportunities for canoeing and sailing. Anglers will find ideal waters and a booklet in English explains what, how and where to go. Full details are available from the local tourist information offices, who also have a broadsheet describing sixteen different cycle tours between Silkeborg and Skanderborg, including a map and an excellent English guide to the more interesting sights. A 55km (34 mile) walking and cycling path from Silkeborg to Horsens is described in the State Forestry Service leaflet *Naturstien Horsens-Silkeborg*, which although in Danish, has a good map showing Youth Hostels, camp sites and parking places. Part of the route follows an old railway track.

ROUTE 14 • AROUND THE LAKES

The route starts in **Silkeborg**, founded in 1846 and grown up around Michael Drewsen's paper mill built to take advantage of the water power available from the Gudenå. The town which makes an excellent base for a country holiday is a thriving shopping and industrial centre, and has a number of educational establishments including catering colleges and course centres.

The square Torvet, is overlooked by the old town hall and a statue of Michael Drewsen. An attractive pedestrian precinct leads down to the new town hall from which there is a good view over the lovely Silkeborg Langsø (Long Lake) with its imposing fountains which are illuminated at night.

Silkeborg Cultural Museum is housed in the town's oldest build-

85

ing, Hovedgården (1767) and is best known for the 2,200-year-old 'Tollund Man' discovered in 1950. Tollund Man together with the body of the 'Elling Woman' found in 1938 less than 1km (half a mile) away, also in a peat bog, have contributed much to the knowledge of their time and way of life.

A modern building in Gudenåvej near the town water works houses the Art Museum with a unique collection of works by Asger Jorn and other modern European artists. At the other end of the town a footbridge near Brugsen's Supermarket leads to a small island where the outline of the walls of a castle dating from the Middle Ages is marked by hedges, but it is possible to see the inner core of the original walls.

A fine walk of about 24km (15 miles) follows the remains of the towpath from Silkeborg northwards to Kongensbro near the southern tip of Tange Sø. Another shorter walk goes from Resenbro some 5km (3 miles) north-east of the town to Fårvang, following the route of the old railway track.

Boat tours through the lakes include a trip in the old coal-fired paddle steamer *Hjejlen* built in 1861 and still going strong. It runs from Silkeborg up the river and across a chain of lakes popular with sailors, ending at a landing stage below the Himmelbjerget. From the landing stage, climb the path to the tower on the top of Himmelbjerget, which was erected to commemorate the signing of the first Danish constitution by King Frederik VII in 1849. From the tower there are

outstanding views. It is possible to land at any of the intermediate stops and catch a later boat after walking in the forests, and leaflets are available describing such walks.

A tour around the lakes takes the visitor through some of the loveliest countryside in Denmark, including its highest point. Leave Silkeborg via Østergade and Århusbakken through Resenbro to Voel. Go through the village and turn left along Amerikavej towards **Gjern** and the Jutland Automobile Museum. Cross the bridge in the village, bear left, then take the next road left through the woods towards Svostrup. The Gjern Bakker have some good waymarked walking routes with fine views over the Gudenå valley from Store Troldhøj. At the crossroads beyond the woods turn right along Sørkelvej to Tvilum Church, once part of a thirteenth-century monastery and now a parish church with a beautifully carved triptych.

Cross the river and turn left towards Svostrup. Along this old 'royal road' several old milestones may be seen. Take the second turning on the right to Grauballe then turn left down the main road to Silkeborg, cross the bridge and continue down Christian 8 Vej and Frederiksberggade to the main Horsens Road 52. At Almind Sø just outside the town there are parking places and an open-air bathing facility on the edge of the lake on the right side of the road and a

Silkeborg town hall

subway under the road leads to woodland walks. There is also a footpath all around the Almind Sø.

Continue towards **Virklund**, turning right at the traffic lights signed to the camp sites, then in the village turn left towards Svejbæk Færge through Sønderskov with many walks and forest trails. Turn left along Svejbækvej to a small parking place about 750m (686yd) down the hill on the left. Walk down the path and round the Slåensø, one of the clearest lakes in Denmark, taking about an hour. From the car park return up the hill and turn left at the first T-junction, following signs to Glarbo and at the main road keep left in the direction of Skanderborg. In Rye Glarbo turn left following signs to Himmelbjerget where the tower may be climbed to enjoy the view.

Return to the main road, turning left then right towards the village of **Gammel Rye**. Immediately turn right again in the direction of Gammel Rye Church built in the fifteenth century to serve the pilgrims visiting Skt Sørens holy spring in the nearby forest. In the village is a restored windmill and Træskomuseet (The Wooden Shoe Museum) with a fully-equipped clog-maker's workshop in the old school.

Go south for about 1½km (a mile) towards Sønder Vissing, and immediately after crossing Rye Bridge turn left along a forest road to the Gudenå Museum with its fine collection of prehistoric implements of hunters and fishermen who lived among the lakes of the middle reaches of the Gudenå river around 6000BC. The museum is at the site of one of the old Stone Age settlements. Return to the major road, turn left then bear left at the bottom of the hill by a timber framed building and go towards Voerladegård through Højlund Skov, emerging to good views over the Mossø. In Voerladegård turn left (signed Strand) through Dørup and Hem to the main road. Turn left for about 1km (half a mile) then in the valley turn right to Ejer Bavnehøj. Follow signs through **Ejer** to Bavnehøj, a high arched tower which stands on what was once thought to be the highest hill in Denmark, 171m (561ft) above sea level.

Continue through the little village of **Ris** and along Ovsted Kirkevej to the highest church in Denmark in a commanding position overlooking the E3 motorway and the country towards Horsens Fjord.

Return to the road from Ris, turn right (signed Horsens) then left (signed Tåning) and at the give way sign turn right under the motorway to Tebstrup. From here it is possible to turn right along Road 170 to join Route 15 in Horsens.

To continue, turn left in Tebstrup along Road 170 and go down the hill, turning right at the motel (signed Hylke) then sharp left under the railway bridge. Take the next turning on the left and continue, with views of Skanderborg Sø, to Ringkloster and the T-junction on the main road. Turn left through Skårup to Skanderborg.

Skanderborg, whose church was part of the royal castle, dates back to the eleventh century. One of the town's statues shows *Dronning Dagmars Dreng* (a page) galloping to Skanderborg for it was here that King Valdemar received the news that Queen Dagmar lay on her death-bed in Ribe. In the town centre is a park overlooking the lake, and the old part of the town is centred around Torvet with the Town Tree and commemorative stone recording the granting of market status in 1583.

Elegant old houses in Adelgade include Amtsgården from 1804

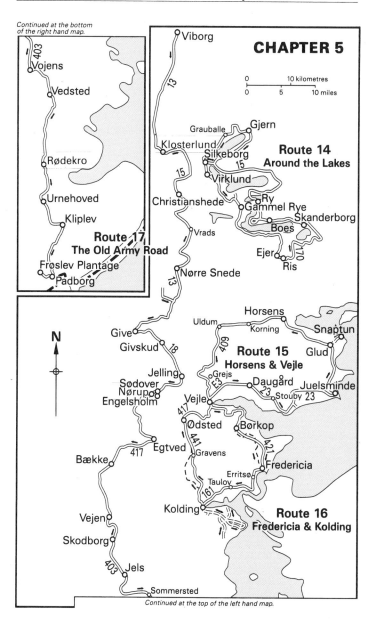

Continued at the bottom of the right hand map.

Viborg

CHAPTER 5

0   10 kilometres
0   5   10 miles

403
Vojens
13
Vedsted

Grauballe   Gjern
Klosterlund
Silkeborg   **Route 14**
Rødekro   **Around the Lakes**
15   15
Virklund
Urnehoved   Christianshede
Ry
Kliplev   Gammel Rye
Skanderborg
Route 17   Boes
The Old Army Road   Vrads
Ejer
Frøslev Plantage   Ris
Padborg   Nørre Snede

N

13
Uldum   Horsens
Korning   Snaptun
Give   409
Givskud   **Route 15**   Glud
18   **Horsens & Vejle**
Jelling   Grejs
Sødover   Daugård   Juelsminde
Nørup   E3   23
Engelsholm   Vejle   Stouby   23
417
Ødsted   Børkop
441
Bække   417   Egtved   421
Gravens
Fredericia
Erritsø
Taulov
161
Vejen   Kolding   **Route 16**
Fredericia & Kolding
Skodborg
403
Jels
Sommersted

Continued at the top of the left hand map.

and Præstegården (The Rectory). Skolegade leads to Borgergade where many of the houses were built of bricks 'rescued' from the demolished castle in the mid-eighteenth century. At the end of the street is the old hospital opposite the town's oldest surviving house built at the beginning of the eighteenth century. Walk back to Adelgade via Louisenlund and turn left along Slotsholmen where the museum in a building from 1888 has collections including articles from local excavations, the main exhibits being related to the town and its castle. Beyond the museum is Slotskirken, erected in 1572 after Frederik II rebuilt the castle as a modern fortress. The royal box was pulled down and new side galleries built in 1801. Jens Nielsen's *Crucifixion* was acquired as an altarpiece when the church was repaired in 1971.

Along Slotsholmen beyond the Slotskirke a car park by the restaurant Capri makes a good starting point for walks through the wooded Dyrehave or Deer Park, originally a royal deer forest fenced in around 1580, but acquired by the municipality in 1886 for forestry and recreational purposes. Two World War II bunkers house the Freedom Museum and some wooden buildings which were originally the officers' mess and the commandant's house now form part of the Skanderborg Youth Hostel. A leaflet in English describes the walks in the area.

At the northern end of the town is Skanderup Church, built around 1050 of limestone. Apart from the tower the original building is intact and the frescoes dating from 1170 are unique in northern Europe.

Leave the town via Banegårdsvej and turn left at the traffic lights along Ryvej under the railway and motorway. Continue through Alken to **Boes** with its lovely little thatched cottages either side of the very twisting road, and on through **Emborg** to Øm Kloster, a Cistercian monastery founded in 1172. The ruins of the abbey are clearly marked to show the positions of the various buildings. During excavations of the foundations between 1911 and 1978 hundreds of skeletons were found under the ruins and in the churchyard and investigations have shown that Øm had a hospital where both medical and surgical treatments were carried out. A small museum and herb garden are on the site and some of the tombs of bishops and abbots have been left visible under protective glass covers.

From Øm Kloster take the road back towards Skanderborg then turn left beside the Gudensø to **Ry** where there is a small Fresh Water Museum in Poul Steffensensvej. A detailed English explanation of the exhibits is available on request. From Ry follow the road between two lakes, the Birksø and Knudsø, towards Alling, then turn right to Tulstrup and Nørre Vissing then left to Låsby. At Låsby turn left onto the main road and return to Silkeborg.

PLACES TO VISIT AROUND SILKEBORG AND THE LAKES

Silkeborg
Cultural Museum
Tollund Man, Art Museum.

Ry
Himmelbjerget
Memorial tower.

Gjern
Jutland Automobile Museum.

Gammel Rye
Fifteenth-century pilgrim church, windmill and Wooden Shoe Museum.

Gudenå Museum
Prehistoric implements from Guden Å area.

Ejer Bavnehøj
Viewpoint tower on Denmark's second highest hill.

Ris
Ovsted Kirke
Highest church in Denmark built in 1200.

Skanderborg
Fine eighteenth- and nineteenth-century houses, local history museum and Slotskirken. Dyrehaven (Deer Park) with walks, Freedom Museum and Youth Hostel. Skanderup Church unaltered since 1050 with unique frescoes.

Øm Kloster
Ruins of Cistercian monastery from 1172 with excavated tombs, herb garden and museum.

ROUTE 15 • HORSENS AND VEJLE

Horsens, reached from Silkeborg via the main Road 52, has a good shopping centre and some interesting buildings, monuments and museums.

A short walk taking in some of the main places of interest starts from the old town hall, built in 1854. The many elegant eighteenth-century façades in Søndergade, the widest main street in Denmark, conceal much older buildings. Go left past Helms Apotek, a lovely baroque building erected in 1736 by a Viborg builder who used stones from a nearby manor house. The apothecary operated under royal licence in former times and was a very important person. This accounts for the very many buildings of great historical or architectural interest in Denmark under the name *apotek* which were both home and place of business. Opposite the *apotek* is Jørgensen's Hotel, formerly Lichtenberg Mansion.

Continue down Søndergade and through Jessens Gade to Vitus Berings Plads with a memorial to the Danish explorer of that name who discovered the Bering Strait separating Alaska from the Soviet Union. Bering was born in Horsens in 1680 and the cannons flanking the memorial, a gift from the Soviet Union, came from the ship in which he made his last voyage in 1741. Return along Søndergade and turn left by Jørgensen's Hotel into Graven, then into Smedegade where one of the five town gates stood just before the end of the first steep rise. Because of the slope many houses have high doorsteps, often with attractive wrought iron handrails. The largest and best preserved merchant's house at the top of the street has been converted into an attractive shopping centre known as Smedetorvet. Nearby is Horsens Theatre and the Galerie Asbæk, an old tobacco factory tastefully converted into a public library and art centre.

Return down Smedegade to Nørregade passing some of the oldest buildings in the town with early seventeenth-century gables. The Flensborg House built in 1790 to accommodate eight widows is an annexe to the Horsens Museum. The iron rings on the door frame were to help the old ladies up the steps! Along Nørregade in Torvet is the oldest building in the town, Vor Frelsers Kirke. It is believed that Valdemar II may have been responsible for the building in 1225 of this very fine brick edifice with its unique triple arch openings under the vaulting of the central nave. The magnificent pulpit was carved in 1670 by a citizen of Horsens, Peder Jensen Kolding. The chancel lighting and altarpiece are modern but blend well with the remainder of the building.

Cross Søndergade and walk down Fugholm past Svaneboligen, small houses built in 1785 as an extension to an existing charitable home for widows, and into Åboulevarden with its old half-timbered warehouse on the site of the original harbour. Past the warehouse is the Klosterkirke or abbey church, the only remaining wing of the Franciscan monastery founded in 1261. It has a lovely interior with misericord seats in the choir dating from the early sixteenth century, chancel gates from 1679 and a carved altarpiece from 1500. The pulpit made in 1610 was originally placed in Vor Frelsers Kirke, while the pulpit now in the latter church belonged to the Klosterkirke. The churchyard leads into Kirkegyde and the eighteenth-century seamens' quarter.

Stjernholmsgade leads to the old electricity works building of 1906 in Gasvej which houses the fascinating Labour, Commerce and Industry Museum. The Horsens Museum in Sundvej at the end of Gasvej has collections relating to the town's history and development together with silverware, pottery, furniture and other items from many of the old buildings in the town. Nearby is the Lunden Art Museum with changing exhibitions and collections of the works of the painter and engraver Mogens Zieler and many examples of Danish nine-teenth- and twentieth-century art.

A public park on the western side of the town was originally the grounds of Bygholm Manor and contains the ruins of King Erik Menved's fourteenth-century castle. The manor house is now an hotel. North of the town near the Nørrestrand Nature Reserve the very fine modern Youth Hostel has superb facilities including seven rooms specially designed for wheelchair users.

Leave Horsens via Bygholm Parkvej and Hattingvej, through Hatting to Korning and Hornborg, then to the T-junction near Uldum. Turn left along Road 409 through Vester Ørum and fork right to Sindbjerg Kirke. Turn left onto the main Road 13 then first right towards Ulkær. At the T-junction turn right, right again just past the dairy (*mejeri*) and go ahead at the next crossroads. The road soon becomes very tortuous with hairpin bends. At the main road turn left towards Vejle down through a wooded gorge, the Grejsdal, acknowledged to be one of the most beautiful parts of the country. Through the valley runs the river Grejs and the railway from Jelling to Vejle on which a steam service operates on summer Sundays, climbing from Vejle on some of the steepest rail tracks in the country.

The history of **Vejle** dates from the end of the twelfth century, its most prosperous period being during the Middle Ages when it was an important commercial, fishing and hop-growing centre. There was a standstill in the town's development until the end of the eighteenth century when Vejle became the new administrative centre for the district. Building of a new harbour and the arrival of the railway in the nineteenth century helped promote the industrial development of the town with cotton mills and iron foundries, and the town spread from the ford by the river to the surrounding hills. Today the town's main industries are connected with food production and information technology.

The main shopping centre in and around Torvegade, Nørregade, Søndergade and Vestergade includes one of the longest pedestrian-only streets in the country. The town is overlooked by the restored white windmill housing an exhibition about watermills and windmills in the area. Vejle museum of history in Flegborg has permanent exhibitions and a selection of drawings of buildings built in the town between 1904 and 1951. An annexe in Den Smidtske Gård, an old merchant's house dating from 1799 in Søndergade, contains a permanent exhibition showing the history of Vejle over 800 years. The Art Museum has one of the largest collections of graphics and drawings in Denmark and a collection of paintings and sculpture from around 1900 to the present day.

The oldest building standing on the highest part of the old town is Skt Nicolai Kirke dating from about 1250. It was enlarged and given a tower in the fourteenth century, but subsequent alterations resulted in the tower being replaced by the present one in 1887. The font is possibly older than the church itself and the pulpit dates from 1576. A coffin in the chapel in the north transept contains a body found in a peat bog in 1835, once thought to be that of the Viking Queen Gunhilde. Recent scientific studies have shown it to be much older,

PLACES TO VISIT IN AND AROUND HORSENS AND VEJLE

Horsens
Vitus Bering Memorial, Vor Frelsers Kirke, Klosterkirke, Industry Museum, Horsens Museum, Lund Art Museum, Bygholm Manor.

Vejle
White windmill with mill museum, Vejle museum of history. Art Museum and Skt Nicolai Kirke from 1250 with preserved body of Iron Age woman from peat bog.

Daugård
Church with frescoes from 1200 and fine carved granite font.

Rosenvold Manor
Built for Karen Gyldenstjerne in 1585.

Juelsminde
Popular holiday resort with good beaches.

Glud
Den Gamle Landsby
Old village museum with Denmark's oldest farmhouse.

dating in fact from the early Iron Age, about 490BC.

Follow the Horsens Road E3 for about 6km (4 miles) then turn right on Road 23 towards Juelsminde. The Romanesque church at **Daugård** has some very early frescoes dating from about 1200 and also contains a very fine granite font with lion carvings. Continue to Stouby, turn right into the village then right again towards Rosenvold

camp site and Renaissance manor house, built in 1585 for Karen Gyldenstjerne. Some good views of Vejle Fjord can be had from here. Continue towards Staksrode and turn right at the T-junction to a car park from which waymarked walks lead through the woods (Staksrode Skov) along the coast and to the site of the small medieval

castle of Stagsevold of which only earth mounds remain.

Return to Staksrode and continue towards Hornsyld, turn right at the main road and continue into **Juelsminde**, a very popular holiday centre with some good sandy beaches. The former ferry service from here to Kalundborg has now been discontinued, the harbour being used solely for freight traffic, fishing vessels and private boats. The coast road continues north through Hosby and Kirkholm to **Glud**,

where the museum Den Gamle Landsby (The Old Village) contains the oldest dated farmhouse in Denmark from 1662. This and other houses and farmhouses from surrounding villages are all furnished and equipped in their original way. An exhibition hall contains a fine collection of furniture, tools, kitchen and domestic equipment from local peasant, fishing and rural communities through the ages. From Glud a diversion may be made to the little fishing hamlet of **Snaptun**, from where ferries operate to the island of Hjarnø in the mouth of

The Valiant Foot Soldier,
Fredericia

Horsens Fjord, and to Endelave, a peaceful island with some lovely bathing beaches situated in the Kattegat, some 70 minutes journey time. Returning to Glud, follow the main road back to Horsens.

ROUTE 16 • FREDERICIA AND KOLDING

This route follows scenic roads from Vejle to Børkop and on to Fredericia and Kolding. Leave Vejle along Toldbodvej and Ibæk Strandvej, signed Havns and Munkebjerg. The road runs beside the fjord under the motorway bridge, and beyond Ibæk it turns right under a very narrow railway bridge with traffic lights and no advance warning. After the bridge hairpin bends lead uphill to the modern Munkebjerg Hotel, situated in what must be one of the finest sites in the country overlooking the fjord. About 1km (half a mile) past the hotel turn left towards Andkær Skovby then left again signed Andkær Vig. The gravelled surface changes to asphalt with hairpin bends going downhill. At the bottom go left along Lodsvej then right on Sellerupstrandvej and continue uphill past the large white institutional buildings on the left and into Brejning Centrum. Go down the hill towards Gauerslund, over the main road and ahead towards the railway. Turn left along Møllegade and continue to **Børkop** Mølle, a lovely old watermill classified as a national monument. The building is now used as a restaurant but there are plans to build a small museum nearby. From Børkop take the main Road 421 into Fredericia. A route is signed along minor roads for cyclists.

Fredericia's importance due to its large modern port complex and proximity to the island of Funen was pre-dated by Frederik III's decision in 1649 to build a fortress to be known as Frederiksodde. In 1644 the King renamed it Fredericia. The statue of *The Valiant Foot Soldier* near Prinsens Port has become the symbol of the town. The ramparts with their bastions, gates, cannon emplacements and powder magazine are considered to be the largest and best pre-served in northern Europe, extending in a semi circle for $5\frac{1}{2}$ km (3 miles) around old Fredericia. The drained moats and ramparts now provide some lovely walks among the trees and along the upper parts with outstanding views. A number of statues and memorials are to be found, including a granite column commemorating the reunion of Denmark with North Slesvig in 1920 and a memorial wall to Danish Railway Freedom Fighters who fell during the German occupation of 1940-5. Just inside the ramparts near their southern end is the 300-year-old Jewish cemetery which is preserved in perpetuity.

 In the town the exterior of Trinitatis Kirke is virtually unchanged since its completion in 1689, and its interior is worth seeing with lovely stained glass windows, an altarpiece from 1691 and baroque pulpit dating from 1690. In the churchyard are the graves of soldiers killed in the defence of the town in 1657 and 1849. The older Skt Michaelis Kirke, consecrated in 1668 was and still is the garrison church, the present building being a reconstruction from 1955 following a disas-trous fire. The oldest house in Fredericia stands at the junction of Kongensgade and Prinsensgade. Known as Nordstjernen (The North Star), it dates from the earliest period of the town, and is probably built from timber brought from the village of Ullerup which was demolished as part of the defence plans.

 Just outside the ramparts in Jernbanegade a fine restored build-ing houses the Fredericia Museum with collections and displays dealing with the wars of 1657, 1848-9 and 1864, and the various refugee communities who settled in the town. There is also a notable collection dealing with the technology of lighting through the ages.

Leave the town via Indre Ringvej in the direction of the Lillebælt bridges, following Strandvejen and Snoghøj Landevej across the motorway with superb views of the new Lillebælt Bridge and the old bridge. At this point, to link with route 21 cross the Lillebælt by the old bridge to Middelfart. Otherwise, turn right before the old bridge onto

Road 161 towards Kolding. This section of the E66 motorway tends to be very busy, and the old main road offers superb views down the Lillebælt to Fænø and the Hindsgavl peninsula of Funen and across to Kolding Fjord.

The town of **Kolding** is dominated by the huge bulk of 'Koldinghus', the old frontier castle built in the mid-thirteenth century following hostilities between the King of Denmark and the Duke of Slesvig.

The earliest part is the west wing built by Queen Margrethe I. After additions by other monarchs, Christian IV built the huge square tower, the chapel and the great hall, later converted by Frederik IV to the baroque style. After a serious fire and many years during which the local population took material for building, reconstruction commenced in 1867, and in 1890 the Koldinghus Museum was founded, since when the board of directors has worked to restore the castle to its former glory. The final phase of the work is now in progress and is expected to be completed in 1990, providing improved cultural facilities. The Castle Museum contains interiors from the sixteenth century to the beginning of the present century, including religious art, handicrafts, porcelain and silverware. Special exhibitions, theatrical and operatic performances and concerts are held in the great hall and courtyard, especially during the Kolding Festival in June.

The town has suffered a number of severe fires and in the sixteenth century most of the buildings were destroyed. The town was rebuilt and the date on the end lintel of number 18 Helligkørsgade facing the street shows it was built in 1589. From 1704 to 1915 it was a shoemaker's shop owned by the same family until the death of shoemaker Peter Møller at the age of 92, and the house, restored inside and out to its original sixteenth-century state, now accommodates the tourist office. The shoemaker's tools are in Koldinghus Museum.

Borchs Gård in Torvegade dates from 1595 and was the old *apotek*, one of the earliest known pharmacies in the Danish provinces and one of the most richly decorated buildings of the period in the whole country.

Not far from the old *apotek* is Skt Nicolai Kirke, built in 1250 and containing some superb wood carvings, notably those of St Nicholas, St George and the Dragon, St Anna and St Olav, and a beautiful altarpiece dating from 1590. The stained glass is modern but very beautiful, while the oak choir stalls from 1529 were originally in the Grey Friars monastery in Kolding.

The Kolding river today is crossed by many bridges, but in earlier times there was just the Sønderbro, originally a wooden structure but replaced in 1806-8 by the present granite bridge.

South of the river is the Geografiske Have or Geographical

Garden, founded in 1920 by a local nurseryman. The 35 acres form one of Scandinavia's largest botanical collections, including the largest bamboo grove in Denmark and one of Europe's finest collections of early blooming rhododendrons.

Along the coast beyond the entrance to Kolding Fjord there are waymarked woodland walks with splendid views in Nørreskov, Midtskov and Sønderskov. There are parking places in each wood and on the coast at Stenderup Hage from where one can see the whole of the southern part of the Lillebælt and the western coastline of Funen, all of which is superb scenery. A leaflet published by the State Forestry Service under the title *Stenderup Skovene Kolding* contains maps and the area may be reached from Kolding by following the road to Sønder Stenderup, then follow signs to Nørreskov and Løver Odde, or to Midtskov and Stenderupstrand. Also from here signs can be followed to Stenderup Hage via Mørkholt and to Sønderskov.

Another diversion from Kolding follows Skamling Vejen to Sønder Bjert and Skamling. Signs show the way to Skamlingsbanke, on the hills on the border with South Jutland. During the years of annexation when South Jutland was part of Germany it played a key role as a gathering place for the Danes opposed to the occupation. It is now a

National Park traversed by numerous paths offering outstanding views over the surrounding countryside and the Lillebælt and includes the highest point in South Jutland, 113m (371ft) above sea

level. A monument 16m (52ft) high built of twenty-five granite blocks stands 'In memory of the champions of the Danish cause in Slesvig'. Other memorials in the neighbourhood include one commemorating the end of the occupation of South Jutland in 1945 and those who lost their lives at that time.

After returning to Kolding, the best route back to Vejle is via Sydbanegade west into Tøndervej, then right at the major junction into Vestre Ringgade, under the railway and continue ahead to Katrinegade. Turn left then bear right along Hans Ludvigs Vej to Vejlevej, Road 170. Follow this to Bramdrupdam where it crosses the motorway then turn left onto Road 441 towards Dons.

Cyclists can use the *natursti* or old railway path which goes through the woods and past the lake of Marielund. After passing Kolding golf course, continue to Bramdrupdam, then under the main road to Bramdrup Mark. The path goes through a tunnel under the motorway then joins Road 441 as above.

Continue through Dons and past Ågård and Gravens to **Ødsted**. The small Romanesque church north of the village on the road to Vesterby is built of travertine and has the original ceiling decorations still intact and there are some very fine carvings on the altarpiece. From here take Road 417 to Jerlev, turn right by the church then left

PLACES TO SEE IN AND AROUND FREDERICIA AND KOLDING

Børkop Mølle
Well preserved geared watermill with two wheels.

Fredericia
Fortress town with museum and Lillebælt bridges.

Kolding
Koldinghus frontier castle.

Sixteenth-century buildings including oldest *apotek*. Urban renewal schemes. Skt Nicolai Kirke, Geografiske Have, Stenderup Skovene, Nørreskov, Midtskov, Sønderskov and Stenderup Hage. Skamlingsbanken and Højen Kirke.

to follow the road to Højen Kirke, also built of travertine hidden behind a layer of brickwork which was added in 1863. Some very early frescoes dating from about 1200 depict the legend of St James, also a calvary frieze. The Renaissance pulpit, old alms boxes and granite font are complemented by a modern altarpiece.

From the church go uphill to the T-junction, turn right and in 1 km (half a mile) turn left to Højen. Continue ahead through the village, turn right under the overhead power lines and in 1 km (half a mile) turn left onto the main road and so into Vejle, passing the white windmill on the right when going down the hill into the town.

ROUTE 17 • THE OLD ARMY ROAD

This journey follows the old military and trading route through varied scenery ranging from heath to forest, marsh and lake, hills, steep valleys and sand dunes, rivers and streams. Many signs of the past such as barrows and passage graves, monuments, old churches, stone bridges and traces of the actual trackways and road can be seen, presenting an overall picture of the history of central and southern Jutland from earliest times to the present day.

What is known as the Hærvej (Army Road) or sometimes the Oksevej (Drove Road), Kongevej (King's Road) or Pilgrimsvej (Pilgrims' Road) originates from prehistoric times and was a system of tracks following a general direction southwards from Viborg to Frøslev on the German border and beyond.

Modern roads follow parts of the old route, and in some places sections of the original tracks remain. There are often diversionary routes, all leading in the same general direction, and it is possible to follow most of the route by bicycle, and much of it by car along roads on or parallel to it.

The route described here generally follows the Hærvej but includes other places of interest near the route. A booklet in Danish illustrated with clear maps describing the route is available from tourist offices, and cycle holidays organised by Dansk Cykelferie (Danish Cycle Holidays) follow much of the old route. People booking for one of their trips receive information and route instructions in English and bookings can be made through the tourist office in Viborg, the starting point.

Road 13 south from Viborg is considered to follow the Hærvej. It does follow one of the tracks from Viborg to Hundshoved, south of Nørre Snede but there are other roads and paths which follow some of the alternative routes used in former times. From Viborg follow Road 13 for 16km (10miles) to Thorning and after another 10km (6 miles) turn left at Klode Mølle following signs to Klosterlund Museum. **Klosterlund** is the oldest settlement in Jutland, 9,500 years old, and a unique collection of flint tools and other finds from the settlement can be seen at Grøndalhus, the white thatched building which is a branch of the National Museum. Continue past the museum, turn left at the T-junction through Kragelund then right along Buskhedevej, another of the old Hærvej routes, towards Funder and Funder Kirkeby. Take the right fork for Funder Kirkeby and continue ahead to main Road 15. Turn right to Hørbylunde Bakker where there is a memorial to the Danish priest and poet Kaj Munk who was murdered here by the Gestapo in January 1944.

Beyond Hørbylunde turn left for **Christianshede** where there is a 'mini-zoo' with a collection of about 300 animals, many of which may be handled under the supervision of the keepers. Continue towards Sepstrup then turn sharp right through heathland, dunes and forest towards Hjøllund. The area has a number of inland dunes resulting from devastating sand drifts in the late Middle Ages. Just before reaching the main road turn sharp left to Vrads near the end of the veteran steam railway line from Bryrup, with a small railway museum and restaurant in the old station building. The railway runs for 5km (3 miles) through some particularly attractive forest scenery including the Snabegård Plantage and several lakes. Much of the remainder of the old rail track has been converted into walking routes.

Return to **Vrads** and just past the church turn left along Torupvej, past three burial mounds to Torup Sø then through Palsgård Skov. Turn left at the T-junction to Boest then right into **Nørre Snede** whose twelfth-century church contains a very fine granite font known as the 'lion font', carved in 1200. The double lions depicted on it are incorporated into the municipal coat of arms. The town is in the centre of the Jutland Highlands and has a small district museum. South-west of the church in Rørbækvej an Iron Age village is being excavated. It dates from about 4-500BC and some of the finds can be seen in Vejle Museum.

One of the finest and best preserved stretches of the Hærvej runs south from Nørre Snede. Follow the main road south for about 4km (2 miles) and at Hundshoved turn right onto a gravel road by two impressive burial mounds. The way is signed and runs for about 5km (3 miles) to Øster Nykirke. There are parking places at intervals with information boards showing footpaths in the area. About 1km (half a mile) after leaving the main road the way crosses a brook, and in about 1½km (a mile) another stream in a culvert where a number of tracks radiate in different directions. Continue along the gravel road for another 1km (half a mile) to a tarred road. Denmark's longest river, the Gudenå, and another river, the Skjern Å, both rise in the vicinity. Turn right along the tarred road towards Vestermølle and at Vester Kirke turn right towards Ballesbækgaard, near the Rørbæk Sø. There is car parking and a visitor centre with information about the Hærvej and the surrounding country. Leaflets are available describing way-marked walks in the area.

Return to the crossroads where the tarred road crosses the gravel road, turn right and continue along the Hærvej to the twelfth-century church at Øster Nykirke standing on a 130m (426ft) high hill and whose tower served as a landmark for travellers. Continue along the tarred road to Nørre Kollemorten, turn right at the T-junction, then left after about 2km (a mile) to Oksenbjerge and **Give**. The district museum here depicts the way of life on old moorland farms in the district, an old school classroom, and other workshops are also featured. The church on the site of an ancient holy well contains murals dating from 1100.

Leave Give along Torvegade to Tykhøjetvej and cross into Øster Hovedvej. Continue to Ris, turn right along the main road to **Givskud** then follow signs to Løvepark or Lion Park, a 400-acre game park which is one of Denmark's noted attractions. Many animals such as lions, zebra, elephants, buffalo etc, and many species of bird roam freely and visitors may drive through in their own cars.

If the diversion to Give is omitted, continue from Nørre Kollemorten along the Hærvej route direct to Givskud then follow Road 18 into **Jelling** where two huge burial mounds are sited one on either side of the church. They are believed to be the burial places of King Gorm the Old and his Queen Thyra. Outside the church are two rune stones, the smaller of which was placed there by King Gorm in memory of his wife. The second stone was erected by Harald Bluetooth in memory of his parents, also to inform succeeding generations of his own important deeds. The inscription 'The Harald who won the whole of Denmark and Norway and made the Danes Christians' lies under the oldest known picture of Christ in Scandinavia, dated AD970. During restoration of the church in 1975-80 a chambered tomb was discovered revealing remains that were almost certainly those of King Gorm. The present church dating from about

AD1100 replaced no less than three wooden churches which had been built on the site, the oldest of which was bigger than the present church and was almost certainly King Harald's 'cathedral'. The frescoes in the chancel are quite unlike any other frescoes found in Danish churches. They are in fact copies, the originals being in the National Museum in Copenhagen. Unfortunately the artist who made the copies confused the original one of St John the Baptist with the Magi!

Leave Jelling by crossing the railway along Fårupvej, following signs to Fårup Sø. In about 2km (a mile) turn right along Gammelbyvej running north of the lake, over a crossroads, then turn left at a T-junction to cross the main Road 441 towards Sødover. Here, turn right and almost immediately left to **Engelsholm** Castle, erected in 1593 by Knud, brother of the noted astronomer Tyge Brahe. In 1730 it was altered to baroque style and is now used as a high school. Pleasant walks through the park and woods are indicated on a map in the car park. The domes and spire of the castle building are repeated on **Nørup** Church on the other side of the lake, reached by returning to Sødover and keeping left around the lake. The north chapel of the church dates from 1621, but the main building was reconstructed in baroque style in 1733, with furnishings to match.

From Nørup follow Schæferhusvej to the T-junction and turn left through Gødding Skov to the main Road 28. Cross over towards Randbøl, passing several burial mounds on the right. This is again on the Hærvej route. Continue through Randbøl and in about 2km (a mile) turn left to Bindeballe. Turn right in the village and keep straight on through Spjarup to join the major Road 176. Turn left in the direction of Egtved, and a short way along on the right will be seen Nybjerg Mølle, a privately owned watermill in beautiful surroundings. It has two undershot wheels and was in use from 1850 to 1934. Overlooking the mill pond is a statue of the Bronze Age 'Egtved Girl'.

Continue towards **Egtved**, and take the first turning on the left (Peder Platzvej), following signs to Egtvedpigens grav (Egtved Girl's Grave). In a small building in a field is an exhibition dealing with the finding of a well preserved body of a Bronze Age girl. In 1921 the farmer, Peder Platz, uncovered a hollowed out oak tree trunk when ploughing out a burial mound and staff from the National Museum realised it was a coffin dating from around 1400BC.

Return down Peder Platzvej to the main road, turn left to go under Road 417 to the T-junction, then turn right to join this road. Turn left to continue through Vester Torsted, and where the road bends to the left it is again following the Hærvej in its southward path. Continue on the major road to Bække and turn right along Klebækvej for about 1km (half a mile) to the Klebæk Høje ship burial site. The Hærvej passed straight through this area. From Bække continue south to

Asbo and turn left to Vejen which grew up as a trading centre for travellers along the Hærvej. The town's symbol is a goblin (*trold*) and outside the museum, the oldest art museum in the country, stands a fountain with a statue of a *trold* by the sculptor N. Hansen Jacobsen.

South from Vejen the route follows the line of Road 403 towards Skodborg . At the crossroads, turn left along main Road 32 in the direction of Kolding, passing the few remains of the medieval castle of Skodborghus. Here was the customs post on the frontier between Germany and Denmark after the annexation of Slesvig after the war of 1864. The next turning on the right leads past the old restored watermill, Knagemølle, on the Konge river. The river valley, Kongeå Dal, was the frontier until 1920, with Danish frontier guards on one side and German frontier guards on the other. It now forms the provincial boundary. Past the mill, turn right across the river and at the next T-junction turn right again into **Skodborg**, whose thirteenth-century cruciform church contains an interesting font of about the same age.

The road continues south to **Jels**, a village in a beautiful location near lakes. The village has one of the best preserved windmills in Denmark and remains of the foundations of a medieval castle. Jels is noted for the Viking pageant which is staged each July in the open-air theatre, details of which are obtainable from the tourist office. Just north of the village the Hærvej route divides, but the branch through the village continues south along Road 403 towards Vojens.

A diversion from Jels follows a minor road towards Klovtoft and Troldeskov. This may be translated as the 'Trolls Forest' and forms part of Stursbøl Plantage. It is an area of strangely twisted and stunted pine trees, and from the car park there are two waymarked trails, one leading past some thirty Bronze Age barrows. From the Troldeskov car park, continue along the minor road, turn left then left again through Stursbøl and Oksenvad (Ox Ford) back to the main Road 403, then turn right to Vojens.

Vojens lies at a road and rail junction with modern features. At the same time it lies on the Hærvej near a number of ancient and historical monuments including remains of a castle at Tørning just to the east of the town and a mill whose working power plant is now a museum. The stable buildings have been restored for use as a vehicle museum. A direct link with Route 18 may be made here.

Near Vojens Church a minor road (Jernhytvej) is signed to Vedsted. After about 2km (a mile) turn left along Tørningvej, then right along Vismarlundvej following signs to Høgelund and Vedsted. In **Vedsted** turn right and immediately left along Langdyssevej, following signs to Gravehøjene. Known as Holmshus Høj, this is the largest Stone Age settlement in South Jutland, with long barrows and passage graves.

PLACES TO VISIT ALONG
THE HÆRVEJ OR MILITARY ROAD

Klosterlund Museum
Finds from oldest settlement in Jutland.

Hørbylunde Bakker
Kaj Munk Memorial.

Christianshede
Mini-Zoo.

Vrads Museum
Also old steam railway to Bryrup.

Nørre Snede
Twelfth-century church. District museum. Iron Age excavation.

Give
Museum of farm life. Church with twelfth-century murals.

Givskud
Løvepark Game Park Free-roaming animals.

Jelling
Viking royal burial place with rune stones, unique twelfth-century church and burial mounds of King Gorm the Old and Queen Thyra.

Engelsholm Castle
Park, walks and Nørup Church.

Egtved
Burial place of Bronze Age girl, with exhibition showing details of clothing, etc.

Vejen
Art Museum.

Skodborg
Knagemølle restored watermill. Former Danish/German frontier on Konge river.

Jels
Well preserved windmill, castle remains, Viking pageant.

Tørning
Castle ruins and mill with power and vehicle museums.

Vedsted
Holmshus Høj Stone Age settlement.

Immervad Bro
Old monolithic bridge on Hærvej. Hærulfsten rune stone on well preserved section of Hærvej.

Damgårde Mølle
Windmill and simple camp site.

Urnehoved
Site of Jutland's ancient court.

Padborg
Bov Museum Exhibits on Hærvej history.

Frøslev
Frøslevlejrens Museum Concentration camp museum.

Return to Vedsted, turn right past the inn, Slukefter Kro, along the main street and turn right towards Skovby, passing a lake with a bathing place. Cross the E3 motorway and just before reaching the main Road 435 on the edge of Skovby turn to the right back across the motorway, then right along the main road. After a few metres turn left following signs for Hærvejen and Hærulfstenen. This stretch of the old Hærvej is preserved almost in its original condition, and in about 2km (a mile) a sign leads to Immervad Bro (Immervad Bridge), a stone bridge beside the road. It is at the oldest crossing point of the

Rune stones at Jelling Church

Sønderå. The present bridge, formed by a single massive granite slab, dates from 1776 and is modelled on older bridges built of tree trunks. Continue through the wooded area and soon the rune stone known as the Hærulfsten appears on the right. This is one of the oldest rune stones in Denmark, bearing the carved runic inscription 'Hærulf', and is one of the stones marking the route through difficult country.

The road continues to Hovslund Stationsby and joins the main Road 24 running south to Rødekro. A short distance after joining the main road a minor road to the right across the railway leads to Damgårde Mølle, a well preserved windmill dating from 1867 by a simple camp site for walkers and cyclists. From the mill either return to main Road 24 and continue to Rødekro or take the road past the mill parallel with the railway, joining Road 24 nearer Rødekro.

Beyond the town, just after the railway crossing, turn left then immediately right in **Rise** where one of the signposts erected by order of King Christian VII stands by the church which dates from 1200. Continue past the church, turn left at the T-junction then right towards Søst and Årslev. Keep straight ahead at the crossroads at Road 443 to join another crossroads about 2km (a mile) after the road makes a large bend to the right. Turn left to the next crossroads at

Urnehoved where, in medieval times, the South Jutland court was held. About 5km (3 miles) further south after crossing Road 42 the road crosses another stone bridge, Povlsbro, of about the same age as Immervad Bro, and reaches the main Road 481. Turn left across the motorway into **Kliplev** with an old medieval pilgrim church dating from about 1500 with a very large choir and the oldest belfry in the country.

Leave Kliplev along Storegade towards Vilsbæk and keep straight ahead parallel to the motorway, then turn right at a T-junction, across the motorway. Turn left to Gejlå, once more on the line of the Hærvej which crossed the river Gejl by another old granite bridge. The way continues south through Bommerlund Plantage and at the T-junction with Road 8 turn left, cross the motorway bridge and turn right. The first turning on the left is Hærvejen, leading into **Padborg**. At a T-junction turn left into Nørregade then sharp right into Bovvej where Oldemorstoft, an old farm dating from 1528, houses Bov Museum with exhibits dealing with the history of the Hærvej.

From Bov Museum return to Nørregade, and continue down the street to cross the railway to the major road. Turn right and keep parallel with the railway to the T-junction where a left turn followed by a right turn leads across the motorway bridge. Follow signs to the right for Frøslevlejrens Museum established in a former German internment camp set up in 1944 to house 1,500 prisoners. From the camp, either return to Frøslev where the motorway E3 crosses the frontier into Germany, or go into Padborg.

The Hærvej originally ended at the Dannevirke, an old defensive earthwork in South Slesvig, formerly part of Denmark but now in Germany.

6

SOUTH JUTLAND
THE BORDERLAND

S outh Jutland consists of the province of North Slesvig and the island of Als, which is connected to the mainland by bridges. Bounded on the north by the Konge river and on the south by Denmark's only land frontier, the people, buildings and customs show the influence of the area's long and turbulent history as a borderland. The scenery ranges from beaches and cliffs to wooded hills and heather-clad moors. Restaurants and inns serve many characteristic local dishes and during the summer there is sure to be an opportunity to see 'Ringridning' or 'Tilting at the Ring', a South Jutland tradition dating from the Middle Ages. The largest festivals take place in Sønderborg, Gråsten and Åbenrå with up to 500 horsemen in traditional costume trying to spear hanging rings with their lances while riding at full gallop. Smaller gatherings take place in towns and villages all over the province.

In the eighth century the mainland border of Denmark ran across the Jutland peninsula near what is now the German town of Slesvig. A wall of earth and wood called the Dannevirke was built to defend the frontier, the vital trade link between the North Sea and the Baltic and the Hærvej trade and military route from North Jutland which terminated at this line. In 810, Charlemagne acknowledged the river Eider just to the south of the Dannevirke as the frontier between Germany and Denmark and it remained so until 1864. During the intervening years power passed back and forth between the Danish monarchy and the German dukes of Slesvig-Holstein and a customs frontier was established in the thirteenth century between North and South Jutland.

In 1848 the duchy of Slesvig-Holstein demanded a free constitution and the incorporation of the Danish province of Slesvig into the German Federation. The province south of Flensborg had become very German-oriented but the northern part was still Danish speaking and inconclusive military confrontation followed in 1848-50. After the death of Frederik VII the new king, Christian IX, signed the law separating Slesvig from Holstein resulting in an ultimatum in 1864 from Bismarck, the new political leader of Prussia, threatening war. A final bloody battle around Dybbøl north-east of Flensborg resulted in defeat for the Danish army and the subsequent occupation of South Jutland as far as a line just south of Ribe and Kolding.

This period was one of great hardship and many Jutlanders emigrated to the USA. Although Denmark remained neutral during World War I, men from occupied North Slesvig were conscripted into the German army and 6,000 of them lost their lives. The Treaty of Versailles confirmed the right of the people of Slesvig to decide their own nationality, and in 1920 a plebiscite returned a 75 per cent majority in favour of the reunification of North Slesvig with Denmark, thus establishing the present Danish/German frontier on a line to the north of Flensborg and south of Tønder. This short historical account may help to understand much of what is seen today in South Jutland.

ROUTE 18 • CHRISTIANSFELD, HADERSLEV AND ÅBENRÅ

Christiansfeld, Haderslev and Åbenrå are three interesting old towns often overlooked by visitors speeding north on the E3 motorway from the German frontier. There is much to see in the area including historic churches and monuments and quiet beaches with views across the Lillebælt to Funen and the smaller islands off the coast.

Christiansfeld, a small town about 15km (9 miles) south of Kolding on Road 170 was founded in 1773 by the Moravian Brethren who were granted a charter by Christian VII. He was impressed by what he saw on a visit to Zeist in Holland where a Moravian Mission had existed since 1745, so he offered to sell them the royal farm Tyrstrupgård. The centre of the town around the church remains almost untouched by the ravages of time, many of the buildings being scheduled monuments.

The town centre, completed in about 1800, is planned in the shape of a cross with Kongensgade running north-south and Linde-gade east-west. The architecture is impressively simple, unlike that of other Danish towns, many of the buildings including the church of the Moravian Brethren being clad in weatherboarding. The Brethren are skilled craftsmen and the whole area gives a lasting impression of these skills. The buildings in Kongensgade were originally used as stables and stores for various groups. The tourist office has good information about the town and the Moravian Mission, written in English. At the corner of Kongensgade and Lindegade is Brødrehuset, the house of the Brethren, where the young unmarried men lived and the first craftsmen had their workshops in the cellars. In the yard stands the unusually large and well preserved pump which

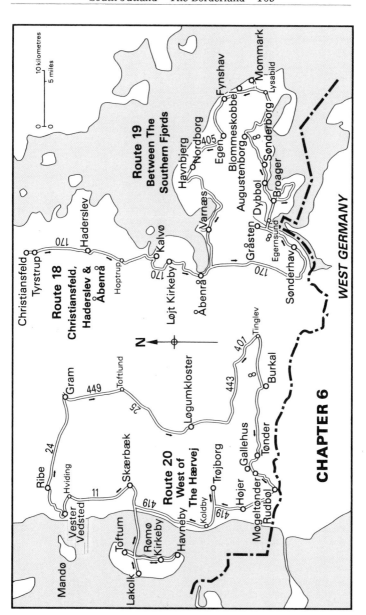

up to the year 1800 supplied water for the house and area. The first factory making stoves covered with glazed tiles was established here and so was the bakery which made Christiansfeld Honey Cakes or Gingerbread. This latter delicacy is still made to an original eighteenth-century recipe and may be bought in the town.

Lindegade, lined by lime trees, has a number of well maintained buildings including the pastor's house with large attic gable and attractive wrought iron railings to the front steps. Opposite is the church square with a beautiful old well and pump which was supplied with water through a 3km (2 mile) long pipe made from hollow oak tree trunks from 1797 until about 1900, when iron pipes were installed. The spring still supplies the town but with modern pumping plant. Facing the square is the church of the Moravian Mission, a very large hall without supporting pillars which can accommodate 1,000 persons. Originally consecrated in 1777, it is notable for its black-tiled roof and copper clad spire, all other houses in the town having red tiles. The interior is marked by its simplicity, being white with only a liturgical table. The only decoration is provided by the old hand-forged chandeliers.

The first house of the town whose foundation stone was laid on 1 April 1773 was the first chapel and now houses the kindergarten. Beyond the attractive tree lined church square in Nørregade are Enkehuset (The Widows' House) and Søsterhuset (The Sisters' House). The former building now contains flats but an extension built in 1799 in Birkevej is the site of the South Jutland Fire Museum and also the Moravian Mission's own museum. The Sisters' House was originally built as a secondary school for young girls in 1777. Parts are still in use as such, the remainder being private dwellings and offices.

From Kongensgade a left turn leads to Genforeningspladsen, the reunion square with a memorial to the reunion of North Slesvig with Denmark in 1920. The square lies between Kongensgade and Gudsageren (God's Field), the cemetery of the Moravian Brethren, consecrated in 1773 and arranged in the shape of a cross with the sisters' graves to the right, the brothers' to the left, all with identical simple tomb stones.

Leave the town via Lindegade then turn right along Gammel Kongevej towards **Tyrstrup** where the original church was built in the thirteenth century but was demolished to make way for a new road. The present building from 1862 incorporates some of the granite from the old church and was the first South Jutland church to be visited by Christian X following the reunion in 1920. Opposite the church is Denmark's first old peoples' home, the Christina-Friedericka Institution named after the benefactress who founded it. It was used as an old peoples' home by the parish until 1977, when it was taken over by the municipality as sheltered accommodation. Past the church, turn right into Kirkealle then left onto the old main Road 170 to Haderslev.

Haderslev on a fording point over the fjord and near the Hærvej became an important trading centre, receiving its first charter in 1292. It was once the seat of Christian IV who was married in the castle, later destroyed during the war with Sweden in 1644. A great benefactor of the town was Duke Hans who built a hospital, dispensary and Latin School. The town centre is one of the oldest in the country, carefully restored so the narrow streets appear as a small village within the heart of the city.

A brief walk can start from the tourist office in Apotekergade. Turn right then right again and through Klosteret into Hægersgade. Go right and on to Præstegade where from the wrought iron gates of the Klosterkirkegård (Convent Churchyard) a fine view of the cathedral can be obtained. Walk through the cemetery to the World War II memorial with a view over the lake park and the inner lake.

Return along Præstegade and across Apotekergade to the cathedral, founded in the twelfth century but destroyed a century later. It was rebuilt of brick and during extensive reconstruction between 1420 and 1440 the church, then a collegiate church of Slesvig diocese, acquired its impressive Gothic nave and choir measuring 22m (72ft) from floor to roof, the tallest in Scandinavia. Its three arched chancel windows 16m (52ft) high give a wonderful impression of light and space. The beautiful bronze font cast in Flensborg in 1485 and the baroque pulpit from 1636 are but two of the treasures to be seen, together with an altar created during restoration between 1941 and 1951. On the altar stands a crucifix from around 1300 and side figures from around 1400. The organ, originally constructed in 1652, is the second largest in Denmark with an international reputation and its baroque front to the top gallery has been preserved.

The Church of Our Lady in Haderslev played an important part in the Reformation, becoming the first Lutheran church in the country. A disastrous fire started by fleeing troops in 1627 destroyed much of the building but restoration was completed in 1650. After reunion in 1920, a new diocese of Haderslev was established in 1922 so the great church became a true cathedral.

The old Latin School lies north of the cathedral and through the mews to the south is an area with many half-timbered houses, including a well restored gabled house in Slotsgade from 1580 housing the Ehler collection of pottery of all kinds from the Middle Ages to about 1900 together with paintings, tapestries and furniture. Across the street at number 25 is a café and craft and graphics workshop with changing art and craft exhibitions. Walk along Slotsgade and Slotsgrunden then right into Naffet, past the old fire station, the old rectory dating from 1591 and the old county administration offices.

Badstuegade on the right leads to Møllepladsen where the old castle watermill building has been converted into a theatre. Cross the bridge to Duke Hans Hospital and chapel, scene of fierce fighting in 1848-9 and again in 1940 on the day of the German invasion. A memorial to the memory of those who fell on 9 April 1940 stands in the grounds. Along the river to the east is a bridge to Sejlstensgyde and the harbour, where the old Haderslev lightship can be visited. The same ticket gives admission to the half-timbered 'Riding House' in Sejlstensgyde, formerly the riding school of the Slesvig Lancers but now home of the unique Slesvig carriage collection.

The Haderslev Museum in Aastrupvej is a modern building containing the principal archaeological collection of this part of Denmark together with local historical exhibits and reconstructions of street scenes and rooms from the late nineteenth century. There is an open-air department with old farm and other buildings and a windmill.

From the lake park reached via Præstegade, Klostervænget and Bisbroen, boat trips go from the inner lake into Haderslev Dam, an extension of the fjord, and up the lake, calling at several places including Søholm Dairy Farm, the first modern dairy farm in Denmark, where visitors are welcome. At the far end of the lake is another landing at Damende where there is a restaurant. A footpath known as Geheimerådens Sti leads back to the town, making a pleasant change to returning by boat.

Alternatively, follow the path from Damende as far as the footbridge over the canal then turn right along the canal towards **Christiansdal**, once the 'cradle of industry' of the duchy of Slesvig. The whole area is situated in a deep wooded valley and the water power of the Tørning river was harnessed as long ago as 1772 to drive factories including a tinplate works; an oil mill, glass and brickworks and saw mills. In 1907 a fire devastated the area leaving only the electricity generating plant still operational. It is the oldest hydro-electric power station in Denmark still generating for the public supply and the buildings have an exhibition dealing with the area. Tørning Mill, which contains a small electricity generating plant, may also be visited together with the old castle mounds. The return to the lake may be made along paths through Pamhule Skov; a leaflet in Danish with a clear map of the paths is published by the State Forestry Service. There are car parks at Damende, near Christiansdal and at Tørning Mill. A direct link with Route 17 may be made here.

Leave Haderslev across the fjord by the inner lake and along Road 170 south to Hoptrup. Just before the Unox garage turn left towards Diernæs and Sønderballe, then ahead to Sønderballe Strand. Turn right at the coast and in about 1km (half a mile) turn sharp left towards Genner Strand and across the causeway to **Kalvø** a small island ship building centre famous for the clipper ships built there around 1850. A small museum in one of the houses contains a fascinating collection of models of ships built during that period together with a display of historical relics and details of the local shipyard, with tools and other items. Before the shipyard was opened in 1847 the island was uninhabited but with the construction of the slipway, houses and other buildings including a forge were built. The yard became the biggest shipyard outside Copenhagen but with the demise of sail it lost its importance early in the present century.

Return over the causeway, turn left to the main road near Genner, turn left towards Åbenrå and in about 2km (a mile) left again to **Løjt Kirkeby**, the principal centre of population for the peninsula of Løjtland, noted for its pleasant hilly countryside and large farms once owned by sea captains. The church dating from about 1100 has a most beautiful carved and painted triptych from the sixteenth century and a very fine model ship.

From the church turn left along Storegade to a signpost to Stollig on the left. Turn along the narrow lane with high hedges, passing several thatched cottages. At Stollig turn right and in about 2km (a mile) turn left towards Dimen and join the main road into **Åbenrå**.

The town of Åbenrå is an important industrial centre with one of the deepest ports in Denmark. Starting as a small fishing hamlet it received its first charter from Valdemar II in 1335 and grew in prosperity during the seventeenth and eighteenth centuries when ships from its port sailed all over the world. The influence of this time can be seen in the many fine houses from 1730 and 1800. The long shopping street is one of the most attractive in the country, but just down the side streets the old town has been carefully preserved.

A short walk around the town can start from the car park near the junction of Madevej and Rådhusgade. Go past the town hall and along the passage Rådhusgangen to Møllegade, then along to a crossing where Persillegade goes up on the right past small houses which were, in the eighteenth century, homes of poor people. At the junction with Nygade turn left then right into the passage called Jomfrugangen leading to Vægterpladsen, a pleasant square which leads to Store Pottergade then through Lille Pottergade to the church square with its World War I memorial.

A fire largely destroyed the town in 1247, after which the Skt Nicolai Kirke was rebuilt of brick. The altarpiece dates from 1642 and the richly decorated pulpit from 1565 although the canopy is not so old. Go through Kirkestien into Nygade, turn left past interesting buildings into Nybro. At the end turn right along Slotsgade to cross Møllemærsk into Ved Slottet by Slotsvandmøllen or the castle watermill, said to date back to 1530-40 and originally forming part of

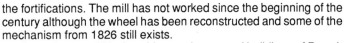

PLACES TO VISIT IN AND AROUND CHRISTIANSFELD, HADERSLEV AND ÅBENRÅ

Christiansfeld
Unaltered eighteenth-century town. Church of Moravian Mission. South Jutland Fire Museum.

Tyrstrup Church
First church visited by Christian X after reunion.

Haderslev
Restored city centre, cathedral, Ehler collection of pottery, old lightship. Riding House, Haderslev Museum, lake boat tours, Søholm Dairy Farm,

Christiansdal eighteenth-century industrial complex. Tørning Mill.

Kalvø
Ship building yard with museum.

Løjt Kirkeby
Peninsula with large sea captains' farms and twelfth-century church.

Åbenrå
Preserved town centre, St Nicholas Church, castle watermill, Brundlund Castle, Åbenrå Museum, Hjælm and Sønderskov with walks.

 the fortifications. The mill has not worked since the beginning of the century although the wheel has been reconstructed and some of the mechanism from 1826 still exists.

 Opposite the mill is the white gatehouse and buildings of Brundlund Castle, built in 1411 in the time of Margrethe I. The original Renaissance building was rebuilt about 1905-8 in its present style and is the official residence of the prefect of South Jutland.

Return across Møllemærsk and up Slotsgade, passing large late eighteenth-century houses then earlier houses with magnificent gables. Turn left along Søndergade and Storetorv then right through Rådhusgade to the junction with H.P. Hanssens Gade near the bus

 station. Turn left and on the right is Åbenrå Museum, the principal maritime museum for South Jutland with one of Denmark's greatest collections of maritime paintings, together with models, navigational instruments, tools and equipment, all relating to the great locally-based shipping industry of the eighteenth and nineteenth centuries. Displays also cover town and local history, prehistory and modern Danish art.

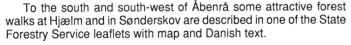 To the south and south-west of Åbenrå some attractive forest walks at Hjælm and in Sønderskov are described in one of the State Forestry Service leaflets with map and Danish text.

ROUTE 19 • BETWEEN THE SOUTHERN FJORDS
(a circular tour)

The peninsula between Åbenrå and Flensborg Fjords has an extremely beautiful coastline along Flensborg Fjord and there are historic places to visit at Gråsten, Sønderborg and the island of Als.

Leave Åbenrå along Kystvej and Flensborgvej (Road 170) along the shore past the marina and sailing club and a large electric power station with one of the deepest harbours in Denmark. Keep straight ahead through Lundsbjerg and Sønder Hostrup, passing a large picnic area beside the road near Hostrup Sø. There is no access to the lakeside but it is possible to drive along some of the forest roads.

Continue past Søgård and Søgård Sø to Kruså. This is a good road but is not busy since completion of the motorway. Turn left at the crossroads in Kruså and in about 500m (457yd) turn right, signed Kollund Strand. Continue beside the beautiful Flensborg Fjord with several parking places. It is worth stopping at **Sønderhav** to admire the view over the fjord with the islands of Lille Okseø and Store Okseø in the foreground. It is said that Queen Margrethe I died of the plague on Store Okseø on her way from Flensborg in 1412. A local ferry boat may be called for a short trip to one of the islands which are very popular with visiting yachtsmen.

The road follows the coast then through Rinkenæs and Alnor with a fine view across the water to the Broager Land peninsula and the twin spires of Broager Church. Turn left in Alnor along Sildekulevej towards **Gråsten**, an attractive little town with extensive woodlands traversed by a number of waymarked paths. The seventeenth-century Gråsten Slot was given to the Danish crown prince and princess (later King Frederik IX and Queen Ingrid) as a wedding present in 1935 and is still used as Queen Ingrid's summer palace. The park and the sixteenth-century baroque palace chapel with its ornate altarpiece are open to the public when the royal family is not in residence, entry being through a small gate in the wall opposite the car park by the bridge at the end of Slotsgade.

Return to Alnor and turn left through Egernsund to **Broager** whose beautiful twelfth-century church contains some interesting murals from the Middle Ages and a very fine fifteenth-century wood carving of St George and the Dragon in the porch. In the churchyard are memorials to soldiers who fell during the wars of 1848-50 and 1864 and nearby is a memorial mound to 189 men from Broager who lost their lives when forced to fight in the German army during World War I. The towers were probably used as observation posts by the Prussians during the bombardment of Dybbøl in 1864. From Broager go through Mølmark, Gammelgab, Skelde and Dynt to the highest point on the peninsula at **Gratelund**, with spectacular views over the landscape of hills and woods, glacial valleys, lanes and beaches.

Return to Broager and take the road north towards Nybøl. From the old ramparts just before Smøl there are spectacular views. Turn right through Smøl to the main road and turn right at the next main crossroads to Dybbøl Banke and Dybbøl Mølle. Park by the mill and walk to the ramparts at **Dybbøl Banke** with magnificent views over Sønderborg Bay and Flensborg Fjord. The whole area is a national monument commemorating the battles fought here for freedom in 1848 and 1864, during which the mill was badly damaged twice. The complex comprises ten sets of gun emplacements and other defence works, and a number of the original cannons used in the battles still stand on the ramparts. A small museum in the mill house describes with illustrations, relics and maps the history of the struggle for control of Slesvig and South Jutland. The mill itself can also be visited. The loss of South Jutland following the defeat of the Danes here in 1864 was finally reversed after 56 years of foreign rule when the population voted for reunion in 1920, and Dybbøl Mill has become a national symbol for the Danish people.

From the mill go down the road into **Sønderborg**, crossing the old lifting bridge over Als Sund. The new main road bridge can be seen to the left and Sønderborg Slot to the right. The town is a good centre for exploring the whole area with good accommodation including Youth Hostels in Sønderborg and Vollerup just outside the town. A large marina caters for visiting yachtsmen and there is a good shopping centre, but the 'gem' of the town is the fine medieval castle founded about 1170 for coastal defence, dominating the town and its natural harbour. Numerous additions were made to the original structure and the castle has been both home and prison for Danish kings. Christian II was imprisoned here by his noblemen in the sixteenth century and the dukes of Augustenborg were governors of the castle for more than a century. In 1568 Queen Dorothea, widow of Christian III, founded a beautiful chapel in the castle notable for being the first royal Protestant church and the earliest Renaissance room in Scandinavia.

Throughout its history the town has had many trading disputes with Flensborg and during the two Prussian wars Sønderborg, Dybbøl and the island of Als were of great military importance. The town was bombarded and suffered much damage during the campaign of 1864 which is why there are so few old buildings, and after the defeat at Dybbøl the town was a naval base for the German Baltic squadron. Following the reunion in 1920 Sønderborg developed rapidly and the population has trebled from 10,000 to 30,000.

The castle became a museum in 1920 with collections relating to South Jutland's history with particular reference to the Slesvig wars and the occupation of 1940-5. There are also cultural collections from Als and Sundeved and a collection of paintings, making it the largest provincial museum in Denmark.

Leave along Alsgade to join the main Road 8 on the outskirts of the town and go in the direction of Fynshav. There is a fine view of **Augustenborg** Fjord to the left and soon the marina and causeway across the inlet appear. Park at the end of the causeway and walk through the main street to Augustenborg Slot, an impressive baroque palace built in 1770 whose main buildings surround a courtyard entered through an arched gatehouse with clock tower. The northern wing contains a beautiful rococo chapel now used as the parish church. The altar, pulpit and organ are constructed one above the other and the marble font was the gift of Tsar Alexander I of Russia in 1807.

From the car park at the causeway continue towards Fynshav then take the next turning on the right to Kirke Hørup where the church on a hill has a very big wooden belfry separate from the main building. Go left along the major road, turn right towards Hørup at the next T-junction then left along Road 427 signed Kegnæs and continue towards Skovby. In about 4km (2 miles) turn left through Vibøge to Lysabild. From this road there are some good views of the island of Ærø. Turn left in Lysabild and follow the main road towards Fynshav. Beyond Lille Mommark turn right at the main road junction. At this point it is possible to go straight on to **Mommark** from where a ferry service to Ærø (Route 32) operates during the summer. Alternatively, from the road junction after turning right towards Mommark turn left almost immediately in the direction of Fynshav and after about 4km (2 miles) look for a tourist sign pointing to the right to **Blommeskobbel**. Follow the signs to a small car park in the woods near one of the largest megalithic monuments consisting of two long barrows, the biggest 53m by 12m (171ft by 39ft) made of sixty-nine stones, together with two round barrows.

Return to the main road and continue to **Fynshav**. At the junction with main Road 8 turn right for the ferry terminal. From here the ferry takes 45 minutes to cross to Bøjden on Funen to join Route 22, an attractive alternative to driving over the road bridge at Middelfart.

Alternatively, continue the tour by turning left at Road 8 and immediately turn right towards Guderup. A small diversion to the right at **Østerholm** leads to the ruins of an old castle dating from 1733 of which only the foundations remain. Near it is an attractive half-timbered thatched building, Østerholm Kro. From here the Nørre-skov, a wooded area along the coast with waymarked walks and car parks, may be visited. A State Forestry Service leaflet with map describes the routes and a number of Stone Age barrows may be seen similar to those at Blommeskobbel.

Continue on the main route to Guderup, passing an attractive restored windmill built in 1888 on the left at Elstrup. At the crossroads

Flensborg Fjord; Store Okseø and Lille Okseø

beyond Elstrup continue ahead to the T-junction at the major road. Turn right and immediately left to **Egen** Church dating from about 1200. The conical wooden bell tower in the churchyard is a memorial to the fallen of World War I. Next to the church are the half-timbered and thatched church stables built in 1700, some of the largest and best preserved in northern Europe.

Return to the main Road 405 and bypassing Guderup continue towards Nordborg. Past the two large Danfoss factories at **Havnbjerg** is Elsmark Mølle, another beautifully preserved windmill built in 1835 in Dutch style with thatched roof and fantail to replace an earlier mill destroyed in a storm in 1776.

The town of **Nordborg** was built around the castle whose origins go back to about 1150. The present picturesque white buildings with black tiled roofs are the work of a German architect who designed them in 1909 as a private school. They are still used as such so are not open but the public may visit the courtyard and gardens. Look across the valley to the church, built around 1250 with a tower dating from 1789. It has a richly carved altarpiece and pulpit and a late Gothic crucifix on the chancel arch. The town was largely destroyed by fire in 1792 so none of the houses are older than that date but in Bækgade and other neighbouring streets there are many quite outstanding house doors which are painted and carved in a most

118

attractive manner.

Return to the main Road 405, cross over and go through Oksbøl and Mjels to **Hardeshøj** where a small car ferry crosses the Als Fjord to Ballebro in Sundeved. From the ferry landing, turn right at the T-junction to **Varnæs** and visit the little Romanesque church built in 1150. It has a fine fifteenth-century triptych and a seventeenth-century carved font canopy. On the large wooden belfry in the churchyard are two iron collars used to punish those who failed to observe church holy days. From the church follow the main road towards Åbenrå and turn right to **Varnæs Vig** on the coast where there is a car park and picnic area. The scenery is particularly attractive and a number of waymarked walks lead along the beach and coast path. The forest lake (*skovsø*) is up to 7m (23ft) deep and surrounded by cliffs up to 30m (98ft) in height, the result of glacial action. An excellent leaflet is available with an English translation and map.

Return to the main road at Varnæs and turn right along the coast road to Åbenrå.

ROUTE 20 • WEST OF THE HÆRVEJ

This route begins at **Tønder**, famous for its lace and its beautiful church. The town lies on the 'Green Coast Road' which runs from Holland along the north-west coast of Europe to the tip of Denmark, across the Skagerrak and up the west coast of Norway.

Tønder claims to be the oldest market town in Denmark by virtue of its first charter granted in 1243, although an earlier reference appears in a work by an Arabian geographer in 1130. A Franciscan monastery was established here in 1238 and from the Middle Ages until the Reformation the town was an important harbour and market centre. In the middle of the fifteenth century dikes and other defences against flooding reduced the importance of the harbour, leading to the growth of the lace making industry for which Tønder is internationally renowned. The rich lace merchants built beautiful town houses notable for the richly decorated front doors and several of these houses have been preserved. They can be seen in Østergade, where the tourist office can be found, and in Uldgade, Storegade and Vestergade. Despite these fine relics from the past Tønder remains a thoroughly modern town with good shops and facilities, and hosts an annual jazz and folk festival every August.

One of the most richly decorated churches in Denmark is Christchurch, built in 1591 on the site of the previous St Nicholas Church. The nave of the earlier church was demolished, and the tower incorporated into the present structure. The upper part of the spire dates from around 1500-20 but the base is older, although the date of the original building is not known. The tower once served as a

PLACES TO VISIT BETWEEN THE SOUTHERN FJORDS

Gråsten
Royal summer palace with chapel, park and woods.

Broager
Interesting twelfth-century church with murals and war memorials.

Gratelund
Highest point on peninsula with fine views.

Dybbøl
Windmill and fortifications, museum and memorials.

Sønderborg
Bridges across Als Sund. Castle with notable chapel and historical connections. Denmark's largest provincial museum.

Augustenborg
Baroque palace with chapel, park and forest open to public.

Blommeskobbel
Large megalithic barrows.

Østerholm
Castle ruins, *kro* and forest walks in Nørreskov.

Elstrup
Restored windmill.

Egen
Interesting church with unique church stables.

Havnbjerg
Elsmark windmill.

Nordborg
Interesting church and castle, now reconstructed as school.

Varnæs
Twelfth-century church with wooden belfry and iron collars for restraining offenders.

Varnæs Vig
Area of natural interest.

navigation mark. Some of the furnishings come from the old church, notably the font (1350) and pulpit (1586) and a very fine rood screen is dated 1625. Kongevej encircles the old town centre on three sides and crosses the river Vid by Bachmanns Vandmølle, a watermill dating from 1598 and now used for music recitals.

A short way along Kongevej beyond the modern town hall is Tønder Museum, in the extended gatehouse of the old castle. This museum contains one of the most important collections relating to the cultural history of South Jutland and Slesvig-Holstein, together with a large collection of Dutch tiles, a fine display of Tønder silverware and an important collection of Tønder lace. Furniture and effects closely linked to the culture of Friesland form an important part of the museum's contents. Next door is the South Jutland Art Museum specialising in works by nineteenth- and twentieth-century Danish artists and sculptors including many lesser known artists not represented elsewhere.

The area around Tønder is quite unlike any other area of Denmark, bearing more resemblance to the low-lying marshy areas of

Christchurch in Tønder from the town square

North Friesland and Groningen in the Netherlands. The Tønder marshes are protected from the sea by a series of dikes first built in the sixteenth century. Some farms are built on artificial mounds and the marshland has been drained, creating polders used for grazing sheep. The Danish word for a polder or reclaimed land is *kog*. The area supports a variety of wildlife including wading birds, storks and lapwings and the marvellous quality of the light is attractive to artists.

From the town centre follow Strucksalle across the railway to Bargumsvej, turn left and go to the T-junction with the main road on the edge of the town. Turn right to the junction with Nordre Landevej, Road 419, and turn left towards Højer. After about 1km (half a mile) turn left towards Møgeltønder. A diversion takes the next turning right towards **Gallehus**, where inscriptions on two stones record the finding in 1639 and 1734 of two twelfth-century golden horns which were sent to a museum in Copenhagen, from where they were stolen in 1802 and melted down.

Continue into **Møgeltønder** which has one of the finest village streets in northern Europe with a row of beautiful thatched Frisian houses. Known as Slotsgade, the street was built in 1680 between Schackenborg Castle and the church. The church is the oldest building in the town, the nave dating from 1175. In 1275 it was enlarged and a tower was added in 1500-35, serving as a navigation mark until it was demolished in a storm in 1628, then rebuilt slightly shorter. The interior is quite outstanding with its gilded altarpiece from 1500 and richly decorated sixteenth-century balcony linked to the pew of the Count of Schackenborg and his family. Murals, some dating from the thirteenth century and a carved pulpit dated 1694 together with many other paintings and decorations in the choir and nave all contribute to the overall effect. The organ is the oldest still in use in a Danish village church and was built in 1679. In the churchyard is a memorial to local men who died in World War I.

 Walking back along Slotsgade towards Schackenborg Castle, the last building on the left is the inn which received its licence in 1687. The first mention of the castle is from 1233, but in 1661 the castle and estate were acquired by Field Marshal Hans Schack and until recently it has been owned and inhabited by members of the Schack family. The present mid-eighteenth-century baroque building is now owned by Prince Joachim, younger son of Queen Margrethe.

The road running south by the church leads to **Rudbøl** on the Danish-German border, and one of the official crossing points. It is only open during the daytime, and the border runs through the centre of the village street. The main part of the village lies on the north side of Rudbøl Sø, where there is a Youth Hostel. Returning from the frontier, bear left on the road towards Højer across marshes and reclaimed *kog* land.

Højer is one of the oldest villages in Denmark and its centre is almost untouched. About 250 houses and farms are the subject of 'Preservation Orders', the major attraction being Højer Mølle, northern Europe's tallest wooden windmill. Of Dutch type, it was built in 1857 and restored in 1976-7 to house a museum dealing with the mill and the marshes of the area. The town has some interesting old buildings including Kiers Gård, a farmhouse dating back to 1400. The church dates from about 1250 and has a Gothic altarpiece from about 1400. The main characteristic of the town is its position in the marshes, often threatened by flood disasters in the past and the mill museum tells of the protective dikes and the Højer Sluse which was built in 1861. Finally an outer dike and Vidå Sluse with locks were completed in 1980 and proved able to withstand the storm floods of 1981. The salt water lake enclosed by the dike and the surrounding marshes provide excellent breeding grounds for wildfowl. An exhibition building is located by the sluices.

From Højer take the main Road 419 north, and at Vester Gammelby turn right towards Visby and Sølsted. After about 4km (2 miles) turn left up a narrow track to the impressive ruins of **Trøjborg**, a castle built in 1580 with four wings and four towers and copper-clad roofs. It stood in a swampy area protected by moats, so well protected that the Swedes in the 1643-5 war could not capture it. It eventually fell

Højer Mølle

into disrepair and was partly demolished around 1851. Return to the main road and cross over towards Hjerpsted. This is the coast road and is still Road 419. Continue through Ballum to the major road junction where the causeway goes left to Rømø Island.

The 10km (6 mile) long causeway built in 1940-8 leads to **Rømø** which is about 9km (5½ miles) long and 6km (4 miles) wide. The western side of the island is open to the North Sea while the eastern shore faces the coast of Jutland and is bounded by tidal shallows . The scenery varies from marshland to heather moors, and from sandy beaches to woodland, supporting a rich variety of wildlife. **Havneby** in the south is a modern fishing port and ferry terminal for the German island of Sylt, while inland are old farms. St Clements Church at **Kirkeby** dates from 1250 and has a fine collection of ship models and unique gravestones of former captains of whaling and other ships. On the west coast at **Lakolk** camp site an old workman's wagon has been set up as a 'mini-museum' showing the geology and natural history of the island, while at **Toftum** the Kommandørgård or

Commander's House contains Rømø Museum. The beautiful interior with painted panels and Dutch tiles shows how the prosperous whaling captains lived in the eighteenth century. Today Rømø is a very popular holiday resort with many beach and holiday houses and Rømø Ny Sommerland family recreation and play park.

Return across the causeway and follow signs into **Skærbæk** where the museum in an old merchant's house has historical and local cultural collections, an archaeological exhibition and a Rømø room with furniture and other objects from about 1800. Follow Road 11 north towards Ribe, but at Egebæk turn left to Vester Vedsted where a tractor bus goes at low tide across the tidal flats to the little island of **Mandø** about 5km (3 miles) away, one of Europe's most important sanctuaries for birds and seals. With about 100 inhabitants it was a self-contained community in former times with its own mill, church and farms. An inner dike built in 1887 was broken by a storm in 1923 but an outer dike constructed in 1936-7 has since protected the island and its inhabitants from the sea. A house built about 1831 preserves the style and furnishings of a captain's home from the days of sail. The single inn on Mandø has limited accommodation for visitors, who are warned not to attempt to drive their own cars across the tidal flats even at low tide along the bus route as it is very dangerous. Information on the times of the tractor bus service are available from the local mainland tourist offices. Return to Vester Vedsted and follow the road through Sønder Farup and Øster Vedsted to Ribe.

Ribe was an important Viking trading centre before the year 800 and one of the first Christian churches in Denmark was built here in 948. During the early Middle Ages it was a focus of trading routes to many countries and was Denmark's most important town. Situated on slightly rising ground in the flat expanse of the meadows and marshes of the coastal plain, Ribe owes its importance to its river, the Ribe Å, which enabled boats to come into the quay to load and unload. This continued until the late Middle Ages when the river began to silt up and the trade routes were diverted. However, the town is still a very lively and progressive centre.

With about 550 buildings scheduled as being of historical or architectural interest Ribe can claim with some justification to be Denmark's oldest town. Even so, the town centre is quite compact and much can be seen during a short walk. The tourist office in Torvet has a number of excellent brochures and booklets in English.

Several late sixteenth- and early seventeenth-century houses face onto the square including the half-timbered inn Weis' Stue. Dominating the square is Ribe Cathedral, or Church of Our Lady. The earliest churches on this site were wooden structures, the first being founded by Ansgar, the apostle of the north, around 860. Building of the present church began between 1150 and 1175, and after many additions and alterations it appears today as Denmark's only five aisled church. The tall red brick tower dates from the fourteenth century and housed the town alarm bell for warning of storms and other hazards. At the top, reached from inside the church, there are extensive views over the surrounding countryside. The Maria Tower contains the carillon bells which play four times daily.

From the cathedral cross to Skolegade to see the old grammar school founded in the early sixteenth century, and Hans Tausens house with an archaeological museum. Cross Sønderportsgade and walk along Puggårdsgade with its cobbled pavement and well preserved old houses from the fifteenth and sixteenth centuries, all lived in and with rich carving and beautiful doors. At the end of the street turn left and left again, returning along Bispegade to Sønderportsgade. Cross to the right then left into Støckens Plads to see Denmark's oldest existing town hall. Built in 1496 the building became the town hall in 1709. The former debtors' prison holds a small collection of items relating to the town's history.

Turn back across Støckens Plads into Dagmarsgade and from Skt Catherinæ Plads the St Catherine Church and abbey can be reached. Founded in 1228 they are, with the cathedral, the only preserved pre-Reformation buildings older than 1536 remaining from Ribe's formerly numerous churches and abbeys. The original church collapsed owing to the soft ground and the present building dates from the fifteenth century. Admittance to the medieval cloister court is through the church but the abbey buildings are an institution for elderly people. The Art Museum in Skt Nicolai Gade may be reached by a footpath leading from the end of Skt Catherinæ Plads and contains works of Danish artists from the early nineteenth century up to the present.

Continue along Skt Nicolai Gade to Nederdammen and go back across the river to Mellemdammen and Quedens Gård, a sixteenth-century merchant's house, now a museum. Turn right along Skibbroen, the harbour quay which is now only used by pleasure craft. Near the end is the flood column which records the height of water during floods in former times. Continue until the road turns left into Korsbrødregade then take the first right into Erik Menveds Vej. This leads to Riberhus Slotsbanke, moated castle mounds with ruins and a statue of Queen Dagmar. The castle was first raised in the early twelfth century but was pulled down in the mid-seventeenth century.

The return to Torvet may be made through Erik Menveds Vej and Grønnegade. Before leaving the town mention should be made of the old custom of the watchman. Every summer evening at 10pm the watchman, dressed in top coat and peaked cap and carrying a lantern and spiked mace, appears outside Weis' Stue in Torvet and patrols around the old town centre singing a traditional song recalling former times when it was vital to check for fires and other dangers during the night. Visitors are welcome to accompany the watchman on his round and he will tell (in English) stories about the town and buildings passed on the route.

Leave Ribe along main Road 24 through an area of forest and heathland to the town of **Gram**. Turn left in the town to Gram Slot, a castle whose history goes back to 1314. The present buildings on an island in a mill pond were built in 1664 by Hans Schack, and are still owned by the same family. The west wing houses the South Jutland Natural History and Geological Museum which includes fossil finds from nearby claypits, notably whale bones 6 million years old. The childrens' department is a particularly good example of the best modern museum technique.

From Gram take Road 449 south to Toftlund in an area of heathland and woods which are ideal for walking and cycling. Continue south on main Road 25 through Nørre Løgum and Løgumgårde to **Løgumkloster** where Cistercian monks came in 1173 to establish a church and monastery which were completed about 200 years later. After careful restoration between 1913 and 1920 the church presents an impressive interior with a remarkable late Gothic altarpiece with rare painted wood carvings. Most of the monastery buildings were demolished after the Reformation, only part of the east wing remaining. Associated with the monastery was the Refugium, a place of retreat which today provides the means for private individuals or groups to enjoy a quiet stress-free stay together with facilities for conferences, meetings and courses in pleasant and peaceful surroundings. Near the church is the Frederik IX bell tower, 25m (82ft) high with a carillon of forty-nine bells, the largest in Scandinavia, associated with a school for carillonneurs. Frequent concerts are given on the bells. The Holmen Museum in the town has exhibitions on local history, monasteries from the Middle Ages and modern religious art and architecture. The *Gøglerstatue* in the market square depicts three travelling showmen, marking the holding of an annual church service for such people during the August market and fair.

Travel south along Dravedvej for about 4km (3 miles) to **Dravedskov**, an area of woods and bog with waymarked walks described in a State Forestry Service leaflet. Continue for another 2km (a mile) beyond the woods to the road junction, turn left along the major road to Road 435 then right at the next T-junction onto Road 443 through Søvang and Sottrup to Bredevad. Turn right onto Road 401 and continue towards Tinglev. Just before reaching the town a turning on the right leads to Sommerland Syd, a family recreation with amusements for all.

PLACES TO VISIT WEST OF THE HÆRVEJ

Tønder
Lace merchants' town houses, Christchurch, Bachmanns Vandmølle, Tønder Museum, South Jutland Art Museum.

Tønder Marshes
Area of reclaimed *kog* land.

Gallehus
Site of finding of twelfth-century golden horns.

Møgeltønder
Finest village street in Denmark. Schackenborg Castle in baroque style. Twelfth-century church with oldest working organ and murals.

Rudbøl
Border village with divided main street.

Højer
Town in dike area with many preserved buildings. Large windmill with museum.
Fine thirteenth-century church.

Vidå Sluse
New flood control sluices on outer sea dike, with exhibition building.

Trøjborg
Castle ruins.

Rømø Island
Causeway to mainland.

Havneby
Fishing port with ferry to Sylt.

Kirkeby
St Clememts Church.

Lakolk
Mini-museum of geology and natural history.

Toftum
Kommanderøgård Museum of life of whaling community. Ny Sommerland (amusement park).

Skærbæk
Museum of daily life, archaeology and Rømø room.

Mandø Island
Tractor bus service. Church, mill, inn and farms within protection of dike.
Preserved sea captain's house.

Ribe
Denmark's oldest town centre, Ribe Cathedral, St Catherine Church and abbey, Skibbroen harbour, Riberhus castle mounds, Quedens Gård (museum), Hans Tausens Hus.

Gram
Castle with combined Natural History and Geological Museum.

Løgumkloster
Cistercian monastery church and Refugium, bell tower, Carillon-neur School, Holmen Museum.

Tinglev
Sommerland Syd (amusement park).

Burkal
Thirteenth-century church with fine paintings and carvings.

In Tinglev turn right following Road 8 in the direction of Tønder. **Burkal** Church is reached after about 10km (6 miles). It has an elaborately carved and painted pulpit, font cover and altarpiece. The ceiling has some particularly fine original paintings which have been well restored. From here continue along Road 8 back to Tønder.

7
FUNEN
DENMARK'S GARDEN

It is said that the island of Funen, or Fyn as it is called in Danish, represents the whole of Denmark. It is also called 'Denmark's garden', and both sayings certainly have a lot of truth in them. The varied and beautiful landscape ranges from hilly areas covered with forest to cliffs and beaches, largely created during the last Ice Age. The coastline is over 1,000km (690 miles) long and provides ideal opportunities for sailing and fishing, yet culture is very much alive. This is not to be wondered at with such famous sons as Hans Andersen and Carl Nielsen who portrayed springtime in Funen in poetry and music. There are almost endless opportunities for exploring Funen by car, cycle, on foot or by rail and bus.

ROUTE 21 • MIDDELFART AND NORTH-WEST FUNEN
This tour begins in Middelfart where Funen is linked to the Jutland mainland by two bridges. The first, built in 1935 to replace the ferry from Strib to Fredericia, was designed to carry the road and railway across the Lillebælt and is more than 1km (half a mile) long. In 1970 Denmark's first suspension bridge was built to the east of the older bridge and carries the E66 motorway from Jutland to Funen.

Middelfart is an old fishing port with a history going back to Viking days and became recognised as a market town in 1496. Attractive old houses in Algade and Brogade include Henner Frisers House, a beautiful half-timbered building which is now the home of the local museum. Near the museum the twelfth-century Skt Nicolai Kirke has a beautiful seventeenth-century baroque altarpiece.

From the church go through the town towards the hospital on the Fredericia road, turn right, then in about 1km (half a mile) turn left following signs to Hindsgavl. Follow the drive to the car park then walk towards the manor, the main building of which dates from 1785. This is now used as a conference centre and is not open to the public, but a museum in the former farm buildings has a permanent exhibition.

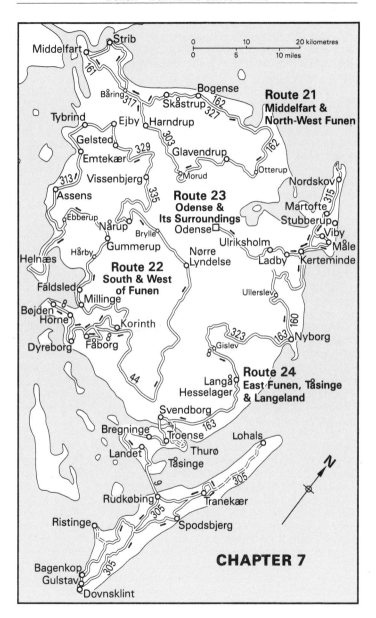

CHAPTER 7

A trail marked with blue signs leads through the estate with several look-out points, some still containing cannon, providing magnificent views over to Kolding Fjord. From one point there is a view of the Slotsbanke, the remains of the earth ramparts of the original thirteenth-century castle.

Return to the main road and leave the town following signs to Odense. Do not go left to the motorway but keep along the old Road 161 for about 2km (a mile) after passing under the railway bridge, then turn left at signs for Bogense and Strib. After passing under the motorway turn right in Stavrby along Road 317 signed Bogense, forking left at Skovs Højrup. After a sharp bend in the road where it crosses the river Stor turn left and follow signs through Bro to Ørbæk and Mejlskov. Follow the very winding road to a T-junction and turn left for **Skåstrup** village where there is an old smithy and other old farm buildings. From here follow signs into Bogense.

The town centre of **Bogense** is very pleasant with picturesque half-timbered buildings and one of the best yacht harbours and marinas in Denmark. Go along Østergade and turn right at the town hall, following the Otterup Road 162. Away to the left can be seen a white windmill, and woods lie to the right. By the turning on the right signed to Smidstrup is the Renaissance mansion and estate of Gyldensten. Continue to Vester Egense, keeping left on Road 162, and after passing through Nørre Nærå turn left at the crossroads to Kørup. Keep straight ahead at the next junctions and about 1km (half a mile) further on there are some interesting cottages belonging to Egebjerggård Manor. Continue around the corner and up the hill to the next junction signed to Otterup, and turn right to Krogsbølle where there is a lovely old farm building. Rejoin the main Road 162 towards Otterup and just after passing through Norup the wooded hill on the left known as Jeppeshøje is the site of the former Ting or council meeting place for North Funen.

Through Otterup turn right for Nislevgård and Bladstrup. Nislevgård Manor was established in the late seventeenth century and the present building is a large nineteenth-century house used as a childrens' home. Continue to Bladstrup, turning right where the major road curves left towards Fremmelev. On reaching the T-junction in Bladstrup turn left, then left again onto Road 327. In about 200m (182yd) take a turning on the right to **Glavendrup**, and at the crossroads go right towards Glavendruplund and Torup. In about 400m (365yd) there is a parking place on the left. Go up a track to the Glavendrupstenen, where there is a boat-shaped long barrow over 100m (328ft) long and a Bronze Age rune stone with the longest runic inscription of any in Denmark. On the site are other memorial stones including a 'Freedom Stone' commemorating 5 May 1945.

Return through Glavendrup to Stensby, turning right at the T-

The old and new Lillebælt bridges

junction then left to **Søndersø**. The attractive building by the lake on the left is Dallund, a moated manor house now used as a convalescent home. Continue through the town and join Road 335 to Vigerslev, where signs are followed left towards Vedby and immediately right towards Tværskov. In a few hundred metres take the unmade road on the left to pass the small manor house of Margård. The present baroque building dates from 1745 but the manor has existed since the fourteenth century. Turn right at the next crossroads and go through Margård Skov to Tværskov. Turn left at the T-junction and in about 500m (547yd) pass the old Tværskov watermill on the right. Continue over the next crossroads and in the woods turn left at the T-junction to reach the main Road 303 opposite Komigen Kro. Cross over and take the left fork.

At the foot of the hill by a stream on the right is Røde Mølle, a watermill first mentioned in 1688 as a grainmill. It was rebuilt as a sawmill after a fire in 1832 and came under a preservation order in 1956. Follow along the road, taking the next turning on the right then right again, descending to Langesø, an eighteenth-century manor house. The house is now owned by the Langesø Foundation and is not open to the public, but the extensive woods and park have waymarked walks described in a free leaflet in Danish, with map. Drive past the entrance gates, down the steep left-hand fork and turn left along the winding road through the woods to Road 335, then turn right to Morud.

At the crossroads in Morud turn left along Road 303 towards Middelfart, and in about 4km (2 miles) the old manor house of Rugård is situated down a side turning on the left. Formerly a medieval royal castle surrounded by moats, the present building was completed in the nineteenth century in Dutch Renaissance style with a tower topped by a spire. On the right of the main road is the so-called 'Ventetornen' or 'Waiting Thorn', a large hawthorn tree which marked the staging post on the main road, known as Rugårdsvej (the ancient royal road from Odense to Middelfart). Local farmers transported the royal baggage from this point. At **Harndrup** there are some particularly nice old houses and the church has an unusual iron-bound door with an inscription dated 1505.

The road continues through Brenderup in an area once famous for hop and tobacco cultivation to join Road 317 running left towards Middelfart over Båring Hill, the old *Ting* Hill for the district. At the junction at the top of the hill beyond the crossroads in Båring turn right towards Båring Mark. This road is nearly 70m (230ft) above sea level and affords magnificent views over Båring inlet, the Røjle peninsula and the Lillebælt bridges. Continue along this road and turn left at the T-junction along Kystvejen, bearing right at the T-junction by the camping sign. At the next T-junction turn right signed to Vejlby Fed and Strib and continue through the summerhouse area in the direction of Røjle. At the next give way sign turn right along Bolsvej to the end, then turn left towards Røjleskov. From the church there are fine views of the sea and the suspension bridge at Middelfart. Take the next turning on the right and follow signs to the car park at Røjle Klint. There is a small promontory with a pleasant view across the Lillebælt to Fredericia and a path also leads down to the shore.

Return to the road junction, turn right, and right again at the next T-junction into **Strib**. Turn right at the first set of traffic lights and follow the road to the car park at Strib Odde, from where the ferries sailed before the building of the first bridge. Return to the main road and turn right to follow the coast road beside the railway and under the end of the suspension bridge into Middelfart.

PLACES TO VISIT AROUND MIDDELFART AND NORTH WEST FUNEN

Middelfart
Lillebælt bridges.
Henner Frisers House, Skt
Nicolai Church.

Hindsgavl
Hindsgavl Manor. Conference
centre with small museum of
local history and the area.
Thirteenth-century Slotsbanke
castle mound.

Bogense
Home of one of best yacht
harbours and marinas in
Denmark. Picturesque half-
timbered houses.

Glavendrup
Rune stone, long barrow and other
memorial stones.

Røde Mølle
Restored mill on 300-year-old site,
now preserved.

Langesø Slot and Lake
Manor, park and woodland with
map and walk descriptions.

Rugård
'Ventetornen' hawthorn marking
royal staging point.

ROUTE 22 • SOUTH AND WEST OF FUNEN

This route starts at Bøjden, the terminus of the car ferry from Fynshav on Als. It takes 45 minutes and is a very pleasant way to get to the south of Funen, especially for those who have driven through Germany.

From the ferry drive over the causeway in the direction of Fåborg. Turn right into **Horne** to see Funen's only round church, one of the seven such buildings in Denmark. It dates from 1100 with later additions and has a high square tower. From Horne Church drive south-east through Bjerne to the attractive fishing village of **Dyreborg** for a good view across the sound towards the islands of Lyø, Avernakø and Bjørnø.

Drive back through the woods and in about 3km (2 miles) turn right to **Fåborg**, an old seaport whose history goes back more than 750 years. The old belfry tower is all that remains of the town's first church, built in the thirteenth century. It forms a fine landmark, especially from the sea, and contains Funen's largest carillon which plays four times a day. The old streets spread out from the market place, with attractive nineteenth-century town houses. A short walk starting from Torvet by the belfry leads down Holkegade past the old Merchant's House, 'Den Gamle Gård'. Built in 1725, it now houses one of the town's museums. Turn right along Havnegade, past the marina and right into Vestergade which leads back through the west gate, Vesterport, the last remaining part of the medieval town fortifications.

Cross over into Grønnegade and about half way along turn left into Klostergade. A right turn along Hospitalsstræde leads to the Helligåndskirke or Church of the Holy Ghost, built in the sixteenth century as a monastery church but becoming the parish church after the Reformation.

From the church go along Kirkestræde back to Grønnegade and turn left. At the far end the Youth Hostel occupies old half-timbered buildings on the right with a 'newer' part on the opposite corner in the former town bath house which later become a cinema! Almost next door is Fåborg Museum, an interesting early twentieth-century building containing paintings and sculpture by Funen artists. Go through the archway opposite the museum into the pedestrianised Østergade, and at the crossing turn left into Tårnstræde. Turn right into Adelgade, a very narrow street with interesting old houses, then into Torvet and follow Strandgade to the harbour and the tourist office, located in the old Toldboden (Customs House). From Fåborg car ferries run to Gelting in Germany, also to the islands of Ærø, Lyø and Avernakø, while a post boat will take foot passengers to Bjørnø.

Leave the town along Banegårdspladsen, turning left before the road goes under the railway into Diernæsvej. Keep left into Prices Havevej and on the right is Kaleko Mølle. The site was in use for a watermill before 1440 and the oldest part of the present building dates from the seventeenth century. The mill contains the oldest milling machinery still in existence in Denmark, and a museum is now housed there.

Continue into Diernæs, turn left on the road to Svanninge, cross the main Road 8 and turn right at the next main road crossing. Park by the old windmill tower and restaurant, a starting point for walking in the Svanninge Bakker (hills). Views over the surrounding countryside can be obtained from the top of the tower, which also contains a small museum devoted to the landscape. Admission is free and much of the area is in the care of the National Trust. A leaflet in Danish with a map describes the walks in the neighbourhood.

From the car park continue north along Road 43 then turn right towards Korinth. In **Gerup** there is a school museum established in one of the oldest schools in Denmark, built in 1784. On reaching Korinth turn left and left again towards Øster Hæsinge, following the road beside Arreskov Sø past Arreskov Manor. In Øster Hæsinge turn left and left again onto Road 43 in the direction of Fåborg. Take the next turning on the right to Gammel Stenderup and turn left in the centre of the village to the main road. Turn left again and take the second turning on the right. Follow the winding road for about 5km (3 miles) to a crossroads then turn left to **Millinge** where there is Legetøjsmuseum (Toy Museum).

Turn right in Millinge along the coast Road 329, passing on the

Gummerup Museum

right the entrance to Steensgård Manor, the oldest part of which
dates from about 1535. The house is now a hotel and restaurant. The
road then runs through **Faldsled**, a fishing village with old home-
steads and fishermans' cottages, also the area's oldest chartered inn
dating from 1744. Beyond the village the road swings away from the
coast through woods, then a turning on the left goes past the entrance
to Damsbo Manor, a single storey building with Renaissance gables
dating from 1656. Continue to Strandby then right to Hårby and rejoin
Road 329 towards Glamsbjerg. In **Gummerup** the West Funen
Home Farm is a small but attractive museum in a farmhouse from
1826. It also includes a rebuilt clockmaker's house from 1776.

At Glamsbjerg turn left onto Road 168 towards Assens, and after
passing Øksnebjerg windmill, a Dutch style mill from 1859 on a hill
beside the road, turn left to Ebberup. Go under the bypass and over
the railway, turn left then right towards Snave. Turn right at the
crossroads into Slots Alle by Hagenskov, a former royal fortress
dating from 1251, replaced by a manor house in 1776. From
Hagenskov turn right along Helnæsvej through Brydegård and
Agernæs and across the narrow causeway of Langøre to the peninsula of **Helnæs** where the 28m (92ft) high lighthouse is open to the
public and provides a fine viewpoint.

Return along Helnæsvej and turn left along Slots Alle and left again into Å Strandvej which runs along the coast to Assens, passing 'De 7 Haver', the Funen Botanic Geographic Garden. The site is one of the warmest spots in Denmark, with beautiful views over the water towards the many islands.

The coast road runs on through Saltofte to **Assens** with its very busy harbour and marina. The old 'cooking house' is where the crews of sailing ships could cook their meals as lighted stoves were forbidden on board when in harbour due to risk of fire. The old custom house has a mark on the wall showing the water level during a great flood in 1872. During 1988 a new carillon was installed in the Church of Our Lady to mark its 500th anniversary, and nearby in a half-timbered house in Damgade is the Mands collection, a cultural-historical museum centred around the articles collected during his lifetime by the blacksmith Anton Mandsbyrd. Willemoesgård in Østergade is another museum specialising in maritime subjects, and sharing the tourist office premises further along Østergade is the Ernst family collection assembled during his lifetime by a local manufacturer.

Leave Assens by Road 313 towards Bogense and Middelfart, and at Sandager turn left to **Emtekær** where there is a memorial to the seven members of an RAF aircrew who crashed here in 1944. Turn left to Wedellsborg, Funen's largest estate with a history going back to the early fourteenth century. The present manor, which includes wings dating from around 1500, is private but the park and woods are open to the public. Follow the road north from the estate entrance across a marshy area to **Tybrind**. In January 1658 the Swedish army of 12,000 men with horses and equipment under King Charles X walked across the frozen water from Jutland and landed here to defeat the Danes. From Tybrind bear right through the woods back to the main road, cross over and follow the road to Ørslev. Turn left to Ejby, cross the railway and turn right to **Gelsted**. On the outskirts of the town, before crossing the railway, turn left on the road towards Grønnemose. At Rørup turn right towards Årup. Just after joining the main Road 329 the manor house of Erholm will be seen on the left. Dating originally from the fourteenth century it was largely reconstructed in the nineteenth century and has beautiful grounds.

Follow Road 329 north across the motorway to Paddesø and turn right following signs to Fyns Akvarium. Continue along the road which bends to the left then right under the motorway, then turn left along Road 161 following signs into **Vissenbjerg**, a large village in the centre of what is known as the 'green spot' of Funen. Vestergade leads into the centre to one of Denmark's largest village churches containing an elaborate carved altarpiece. Near the church is an interesting terrarium with Scandinavia's largest collection of reptiles. From it a path leads to the viewpoint on the top of a very long narrow

PLACES TO VISIT
SOUTH AND WEST OF FUNEN

Fåborg
Old seaport town with ferries to islands and Germany, belfry with Funen' s largest carillon, 'Den Gamle Gaard' housing the town museum, Helligåndskirke, Youth Hostel.

Kaleko Mølle
Watermill, machinery and museum.

Faldsled
Unspoilt fishing village with old inn.

Gummerup
West Funen Home Farm museum.

Helnæs
Peninsula with 28m (92ft) high lighthouse viewpoint.

Assens
Harbour with cooking and custom house, Mands collection, a cultural-historical museum, Willemoesgård Maritime History

Museum, Ernst collection.

Wedellsborg
Funen's largest estate.

Erholm Manor
English style gardens and park.

Vissenbjerg
Centre of geologically important area, Terrarium reptile collection. Funen aquarium.

Frøbjerg Bavnehøj
Highest point in Funen, with memorials.

Krengerup Manor
Fine neo-classical mansion with concerts in summer.

Nørre Lyndelse
Birthplace of Carl Nielsen with museum.

Egeskov
Beautiful castle with extensive park and gardens. Veteran Museum.

ridge with extremely steep slopes cut by steep narrow ravines, all the result of ice action over 15,000 years ago. A path runs along the ridge through the woods, with views over the village and the valley of the river Brænde. It is possible to make a circular walk, going down the slope at one end and returning along the valley with a stiff climb back at the other end. To the south of the viewpoint is what is known locally as the 'Abyss', a ravine that drops from 128m (420ft) to 16m (52ft) above sea level in a very short distance. A number of waymarked paths and cycle routes are described in a leaflet with Danish text and map.

From Vissenbjerg go down the steep winding hill to Tommerup Stationsby and in the centre of the village turn right in the direction of Lilleskov. Turn right at the T-junction to the large brickworks on the right which is currently being converted into a museum of tile making. Continue along the undulating road towards Frøbjerg, turning right at the T-junction after about 2km (a mile). Soon a sign on the right points

Many manor houses, although privately owned, can be seen from the nearby public road. This is Krengerup, in Funen

to a car park from which footpaths lead up onto Frøbjerg Bavnehøj, which at 131m (430ft) above sea level is Funen's highest point, affording magnificent views over a wide area. On top of the main peak is Denmark's oldest monument to the constitution while on the neighbouring hill is a large memorial dedicated to members of the Resistance who were killed during World War II. Nearby is an amphitheatre where open-air performances take place.

Back on the road turn right to Frøbjerg and take the first turn on the left along a winding road, then turn left at crossroads through Nyrup. At the next crossroads keep straight ahead through a gateway where the public road goes through the cobbled courtyard and estate of Krengerup Manor, one of the most distinguished of Funen's neo-classical manor houses from the late eighteenth century. Follow the road for 2km (a mile) through the wooded estate then turn left and left again, coming to a T-junction where a left turn leads towards **Nårup**. Turn right at the next T-junction and in Nårup village turn left at the crossroads following signs to Frydenlund Fuglepark or Bird Garden.

Beyond the Bird Garden turn right at the T-junction and follow signs through Tommerup and Brylle to cross the main Road 168 to Borreby where the Odense river is crossed. Continue to Fangel and go through the village and on through Dømmerstrup to **Nørre**

Odense town hall and Skt Knud's Kirke

Lyndelse, the birthplace of Carl Nielsen, the famous Danish composer. A small museum is established in his childhood home and a memorial sculpted by his wife stands near the church. Opposite the church take the road to Lumby and continue to Freltofte and on towards Gestelev passing the privately owned eighteenth-century moated manor of Nordskov.

Beyond Gestelev cross Road 323 and continue through Herringe and Rudme, crossing the railway into Volstrup. Turn right and after re-crossing the railway turn right again to Egeskov, one of Denmark's most beautiful castles. The sixteenth-century Renaissance fortress was built on oak piles and rises sheer from the water. The Veteran Museum in farm buildings has an interesting collection of carriages, cars, motorcycles and aeroplanes.

Turn left from the car park to main Road 8 then right towards Fåborg. In about 500m (547yd) turn left past Egeskov windmill and left at the next junction past Stenstrup Church to Kirkeby. Just before Kirkeby Church, near the bend in the road, turn right and follow the road through the woods to the main Road 44 and turn right. There is a good view of Hvidkilde, the white baroque manor house by the lake. The house is not open to the public but from the car park waymarked walks can be followed through the park into the forest. A leaflet in Danish with map is available. Along the main road past the lake is

Røde Mølle restaurant and the road continues towards Vester Åby. Immediately after a sharp bend across the Hundstrup river take the second turning on the right and follow the road through the woods to Brændegård Sø. Continue along the edge of the lake, keeping straight ahead at the next junction then taking the right fork past the end of Nørresø to the main Road 8. Turn left to the manor of Brahetrolleborg, originally a Cistercian monastery but which has been much altered. It is private but the north wing, formerly the monastery chapel, is now the parish church. Continue along the main road back to Fåborg.

ROUTE 23 • ODENSE AND ITS SURROUNDINGS

Odense is the capital of Funen, the third largest city in Denmark, one of Denmark's oldest cities and a place of pilgrimage in the Middle Ages. With the existence of churches and monasteries, it became a centre for artists, architects and craftsmen including some of the earliest printers.

Several free car parks are available within easy reach of the city hall which houses the tourist office. The city hall may be visited before starting a walk around the city. Cross Flakhaven to Skt Knuds Kirke, the cathedral dedicated to the martyred King Canute and whose spire dominates the city. The present fine brick-built Gothic structure was erected on an original eleventh-century church destroyed by fire in 1247, of which only the crypt remains. Two shrines in the crypt are supposed to contain the remains of King Knud himself and possibly those of the English St Alban. The finest adornment of the cathedral is the carved and gilded altarpiece made in 1520 for the Grey Friars Church and moved to Vor Frue Kirke in 1800 and then to Skt Knud's in 1874. The font, pulpit and organ all date from the restoration of the church, completed in 1754, and the overall effect of the interior is most impressive.

From the cathedral a footbridge leads into H.C. Andersen-Haven, a pleasant garden by the river overlooked by a statue of the writer. Keep around to the right to another footbridge leading back through Kloster Haven into Klosterbakken. Turn left and take the first turning on the right up Munkemøllestræde, near the top of which on the left will be seen Hans Andersen's childhood home, a little house where he lived with his parents from the age of 2 to 14. Turn back down the street, cut through on the right to Klaregade, turn left down to the bridge over the Odense river, cross over and turn right alongside the river on footpaths through Munke Mose Gardens to another bridge carrying a footpath and cycle path back across the river. On the other side, river cruises can be booked and boats hired. Cross the road and go ahead along Ny Vestergade, turn right along Vestergade and then left into Brandts Passage, leading to the former Brandt Klædefabrik

(Cloth Mill) which now accommodates a Graphic Museum, an art gallery with changing exhibitions of contemporary art, architecture and handicraft, and a Photographic Art Museum.

The area between the old factory and Kongensgade has been cleared, has a car park, shops and courtyard with trees, making a pleasant spot to rest and have some refreshment before continuing to the left along Kongensgade. Turn right at the crossroads into Vindegade and left along Klostervej to the Falck Museum which depicts the history of this unique rescue corps founded in 1906 by Sophus Falck as a rescue service at fires.

Continue to the end of Klostervej, turn right along Østre Stations-vej then right into Kongens Have. Pass the equestrian statue of Christian IX and continue towards the castle, now used as the residence of the royal Governor of Funen. Adjacent to the castle is Skt Hans Kirke, begun in the thirteenth century as an abbey church and having an external pulpit. Turn right into Vindegade then left into Jernbanegade to the Funen Art Museum and Prehistoric Museum on the left.

From the museum continue down Jernbanegade then left along Skt Gertruds Stræde through Gråbrødreplads, the site of the Francis-can monastery established in 1279 whose church preceded Skt Knuds as the parish church. At the end turn left along Asylgade then right along Gravene, across Nørregade and through to Thomas B Thriges Gade. Cross over to an area of older houses which is one of the city preservation areas. Ahead in Hans Jensens Stræde is the house where Hans Andersen was born, and which now provides the setting for the H.C. Andersen Museum with its unique collection displayed to illustrate the life and work of this well known and well loved character. The surroundings include many eighteenth- and early nineteenth-century houses, all subject to preservation orders but still lived in. At the end of the street beyond Claus Bergs Gade is the fine modern concert hall complex, the equal of any in Europe, which incorporates a museum devoted to composer Carl Nielsen and his sculptress wife Anne Marie.

Claus Bergs Gade leads from the concert hall into Overgade, and to the left is Møntergården, a collection of sixteenth- and seven-teenth-century urban dwellings preserved and furnished in period style, which also provide the setting for changing exhibitions. At the end of Overgade turn right along Frue Kirkestræde past Vor Frue Kirke which for a time housed the altarpiece now in Skt Knuds Cathedral. Turn right along Nedergade past more houses coming under the city preservation plans, rejoin Overgade and cross Torve-gade into Vestergade, one of the traffic-free main shopping streets of the city. Here a return can be made to the starting point of the walk at the tourist office.

Funen village

Beyond the railway station on the north side of the city centre is the Jernbanemuseum or Railway Museum, one of Europe's largest, based on the old locomotive 'round-house' near the railway and bus station.

From the Munke Mose landing stage on Filosofgangen boat trips along the river visit the Funen Tivoli Amusement Park and pleasure ground, which is next door to the Zoological Gardens, one of Denmark's most attractive zoos. To the south of the city centre via Albanigade and Hjallesevej and taking the left fork along Munkebjergvej the modern Munkebjerg Church may be seen. The nearby

Youth Hostel is in part of the former manor farm of Kragsbjerggården, the hostel buildings forming three sides of a hollow square, entered through an arched gateway. The fourth side is the manor house itself which is government property.

By continuing along Munkebjergvej, turning right along the ring road to the crossroads at Læssøegade and turning left, signs may be followed to Den Fynske Landsby or Funen Village, one of the country's largest open-air museums with over twenty farms, houses and other buildings from various parts of Funen dating from the eighteenth and nineteenth centuries, and re-erected to form a complete village.

Risinge Slot, near Kerteminde

ROUTE 24 • EAST FUNEN, TÅSINGE AND LANGELAND

This route covers the whole of Funen east of the Odense to Svendborg road, and the islands of Tåsinge and Langeland which are linked to Funen by bridges. For convenience the route described starts at Odense and finishes at Rudkøbing in Langeland, but shorter circular routes can easily be made by linking with Route 23 at Odense and with Road 9 at Ringe or Svendborg.

Leave Odense city centre via Overgade, Skt Jørgensgade and Åsumvej. At Åsum where the main road turns left, keep straight on up the hill in the direction of Bækskov and Marslev. After passing through Rågelund bear right and continue through Marslev keeping left at the church, and at the T-junction turn left on the main road towards Kerteminde. After a sharp right-angled bend to the right, turn left opposite an inn, signed to **Ulriksholm**. The Renaissance manor house dating from 1636 stands in a superb position on the edge of Kertinge Nor and is now an hotel and restaurant. Take the next turning left along Ulriksholmvej to Kølstrup Church, dating from 1100. In the car park from which there is a fine view across the water towards the mansion is a 'freedom stone' commemorating the liberation of Denmark in 1945.

Continuing through the pretty and popular holiday village of Kertinge, turn right to **Ladby** and as soon as the first houses are

PLACES TO VISIT IN AND AROUND ODENSE

Skt Knuds Kirke
Gothic cathedral with shrine of martyred King Canute and fine gilded altarpiece.

H.C. Andersen-Haven
Memorial garden with statue of Hans Andersen.

Hans Andersen's Childhood Home
Cottage of Hans Andersen's parents.

Brandt Klædefabrik
Former cloth mill with Graphic Museum, an art gallery and Photographic Art Museum.

Falck Museum
History and development of Falck rescue corps.

Funen Art and Prehistoric Museum
Including paintings of Funen

School, and prehistoric culture of Funen.

H.C. Andersen Museum
Material on life and work of the writer.

Odense Concert Hall
Including Carl Nielsen Museum.

Møntergården
Museum collection of sixteenth- and seventeenth-century houses. Exhibition venue.

Jernbanemuseum
Railway Museum
Working model railway layout and display material.

Munke Mose
River trip to Tivoli Amusement Park and Zoological Gardens.

Den Fynske Landsby
Open-air museum village.

reached at the bend in the road, turn left and follow the sign 'Vikingskibet' to a small car park by a thatched cottage. Tickets can be obtained here to view the only known Viking grave in Denmark in which a chieftain was buried in his own ship together with his horses and hunting dogs. A path behind the cottage leads to the grave mound commanding an extensive view over the fjord. A farmer found it by chance in 1935 and fortunately the people immediately concerned took steps to cover and preserve the wooden ship whose hull can now be seen in a protective chamber built inside the original mound. It is in the care of the National Museum and information on the discovery is displayed in the cottage.

Continue through Ladby village following signs to **Kerteminde**, entering the town by the Langebro, the bridge across the entrance to Kerteminde Fjord. The old fishing village with its red-roofed houses lies along the shore at the entrance to the fjord and facing out over the Storebælt beyond the harbour entrance is the modern yacht marina. The parish church of Skt Laurentius in Langegade dates from the thirteenth century and contains relics of the Swedish war of 1658-9 in which Kerteminde suffered severely. Adjacent to the church is the tourist office and in the next road, Strandgade, the old fifteenth-century custom house contains exhibitions of the works of local artists. Further along Langegade is Farvergården, the oldest house in the town, a half-timbered building dating from 1630 now containing the Historic Museum. Around the corner to the right in Trollegade is the Høkeren (Museum Shop). This is a re-constructed shop from about 1900 established in a building dating from 1700, and goods and office furniture typical of the time are on display.

Leave the town centre along Langegade, away from the bridge over the fjord entrance, and just after joining Hindsholmvej opposite the Marina, park in the car park on the right and walk up Møllebakken on the left. The Svanemølle windmill stands on a site occupied by windmills since 1600. The present structure dates from 1853 and has been completely restored. Opposite the mill is the former home of Johannes Larsen, a painter of bird life and Danish landscapes, known also for his woodcuts and book illustrations. Larsen designed the house and gardens, and lived here for 60 years until his death in 1961 at the age of 94, and the property is maintained as a museum containing works by Larsen and many other artists.

Continue north along Road 315, and where it bends sharply left at a speed restriction sign, go ahead towards Måle, passing the Hverringe estate with a very large farm on the left and a late eighteenth-century moated Palladian manor house on the right. **Måle** itself is an attractive village with many old half-timbered houses and large thatched farms and fine views over to Romsø Island. Continue to **Viby**, another attractive village with a recently restored stage mill and a very interesting Gothic church with a half-timbered tower added in 1718. Attached to the church is a large mausoleum, the chapel of the Juel family from Hverringe. From Viby take the road past the mill to Salby, turn right at the main road and continue through Messinge and Dalby to Scheelenborg Manor, where the road turns sharply to the right towards **Stubberup**. Enter the village whose Romanesque church, often called locally the 'White Virgin', was enlarged in the fifteenth and sixteenth centuries. The pulpit dates from that time but the altarpiece is from 1632.

Rejoin the main road and beyond **Martofte** village turn right along Snavevej following signs to Jættestuen. A small signpost on the left marks a lay-by from which a path leads across the field to a high mound containing one of the largest single-chamber passage graves in Denmark with a main chamber over 10m (33ft) long with full standing headroom. A torch is necessary to view the interior. Return to the main road from which a number of large grave mounds can be seen and continue north past orchards and through the village of Nordskov to **Kørshavn** where there is a pretty harbour and a large car park in a popular holiday area. It is possible to walk to Fyns Hoved,

Nyborg Museum

the outermost tip of the Hindsholm peninsula, taking about 40 minutes there and back. A visit to this area is worth the effort and would repay a longer stay.

From Kørshavn return south along the main Road 315 through Dalby and Salby to Kerteminde, going through the town to Langebro and across the fjord. On the far side, on the right of the road, is the statue of a fisher-girl known as *Amanda* who is supposed to represent a local girl Sophie Krag who became an actress but suffered an unhappy love affair. Where the road forks by a factory on the left, go left into Klintevej then immediately take a right turn along Skovvej which leads through the woods past the Youth Hostel on the right and the pavilion on the left before curving left to rejoin Klintevej, Road 165. Turn right along the coast road with outstanding views over the Storebælt. After passing Risinge Slot, a most unusual eighteenth-century black and white timber-framed manor house with a large square tower, take the next turning on the right signed to Kissendrup, noting the large farm houses with ornamental patterned brickwork as well as traditional thatched houses. Turn right at the give way sign in Kissendrup, pass a pond on the left, and continue through Langtved and Mullerup, turning right along the main Road 315 towards Kerteminde. Take the next turning on the left to Hannesborg then turn right along Skovsbovej. In the trees on the right is the manor house of Skovsbo dating from about 1400, and in a field to the left is a large early seventeenth-century wayside crucifix belonging to the estate, an unusual sight for Denmark.

Continue to **Rynkeby**, and at the beginning of the village turn right to the church. The original twelfth-century building has had many additions. Beyond the church turn left and left again to rejoin the road back past the Skovsbo crucifix. Turn right along Bøgeskovvej past small farms and orchards, and at the main Road 160 in Ullerslev turn left past the church then right on Road 315 signed to Ørbæk. Just across the railway is the lovely manor house of Hindemæ, one of the finest classical residences in Funen, built in 1787. The interior decoration is original, and the furnishings are from the seventeenth, eighteenth and nineteenth centuries. The house may be visited to view the contents, and exhibitions and sales of antiques are held.

Turn right from the manor and keep straight ahead where the main road bends right. Follow the road across the railway bridge and back to main Road 160, turn right and passing Avnslev Church to the right continue into Nyborg.

From about 1200 to 1413 **Nyborg** was the home of the Danehof or Danish parliament, with many buildings from the Middle Ages remaining. In the centre of the town are the remains of the castle built in 1170 which was restored in 1917. In nearby Kongegade is Mads Lerkes Gård, a fine fifteenth-century merchant's family home, now a museum. At the other end of Kongegade is the late fourteenth-century Church of Our Lady with a fine fourteenth-century Gothic chandelier and four ship models, the oldest being *Staden Nyborg* from 1774. A group of pipes in the organ are the oldest pipes still in use in Denmark, having come from the original organ installed in 1596. Forming part of the original ramparts from 1660 is the oldest existing landport or fortress gate in Denmark, and a pleasant walk around the ramparts encircling the town terminates at Den Hvide Jomfru, a white-washed brick tower built in 1660. From the harbour both a car ferry and a train ferry go to Korsør in Sealand and from Knudshoved harbour to the east of the town where the motorway ends another car ferry service connects with Halsskov on Sealand.

From Nyborg town centre take Strandvejen and Dyrehavevej on Road 163, passing an interesting windmill on the right, cross Nyborg Fjord past a good picnic area and the beautiful early seventeenth-century manor of Holckenhavn on the left, then immediately turn right towards Kogsbølle. Go straight ahead at the next three junctions through Sulkendrup in the direction of Refsvindinge. The road is undulating, attractive, and passes Lillemølle watermill on the right, opposite its mill pond. The mill is private but can be seen from the road. In Refsvindinge turn left onto Road 8 and in Ørbæk turn right on Road 323 in the direction of Ellested and Fjellerup. On the right a rough track leads to a very small car park at Lindeskov Dolmens, by a long barrow, beyond which more dolmens may be seen in the woods. In Ellested turn right in the direction of Måre and beyond a church and bridge over a stream turn left along the narrow winding Åsvej. At a T-junction by a yellow house turn left to Ravnholt, an attractive little seventeenth-century manor whose park is open to the public.

Continue to the T-junction and turn left on main Road 323 through Fjellerup to Gislev. Turn left through the town and then right. At the next crossroads go left to Svindinge past the church with a tower and spire, then turn right and left again towards the sixteenth-century Glorup Manor whose great park and gardens are open to the public. The road encircles the manor before continuing into **Langå** whose church contains some sixteenth-century frescoes, and join main Road 163. Turn right and just after the end of the bypass turn left beyond a white house towards Vormark. In about 1km (half a mile) turn right towards **Hesselager** then in 500m (547yd) follow signs left to the *Dammestenen*, an enormous erratic boulder from Norway left by the retreating ice. Return to the road and turn left, then in Hesselager turn left again to pass Hesselagergård, a most impressive sixteenth-century brick-built moated mansion.

Turn right at the next crossroads then left at the main road towards Svendborg through Oure and Vejstrup. Just beyond Vejstrup on the

Typical Danish church at Rynkeby, Funen

right of the road where it crosses the stream is a beautifully-preserved watermill. The road continues through Skårup then runs down Nyborgvej into **Svendborg**. Follow Nordre Havnvej into Havnegade and Toldbodvej where parking is possible. From the tourist office in Torvet walk up steps leading to Vor Frue Kirke built on a rise overlooking the old town and harbour. Originally built in 1253-79, it was rebuilt in the Middle Ages and has a carillon made in Holland. The church path leads left to Fruestræde and Anne Hvides Gård, the oldest half-timbered house in the town, built around 1560 and now a museum. Along the street on the right is Pistolstræde, leading to Møllergade, then Tullebrinke. Møllesti, a path on the left, crosses a big parking area on the right to join Dronningemaen which is followed uphill to the left. On the right is the Zoological Museum. Turn left into Grubbemøllevej, and at its junction with Svinget the former workhouse, Viebæltegård is another museum with old craft workshops and archaeological collections from Svendborg and south Funen.

From Svinget the footpath Studiegangen leads to Viebæltet. Turn left past the library and bear left again down Bagergade, a street with some of the oldest houses in Svendborg. To the right along Fruestræde and across Torvet is Skt Nicolai Gade with Skt Nicolai Kirke, Svendborg's oldest church dating from before 1200 which has a sixteenth-century tower. A number of boat trips including a tour of

Ravnholt, Funen, is one of the many estates open to the public

the sound by an old steamer, *Helge* built in 1924, and ferry services to the island of Ærø start from the harbour.

The pleasant island of **Thurø** can be visited via Christiansminde-vej, past the Youth Hostel, to the causeway across Skårupøre Sund. Cyclists can follow the path along the shore to the causeway. The island of **Tåsinge** is joined to the 'mainland' of Funen by the Svendborgsund Bridge, built in 1966 to carry the main road. Outstanding views of the bridge and Svendborg sound can be obtained from the old Skt Jørgens Kirke, reached along Strandvej and under the end of the bridge.

Leave Svendborg town centre via Vestergade and Johannes Jørgensens Vej and take the slip-road onto Sundbrovej and across the bridge, which is over 1km (half a mile) long and has a clearance of 33m (108ft) for vessels passing through the sound. At the first junction on the Tåsinge side, turn left and left again down Bregningevej towards the waterside. Turn right along Troensevej and follow signs to the attractive village of **Troense**, once the home port of sailing ships and now providing facilities for visiting yachts. The old village school in Strandgade provides a home for the Troense Maritime Collection, a fascinating museum dealing with the history of the shipping trade from the nineteenth century in what was the largest and busiest port area outside Copenhagen.

From Troense follow Slotsalleen, an avenue of lime trees leading to the arched gateway of Valdemars Slot, the grandiose mansion and estate designed and built in 1754-6 by the grandson of Danish naval hero Niels Juel who purchased the estate in 1678. The original castle was built by Christian IV in 1639-44 for his son Valdemar, hence the name. The public road passes through identical gatehouses at each end of the courtyard from which the lake and formal gardens may be seen.

From the castle turn right by two thatched cottages and left at the next junction to **Bregninge**. The church stands on the summit of the Bregninge Hills, commanding a magnificent view over south Funen and the islands. Tradition says that the 1727 ship model in the church is a copy of Niels Juel's flagship. Opposite the church is the Tåsinge folklore collection and shipmaster's home. One building has been fitted up and furnished as an exact replica of a shipmaster's home from about 1860, and the nearby windmill has been converted into a restaurant.

From the village turn left at the main road then right towards Nørre Vornæs. Drive around Vornæs Skov with views out towards the other islands, then back across Veijlen, a marshy area rich in wild fowl, to the Mechanical Doll Museum at Vejlegården. Other displays, an antique shop and 'fleamarket' can be visited. Continue south, taking the next turning left to Gesinge then left to **Landet**, where the medieval church of Skt Jørgen has graves of two English airmen who came down at Vornæs in 1944. At the main Road 9 turn right then take the next turning left and follow the road along the shore through the woods towards Vemmenæs. Turn right before the village sign to rejoin the main road and turn left to cross the bridge to the small island of Siø. Opposite the farm are three large wind generators and the windmill at Rudkøbing can be seen ahead.

Continue up the steep slope of the bridge to Langeland Island, a hard pull for cyclists, and turn right into **Rudkøbing** following the ferry signs for Marstal on Ærø Island and the small neighbouring island of Strynø. The centre of the town has some interesting old houses and the museum in Jens Winthersvej contains finds from Stone Age habitations on the island and from underwater archaeological research. Viking artefacts and exhibits from later periods are included, and of particular interest are displays relating to the brothers Ørsted, one noted for research into electromagnetism and the other a leading jurist and statesman. They were born in the local *apotek* in Brogade.

Leave the town past the museum and along Humblevej to Road 305 and turn right. A Dutch style windmill with fantail stands among trees on a hill to the left at Lindelse. Turn right at the church towards Bogø. Keep right at the first junction down a narrow twisting road to Kædeby Haver and turn left at Langøvej, passing some wind genera-

Nyborg Slot

tors and numerous rounded hills. Go through Kædeby village to the main road, turn right and go through Humble. Turn right beyond the village, signed to Ristinge. At Hesselbjerg a diversion can be made to **Ristinge**, on a peninsula with bathing beaches, holiday huts and views over to Ærø. In Hesselbjerg turn left signed Nørreballe, past a long barrow on the right, keep right at the top of the hill by a thatched cottage and continue along a narrow road through Kinderballe and Ormstrup, passing a dolmen on the right. Keep straight ahead to a T-junction then turn right towards Vesteregn and left towards Bagenkop with views of the sea among rounded low hills on the right. At the main road turn right into **Bagenkop**, a fishing harbour and ferry terminal for Kiel in Germany.

From the harbour go right then left along a street with thatched houses and take the road towards Søgård, a passage grave near one of the prominent rounded hills which are a feature of the Langeland landscape. Looking like round barrows, they are in fact a result of ice

Troense Søfærts Museum

Valdemars Slot, the gate house

PLACES TO VISIT IN EAST FUNEN, TÅSINGE AND LANGELAND

East Funen

Ulriksholm
Seventeenth-century mansion open as hotel and restaurant.

Kerteminde
Old fishing village with marina, thirteenth-century church, art exhibitions in custom house, historic museum in Farvergård, Høkeren Museum Shop, Svannemølle windmill, Johannes Larsen House and museum with paintings.

Viby
Restored windmill and Gothic church with half-timbered tower.

Stubberup
Romanesque church known as 'White Virgin'.

Martofte
Snave Jættestuen, Denmark's largest passage grave.

Rynkeby
Church with sixteenth-century murals of angel orchestra.

Hindemæ Manor
Seventeenth- to nineteenth-century interiors and antique sales and exhibitions.

Nyborg
Site of former *Danehof*, museum in fifteenth-century merchant's home, church with old organ pipes and fine ship models.

Langå
Church with sixteenth-century frescoes.

Hesselager
Dammestenen, Denmark's largest erratic boulder.

Svendborg
Vor Frue Kirke with Dutch carillon, museum in Anne Hvides Gård, Zoological Museum, Viebæltegård Craft and Archaeological Museum, Skt Nicolai Kirke from 1200, Skt Jørgens Kirke with views of bridge and sound.

Tåsinge

Troense
Troense Maritime Collection. Valdemars Slot Mansion and chapel.

Bregninge
Church with viewpoint. Bregninge mill, now a restaurant.

Veijen
Wildlife Reserve and Mechanical Doll Museum.

Langeland

Rudkøbing
Old houses, museum and ferry terminal.

Bagenkop
Fishing and ferry port.

Gulstav and Dovnsklint
Bird reserves and Ice Age scenery.

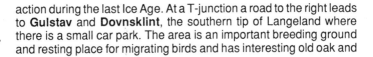

action during the last Ice Age. At a T-junction a road to the right leads to **Gulstav** and **Dovnsklint**, the southern tip of Langeland where there is a small car park. The area is an important breeding ground and resting place for migrating birds and has interesting old oak and beech woods. Return to the road junction and keep ahead to reach the main road out from Bagenkop. Follow the road to Tryggelev, turn right immediately after the church and follow signs to Ore and continue ahead to Brandsby. Turn right at the T-junction then left to Hennetved, passing an unusual windmill on the right. Follow the road to Lindelse, turn right at the main road then keep ahead on the minor road signed to Illebølle. Take the left fork following signs to Fuglsbølle, then bear right past the church and follow signs to **Spodsbjerg**, where there are good beaches and a harbour from which the ferry sails to Tårs in Lolland.

Leave Spodsbjerg by the main Road 9 signed to Svendborg, and turn right towards Tranekær, passing through Løkkeby and joining the main Road 305 at Frellesvig. Through **Tranekær** the road bends sharply before reaching Tranekær Slot, high on a castle mound on the right. Parts date from 1160, with remains of a medieval royal castle, but the large structure is mainly from 1863. A footpath runs from the car park around the lake and part of the park outside the moat is open to the public. Beyond the castle the road passes an old Dutch type windmill from 1846 which is now a museum. The route may be extended north to **Lohals**, the terminal for the ferry to Korsør on Sealand, to join Route 26 at Korsør. The return route follows the main Road 305 back to Rudkøbing.

8

SOUTH SEALAND
THE STORSTRØM COUNTY

The Storstrøm County, or Storstrøms Amt comprises the southern part of the island of Sealand together with the smaller islands of Lolland, Falster and Møn, all of which are now linked together by road and rail bridges and tunnels. Each of these three islands has its own distinctive character. Lolland has some of Denmark's richest farmland and a number of manor houses. Tårs is the terminal for the ferry from Spodsbjerg on Langeland, a useful service if coming from the south and less busy than the Storebælt ferries further north. For convenience, all that part of Sealand which lies south of the E66 motorway from Korsør to Køge, as well as the towns of Korsør, Slagelse, Sorø and Ringsted is included. Køge is included in chapter 10 as it is part of Greater Copenhagen.

ROUTE 25 • LOLLAND, FALSTER AND MØN

Nakskov, just south of Tårs, is an interesting town with narrow medieval streets, merchants' yards and many half-timbered buildings between the town square, Axeltorv, and the harbour. Chartered as a market town in 1266, it was badly damaged during the Swedish wars in the seventeenth century but recovered, and in 1882 Denmark's largest sugar factory was established here. In the square an equestrian statue of Christian X erected in 1952 commemorates the 1945 Liberation. The old *apotek*, founded in 1645, still occupies the original building and a nearby archway leads into Theisens Gård, a merchant's yard with a house dating from 1786. In the chancel arch of Skt Nicolai Kirke, whose tall spire overlooks the town, a Swedish cannon ball fired in 1659 can be seen. Near the church, in Tilegade, an old smithy has been restored as a working museum. Walk down Søndergade from a square to an alley on the left, with several fascinating old buildings including a watchmaker's shop and shoemaker's shop, all with old signs. From Søndergade, Dronningensstræde leads down towards the harbour where the early seven-

Nakskov Church and square

teenth-century Dronningens Pakhus or Queen's Warehouse can be seen. Passengers are carried by the mailboat on its daily sailings around Nakskov Fjord.

Leave the town via Maribovej to the roundabout and ahead to the main Road 9. Turn right towards Halsted Kloster whose park is open to the public then turn left to Horslunde and follow signs to Pederstrup and Reventlow Park. This beautiful park was laid out in English style in 1858. The impressive mansion contains a museum in memory of the former prime minister C.D.F. Reventlow (1748-1827).

Take the road opposite the park entrance towards Magletving then turn left to Torrig. At the main road turn right and in 1½ km (a mile) turn left to **Kragenæs**. Go down to the ferry terminal for boats to the small islands of Fejø and Femø. Otherwise turn right at the sign to Ravnsby Bakker. From the car park walk to the highest point on Lolland, offering superb views over the neighbouring islands. The landscape here is the result of the melting of the ice sheet after the last Ice Age. Near the coast are the embankments of Ravnsborg, a fortress built in 1330, and in the area is a well preserved passage grave known as Glentehøj.

Leave the car park, turn left to the main road and left again towards Maribo. From **Bandholm** harbour a ferry sails to the little island of Askø. It is also the terminus of the veteran steam railway from Maribo, which runs along the 7½km (5 mile) route of Denmark's oldest private railway, opened in 1869. Not far from the rail terminus at Bandholm harbour is the entrance to Knuthenborg Safari Park, in the grounds of a nineteenth-century manor house. A 7½km (5 mile) long wall encloses the park, laid out in 1862-74 by the English landscape architect Milne.

Drive towards **Maribo** and after crossing the veteran railway turn left towards Hunseby. Turn right at the T-junction and follow the road under the motorway to enter the town near the main railway station. Maribo grew up around a Birgittine abbey consecrated in 1416 but after a fire the big abbey church became the parish church of Maribo. After major restoration during the nineteenth century, the church became the cathedral for the new Lolland-Falster diocese in 1924. The impressive interior is dominated by the high altar dating from 1641 and the earlier Renaissance pulpit. A showcase on the wall contains holy relics presented to the abbey in 1455. The abbey ruins consisting of outlines of the kitchen and refectory are situated to the north of the cathedral near the shore of the lake Søndersø.

From Vesterbrogade which crosses the short stretch of water linking Søndersø with the smaller Nørresø, Bangshavevej leads to the left towards the Frilandsmuseum, an open-air museum with old farm and other buildings from Lolland-Falster, re-erected and furnished in typical eighteenth- and nineteenth-century style. Another museum is the Lolland-Falsters Stiftsmuseum (County Museum) with exhibits showing everyday life from Stone Age times to the present, combined with the Lolland-Falsters Kunstmuseum with collections of Danish painting and graphic art. These museums are situated in Jernbanegade near the station.

Leave the town along Østergade and Road 153 to **Rødby**, once an old sea port but now 5km (3 miles) inland from the coast. The fjord was reclaimed during the nineteenth century but an old warehouse in Østergade is a reminder of the days when ships could moor alongside. A museum, workshop and shop are devoted to the polishing and mounting of amber. In 1872 a great flood inundated the town and a column in Nørregade recalls the height reached by the water. Today the new port is at Rødbyhavn from where regular ferries sail to Puttgarden in West Germany. The coastal region is now being developed with a number of holiday villages.

Take the road east from Rødby across the motorway to Ringsebølle then turn right towards Errindlev. After about 5km (3 miles) the manor house of Lungholm is on the left. The main building dates from 1853 and the park with rare trees and a lime avenue was laid out in 1860. In the estate is a riding stable and international riding school, also a wolf park with associated Wolf Museum. Continue to **Errindlev**, an attractive village with a pond and old houses and a

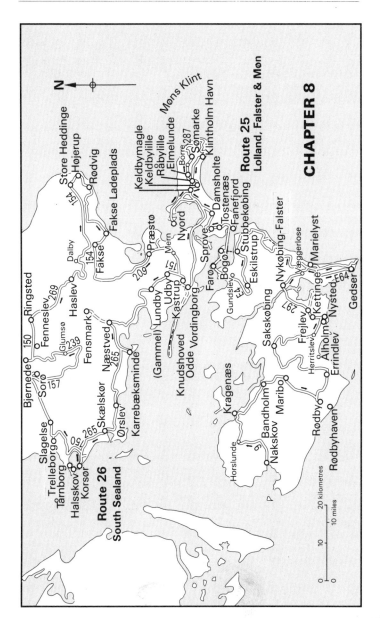

church without a tower, which is unusual for this part of Denmark. Bear right beyond the church towards Egelund and there turn left, following the twisting road towards Fuglse, passing the beautiful moated manor of Kærstrup. Continue under the railway and to the main road. Cross over and into Fuglse, turn right to Bøsserup then left to Søholt. Turn right at the T-junction and on the left is Søholt Manor, an attractive white building with Flemish gables and a tower. The main building dates from 1804 and the formal gardens have walks with high trimmed hedges. Opposite is the impressive home farm. The road continues ahead passing some thatched cottages, and through woods. Turn left at the next junction towards Maribo, through more woods and skirting lakes until signs to **Engestofte** Kirke are seen. The white building of the church, with a spire, stands by an attractive manor house and very large estate farm. In the porch is a war memorial to Monica Wichfeld, a member of the family who own the estate. There is also a lovely little rose window in the chancel and fine wrought iron gates with family crests.

From Engestofte continue to the main road and turn left towards Maribo. At the T-junction turn right along main Road 153 to **Sakskøbing**, situated at the head of an inlet where the two most important roads across Lolland met in the Middle Ages. Commerce and industry contribute to the town's importance, including one of Europe's largest and most modern sugar factories. The beet-growing industry is marked by the bronze sculpture *The Beet Girls* in the main square. The earliest church building dates from 1200, and the present Skt Pauls Kirke in late Romanesque style has a beautiful altarpiece and a fine carved pulpit from 1620. There are plenty of walking routes in the neighbouring woods and along the inlet, and overlooking the town is the watertower which has been painted with an amusing smiling face.

The direct route from Lolland to the southern part of Sealand is from Sakskøbing along the E4 motorway through the recently-opened tunnel under the Guldborg sound to Falster, then across the Farø motorway bridges. The older route from Sakskøbing follows Road 153 to Guldborg where it crosses the sound by a bascule bridge built in 1934 then continues north to cross the 4km (2 mile) long Storstrøms Bridge which, when built in 1937, was the longest in Europe. It carries the road, railway and a cycle path, and cyclists wanting the most direct route between Lolland, Falster and Sealand will have to use this bridge.

To continue the tour of Lolland, leave Sakskøbing by main Road 9 towards Nykøbing, turn right in Radsted and pass the entrance to Krenkerup Mansion whose oldest wing dates from about 1500. At the next T-junction turn left along road 283 to Herritslev. Turn left following signs to Nysted and in about 4km (2 miles) turn right, following signs to **Ålholm** Castle and museum. The castle is one of the oldest inhabited castles in the world, dating back to the twelfth century. Extensions and improvements have been made to the former royal fortress and today the castle kitchen and some rooms with collections of furniture, paintings and weapons are open to the public. A further attraction is the Automobile Museum, one of the biggest in Europe. From the museum, situated in the grounds of the castle, a veteran steam train runs to and from the beach.

From Ålholm continue into **Nysted**, Lolland's smallest town set among trees with pleasant streets sloping down to the natural harbour, now mainly used by visiting yachts. Overlooking the town is the spire of the church, and outstanding views are possible from the old watertower. Take the road leading north from the town to **Kettinge**, where a Dutch type windmill is open to the public and the thirteenth-century church contains numerous frescoes. At the junction with main Road 297 turn right towards Nykøbing-Falster, more often written Nykøbing-F to distinguish it from other towns of the same name. At **Frejlev** a diversion may be made to the right along Enghavevej to Frejlev Skov, a wooded area along the shore of Guldborgsund. Within these woods are over 100 prehistoric monuments ranging from dolmens and barrows to passage graves, showing occupation from the Stone Age through the Bronze Age to the Iron Age. Leaflets with maps are available in Danish showing the various finds. Return to Frejlev and continue along the main road to the right, and soon Fuglsang Manor will be seen with its English style park. The estate dates from 1368 but the main building in Gothic revival style was built in 1869. The manor is now a retreat house and study centre connected with the established church.

Return to the main road and continue right to join main Road 9 and cross the bridge to the island of Falster and into the town of **Nykøbing**. It is the principal town of Falster with a history going back to before 1231. The late twelfth-century castle was destroyed, with the town, by fire in 1253. It was rebuilt and after a varied existence was demolished at the end of the eighteenth century, only part of one tower and some signs remaining to show its original size and position. In 1532 the large Gothic brick-built church of the Franciscan abbey became the parish church and is worth visiting. There is an interesting medicinal herb garden by the church. Among old buildings which have survived various fires the Czarens Hus, so-called after the visit by Czar Peter the Great in 1716, houses the Falsters Minder Museum containing cultural, historical and archaeological collections. In the same part of the town are several houses from the sixteenth and seventeenth centuries. The watertower, built in 1908, is Denmark's first ferro-concrete structure of this size, and offers good views from the top.

Leave the town along Vesterskovvej, the main E64 road towards Gedser, and after passing the race track turn left into Væggerløse then left again to Stovby, past the newly restored post mill. Turn right past the mill and left at the next T-junction into **Marielyst**, a very extensive holiday area on the popular Baltic coast including among its attractions Sommerland Falster, a large recreation and amusement park for all the family. Return to the main road and continue south to the port of **Gedser** whose importance is based on the ferry services to Warnemünde in East Germany and Travemünde in West Germany. The harbour is also a popular yachting centre. Ferie Park Gedser is a modern holiday complex with sub-tropical swimming facilities under a massive dome. A short distance beyond the town is Gedser Odde, the southernmost point of Denmark. The lighthouse may be visited and on a clear day the coast of Germany can be seen from the tower.

Return north through Marielyst to Idestrup, then through Sønder Ørslev to Ulslev. Turn left to Sønder Alslev and take the second turning right to Korselitse. Turn right past the manor house and continue to the coast, then left at Tromnæs and along the coast road, eventually turning left through Tunderup to Karleby. Cyclists may keep to the forest road along the coast. At Karleby turn right towards Horbelev, and at Meelse turn right towards **Bregninge**. At the end of this attractive village with its pond follow signs to Halskov Vænge and take the next junction on the right. Opposite a thatched building is a sign 'Fortidsminder Skoven Naturmuseum' and a car park with information boards. A pleasant walk through the woods leads to a small natural history museum with toilets and a study centre. Among the trees are good examples of long barrows and dolmens from the late Stone Age and Bronze Age.

From the car park return towards Bregninge, turn right at the T-junction and follow the road into Hesnæs, a village with attractive cottages with thatched roofs and straw-thatched walls. There are many picnic areas with views over the Baltic. Continue through the village and through Korselitse Østerskov. Near the far edge of the woods, after a sharp right angle bend to the left, take the next turning on the right and follow signs to **Stubbekøbing**, the oldest town on the island of Falster. It began as a fishing village whose oldest known municipal privileges go back to 1354 but fires and storms through the ages led to its decline until the nineteenth century when the harbour was improved. Now with its interesting 80-year-old church, old merchants' houses, fishing and yachting harbours, the town has revived and is especially noted for the large Vintage Motor Cycle Museum. Falster is now connected to Møn via a new motorway bridge to the little island of Farø then across a causeway to Bogø Island, which in turn is linked by causeway to Møn. However, the only route for cyclists coming from the south is via the old ferry from Stubbekøbing to Bogø, which also takes cars.

From Stubbekøbing take the Road 271 south to Maglebrænde, turn right past the church, then through Torkilstrup and Gundslevmagle to **Eskilstrup** where there is the Lolland-Falster Tractor and Motor Museum. Beyond the village, turn right at the T-junction onto Road E64 then join the E4 motorway towards Copenhagen. This leads across the Farø-Falster Bridge, a remarkable piece of engineering opened in 1985. On the small island of **Farø** lying to the west of Bogø there is a rest area and restaurant providing good views of both the Falster Bridge and the northern bridge connecting Farø to Sealand.

Leave the motorway and join main Road 287 from Farø across the causeway to **Bogø**, where the village church with its medieval nave has traces of late fifteenth-century murals. Formerly a navigation school was in the village and on the left of the main road is a well preserved windmill from 1852, with stage and fantail. The road continues across the causeway to Møn, one of Denmark's loveliest and most interesting islands. Take the first turning on the right to **Fanefjord** Church, a beautiful whitewashed building with a red tiled roof overlooking Fanefjord, an inlet from the Grønsund. Long before the church was built, a large long barrow was raised which contains the 4,000-year-old tomb of Queen Fane after whom the fjord gets its name. The most interesting features are outstanding frescoes from two distinct periods. The oldest are from about 1350, while the others are about 100 years later, and their quality and extent is remarkable. The richly carved altarpiece is dated 1634, and the pulpit is from the same period, while the marble font is from about 1300. A number of small holes in walls and pillars were made to improve the acoustics of the building, a feature seen in a number of these old churches.

From the church go towards Kokseby and Store Damme, and in Kokseby turn left at the T-junction then right to the main road. Cross over in the direction of Røddinge. On the left at Tostenæs is a white windmill. In the village turn right, still following signs to Røddinge, passing on the right the mound of the Klekkendehøj, a passage grave with double chamber and two entrances. Go through Røddinge to **Sprove** where the turning to the left signed 'Kong Askers Høj' leads to a small lay-by with a sign 'Jættestuerne'. The mound covers Denmark's largest passage grave from the top of which there is a superb view as far as the Queen Alexandrine Bridge over the Ulvsund to the east and the new Farø Bridges to the west. Continue along the coast road through Borren and turn right at the T-junction, through Store Lind towards **Damsholte**, passing the distinctive Marienborg Manor. At the main road turn right and Damsholte Church is on the right. It is the only church on Møn which does not date back to

PLACES TO VISIT ON LOLLAND, FALSTER AND MØN

Lolland

Nakskov
Merchants' houses, Skt Nicolai Kirke, Working smithy.

Reventlow Park
English style park. Museum in mansion.

Kragenæs
Ferries to Fejø and Femø Islands.

Ravnsby Bakker
Ravnsborg Castle ramparts and prehistoric passage grave.

Bandholm
Terminus of veteran steam railway. Knuthenborg Safari Park.

Maribo
Impressive cathedral, Frilandsmuseum, Lolland-Falster County Museum and Art Gallery.

Rødby
Former sea port on reclaimed land. Amber Museum and workshop.

Lungholm
Manor and park. Riding stables and school. Wolf park with museum.

Søholt
Manor and formal gardens.

Engestofte
Church and memorial to patriotic woman who died in Nazi camp.

Sakskøbing
Centre of sugar beet industry. Interesting church. Water tower with smiling face.

Ålholm
Oldest inhabited castle. Automobile Museum. Veteran steam train.

Nysted
Small port with old houses. Water tower with viewpoint.

Kettinge
Windmill. Thirteenth-century church with frescoes.

Frejlev Skov
Woodland walks. Concentration of prehistoric remains.

Fuglsang
Manor, retreat and study centre. Beautiful park.

Falster

Nykøbing-Falster
Former abbey church, Czarens Hus with museum, Ferro-concrete water tower.

Marielyst
Extensive resort on Baltic coast.

medieval times, having been consecrated in 1743. Built of yellow bricks, and with a small octagonal tower topped with an onion-shaped spire, the interior is very simple with the pulpit above the altar.

Turn back through Damsholte village and follow the main road to **Stege**, the 'capital' of Møn, passing through the industrial and residential suburb of Lendemark and across the bridge over the Stege Nor into Storegade. Stege is one of the few towns with fully preserved ramparts which are laid out with the dried up moat as a green park around the town. It is a busy town with good shops and

Sommerland Falster, a recreation and amusement park.

Gedser
Old fishing port. Ferries to East and West Germany, holiday park, Gedser Odde Lighthouse.

Halskov Vænge
Woods with natural history museum and prehistoric remains.

Stubbekøbing
Oldest town on Falster. 800-year-old church, old merchants' houses, Vintage Motor Cycle Museum, Ferry to Bogø.

Eskilstrup
Tractor and Motor Museum.

Farø
Island between motorway bridges from Falster to Sealand.

Bogø
Island between Farø and Møn. Village church with fifteenth-century murals. Windmill.

Møn

Fanefjord
Church with fine fourteenth-century frescoes. Long barrow.

Tostenæs
Klekkendehøj passage grave with two chambers.

Sprove
Kong Askers Høj, largest passage grave in Denmark.

Damsholte
Eighteenth-century church.

Stege
Fifteenth-century ramparts with Mølleport, large church, Møns Museum in Empiregården.

Keldby
Church with outstanding frescoes.

Keldbylille
Hans Hansens Gård Farm Museum.

Elmelunde
Oldest stone church on Møn.

Sømarke
Large dolmen.

Liselund
Thatched manor house in park with summer houses.

Møns Klint
Unique chalk cliff landscape with forest walks.

Klintholm Havn
Fishing harbour with holiday hotel.

Ulvshale
Nature reserve.

Nyord
Island with village banned to cars.

a number of protected buildings in and around the centre. Skt Hans Kirke was started in the early thirteenth century. Like most of the old churches on Møn, it contains frescoes, here dated 1494. The main street, Storegade, runs through Torvet, and continues to the far side of the ramparts, where the old Mølleport (Town Gate) dating from 1480 still stands next to Empiregården, a rather elegant house containing the Møns Museum which gives an overall picture of Møns history and culture.

From the Mølleport continue on the main road to **Keldbymagle**.

Keldby Church on the right of the road originates from the early thirteenth century. The chancel walls are decorated with friezes dating from about 1275 and others from around 1325-40. Finally the latter part of the fifteenth century saw work by the so-called 'Elmelunde masters', a craftsman or group of craftsmen whose outstanding work can be seen in a number of Møn churches. Beyond the church turn right to **Keldbylille**, and through the village a turning on the right leads to Hans Hansens Gård, an old farm which is now an open-air museum illustrating customs and life from the nineteenth century to the present day. Continue on from the museum turning, keeping to the left to **Råbylille** which has a small art centre. Turn right along the main road to **Elmelunde**, which has the oldest stone church on Møn. The nave and lower part of the tower date from around 1300, but the outstanding feature of the church is the wonderful painting on the vaulted ceiling carried out by the Elmelunde masters at the beginning of the sixteenth century. In common with the frescoes in Fanefjord and Keldby, they give a fascinating picture of great social and historical interest. The carved pulpit, built in 1649, is supported entirely on a figure of Peter the apostle. The altarpiece from the same period has a figure of a cherub climbing a ladder to heaven, the figure and the ladder being carved from wood.

The main Road 287 continues through Borre with its early thirteenth-century brick-built church to Magleby. Through the village turn left to **Sømarke** where a road to the right goes to the Sømarkedyssen, a large well preserved round dolmen with a huge capstone over the open chamber and an unusual smaller capstone over the entrance passage. In fine weather there is a superb view over the whole island and beyond. The road continues past the dolmen then turns left up a very narrow lane. At the top, turn right along the road for about 750m (820yd) to the entrance to Liselund, the thatched mansion or mini-chateau built in 1795, once called a Danish 'Petit Trianon'. Its interior is tastefully furnished and decorated and the lovely park in which it stands contains three eighteenth-century summer houses, the 'Chinese House', 'Norwegian House' and 'Swiss Cottage', the latter now being a restaurant.

From Liselund continue down the road to join the major road by a camp site and a former hotel, Hunosøgård, now the Youth Hostel. Turn left to the end of the road and follow signs through the forest for **Møns Klint**. At the end of the track is a car park (fee payable) and hotel. Numerous walks go along the cliffs, through the forests and down flights of steps to the beach. The whole area is unique to Denmark, with high steep chalk cliffs intersected by steep cuttings and wooded slopes. The highest point along the cliffs is 128m (420ft) above sea level, and many of the peaks rise well over 100m (328ft). The chalk cliffs are unstable and dangerous to climb, but a good impression of the scenery can be gained from the cliff walks or along the beach, where fossils may be found. Many waymarked walks lead through the woods.

From the car park go south along the forest road Sandvej, and turn right at the T-junction towards Mandemarke. From the road there are superb views. Just before the village turn left down a lane towards the coast and turn right at the bottom. At the main road turn left to **Klintholm Havn**, an old village with a busy fishing harbour and a modern marina and holiday hotel. Return up the road to Busemarke, turn left and continue through Råbymagle and Råbylille to join the main Road 287. Turn left and continue through Keldbymagle, then turn right, following signs through Udby to Ulvshale, site of Denmark's first nature reserve. The road passes holiday cottages screened among the trees but much of the peninsula is covered by natural woodland and saltmarsh, providing one of Europe's most important wetlands and breeding grounds for birds, as well as a halting place for migrants. The road continues beyond the woods to cross a narrow bridge and causeway on to the island of **Nyord**, also a nature reserve, where the only houses are concentrated in the little village of the same name at the western end of the island. Cars are not allowed into the village so must be left in the car park. The very simple octagonal church dates from 1846, and has a small spire in which the bell used to hang. Now there is a separate bell tower. The village shop built in 1774 is still owned by the family who founded it.

From Nyord return through Ulvshale and follow signs to Stege. Cross the harbour bridge and follow the main Road 59 signed to Kalvehave. Cross the Queen Alexandrine Bridge towards Vordingborg.

ROUTE 26 • SOUTH SEALAND

This route explores the area of Sealand south of the E66 motorway, starting at **Vordingborg** easily reached by the bridges from Falster and Møn. It is an old town situated at a natural crossing place to Falster. The ferry service was terminated by the building of the Storstrøms Bridge in 1938, providing both road and rail connections. In the centre of the town are the ruins of King Valdemar Atterdag's Castle with one remaining tower, the Goose Tower, so called because Valdemar topped it with a golden goose in defiance of the German Hanseatic states. From it there is a spectacular view of the surrounding town and country. The castle fell into disrepair after the Swedish war of 1660 and was replaced by a new fort and cavalry barracks, one of whose buildings forms part of the South Sealand Museum. Near the museum is the Historical Botanic Garden established in 1921 also containing a small zoo. The church, started in about 1400 stands on what was formerly the town moat. Inside are

Møns Klint, on the Baltic coast

some fine frescoes from about 1470 and a carved altarpiece from 1641. The acoustics of the church are particularly noteworthy. In the town modern shops intermingle with older buildings from the eighteenth and nineteenth centuries, and below the rising ground of the castle ruins lies the harbour, sheltered by the Oringe peninsula and protected against enemy attack in Viking times by wooden piles.

From Vordingborg the long narrow tongue of land known as **Knudshoved Odde** to the west of the town is reached by going along Algade, crossing the railway by the station and turning left along Kuskevej to Rosenfelt Manor built about 1868. The stud farm is about 100 years older and includes bricks salvaged from the ruins of Vordingborg Castle. Beyond the manor the road continues towards Knudsskov. Cars must be left at the car park at the beginning of the woods which are completely natural and untouched. To reach the tip of the peninsula involves a walk of about 7km (4 miles) each way, through thick woods and grassland with salt-water ponds and Stone Age remains.

Return to Vordingborg, and just before the railway turn left onto Næstvedvej (Road 22). Immediately after the flyover turn right along Krondrevet past the Youth Hostel towards **Kastrup**, whose church stands on open ground above the village. Built about 1100, of granite boulders, it has a granite font from about the same period and fine

The view from the top of the Goose Tower in Vordingborg

carved pulpit and altarpiece from the fifteenth century. The porch door is made from wood salvaged from the frigate *Sjælland*.

From Kastrup, go east through the village of Ornebjerg, turn left at the T-junction onto Road 151 and continue for about 5km (3 miles). Turn left before the motorway junction into **Udby** where the twelfth-century church has frescoes from the thirteenth, fifteenth and sixteenth centuries. A memorial stone in the churchyard and memorial rooms in the rectory recall the noted poet, hymn writer and social reformer N.F.S. Grundtvig who founded adult further education schools. He was born in Udby in 1783.

Follow the road parallel to the motorway through Grumløse to **Gammel Lundby**, turning left at the T-junction then right past the church to Lundbygård Manor where the main house dating from 1815 contains a collection of antiquities. Go left at the T-junction beyond the estate to Hammer-Torup. Turn left to Hammer, then left past the church. Take the right fork and continue until a right turn across the railway leads through Ring to Road 22 by Dybsø Fjord. Turn right, then left in Vester Egesborg through Svenstrup to Vejlø. Turn right and immediately left across marshland, then bear left to Gavnø Manor on the site of a thirteenth-century royal stronghold and hunting lodge. In 1402 Queen Margrethe I had it replaced by a convent. The main house reached its present appearance in the mid-eighteenth century and the gardens were laid out to provide one of Denmark's most beautiful parks and gardens. The house includes the former convent church and contains an outstanding collection of paintings. Recently a section of the Falck Museum from Odense has been established at Gavnø.

Leave the grounds and turn left following signs to **Næstved** *centrum* (centre). Situated at the mouth of a navigable river with access through a sheltered fjord to the sea, the town's development really began in 1135 with the founding of Skt Peders Kirke and a Benedictine monastery. From the car park in Farimagsvej near the station walk along Jernbanegade to Skt Mortens Kirke, first mentioned in 1292, but which underwent major restoration in the nineteenth century. Many old memorials were preserved, also two fourteenth-century frescoes and the sixteenth-century altarpiece, crucifix and an unusual metal font.

In Riddergade many of the houses are scheduled buildings ranging from the sixteenth to the nineteenth century. Turn right along Købmagergade then left into Kompagnistræde where the sixteenth-century Kompagnihus was a meeting place for a merchants' guild. On the south side of Skt Peders Kirkeplads a group of fifteenth-century buildings, known as Stenboderne, house an annex of Næstved Museum. Skt Peders Kirke in its present form was built between 1375 and 1500, although remains of an earlier building from about 1250 have been found.

The surrounding streets contain more medieval houses and one of the town's finest medieval gables is on the Helligåndshus (House of the Holy Spirit) in Ringstedgade. This was an institution for the old and sick in the fifteenth century and now houses the Næstved Museum showing the history and growth of the town. The old cavalry barracks in Grønnegade were first established in 1799. The cobbled roads lead to the old Riding School, Fencing Hall, stables and other buildings, all of which have been restored.

A park along the bank of the Suså extends to Herlufsholm, founded as a monastery in 1135. It has been a boarding school since the Reformation. In 1261 the monastery church was restored and enlarged after a fire, and contains many fine historical effects and memorials, notably an ivory crucifix from the north of France, dating from about 1220.

From Næstved a diversion can be made to the famous Holmegårds Glassworks at **Fensmark**. First established in 1825, production was for many years mainly in the hands of foreign workers including Norwegians, Swedes and Germans who formed a closed community, and even today the town of Fensmark is very much dependent upon the factory and the Holmegård designs are world famous. A museum is attached to the factory.

Leave Næstved along Karrebækvej to **Karrebæksminde**, an old fishing port with attractive old houses and harbour with a lifting bascule bridge. It is a popular yachting centre. Return towards Næstved and just before Nybro turn left on Road 265 towards Skælskør, turning left at Rude to Holsteinborg Manor whose main building is a four-winged complex in Renaissance style from 1598 to 1651. Turn right along the long chestnut avenue to **Ørslev** whose church has many frescoes, notably that known as the *Dansefrise* dating from about 1350 and depicting young noblemen and crowned young women in a ring dance. Continue through Vedskølle to Magleby, turning left in the village to reach the main road. Cross and go on to the beautiful manor of Borreby, built in 1556. Turn right at the T-junction into **Skælskør** with narrow streets and attractive sixteenth- and seventeenth-century houses at the head of a long sheltered inlet with a modern marina and old harbour. On the other side of the harbour are more old buildings including the thirteenth-century church and tithe barn beyond which a road leads out of town to Møllebakken, a Bronze Age mound offering imposing views over the inlet and neighbouring islands.

Follow Road 265 north to Korsør and Halsskov. First mentioned in 1241, **Korsør** is an old market town, chartered in 1425 as a small ferry port and harbour. After the coming of the railway in 1856 it grew to an important industrial and commercial town with a large modern harbour. **Halsskov** lies on the other side of the entrance to Korsør Nor, and the importance of the twin towns is mainly due to the ferry services linking Sealand with Funen across the Storebælt on the main route between Copenhagen and Jutland. The E66 motorway comes into Halsskov to connect with the car ferry to Knudshoved, and trains run right down to the harbour and are shunted onto train ferries linking with Nyborg. A car ferry also goes to Lohals on Langeland. The oldest part of Korsør is near Skt Povls Kirke, built in 1869, and has some attractive old houses and more elegant merchants' houses, particularly in Algade. Of special interest are Kongegården (1761), intended to house an exhibition of the works of sculptor Harald Isenstein, and Stapelsgård (1667). Overlooking the old fishing harbour and harbour entrance is the fourteenth-century fortress of which little remains other than the ramparts. One building, a gun hall dating from 1825, is now used as Korsør Town and Ferry Service Museum dealing with the history and development of the ferries and their importance to the town's growth and prosperity.

The future of Korsør-Halsskov as a ferry terminal is bound to be affected by the Storebælt Link joining Sealand with Funen by combined bridges and tunnels carrying road and rail traffic. This massive project due for completion by 1996 will run north of the small island of Sprogø, using an artificial island as a 'stepping stone'. The

Stenboderne, fifteenth-century houses in Næstved

scheme should speed up travel between Copenhagen and the rest of Denmark and Europe.

From Korsør, go along Skovvej, Road 265, and turn right through the woods along Bonderupvej leading to Klarskovgård and the Savings Bank Museum. Return to the main road and turn right, then take a left turn onto Road 150, signed to Vemmelev. In about 3km (2 miles) turn left to **Tårnborg**, passing the ruins of Korsør's first fortress at Tårnborg Banke. Recent excavations have revealed traces of a previously unknown medieval town. Continue beside Korsør Nor to Halseby, then turn right through Tjæreby to Vemmelev. Join the main Road 150 going left over the motorway towards Slagelse, and in about 2km (a mile) turn left along a very winding road towards Hejninge and look for signs on the left to **Trelleborg**, a circular fortified Viking camp, the ramparts of which have been reconstructed. A reproduction of one of the long houses has been built at the site together with a scale model of the complete moat, circular rampart and buildings the size and design of which give an insight into the organisation of the Vikings at that time.

Leave the fort, continue along the road to Hejninge, then turn right into **Slagelse**, one of the oldest towns in the country, having acquired its first charter in 1288. Its existence dates from pre-Christian times and coins were minted here in 1000. In the twelfth century the town had two churches which still exist, and since the nineteenth century the town has grown in commercial and industrial importance. The oldest building is Skt Peders Kirke, at the junction of Bredegade and Herrestræde, built in the middle of the twelfth century. Near the church, in Bredegade, is the Slagelse Museum with collections dealing with local history, trade and handicrafts and including a number of workshops and an old grocer's shop. Further along Bredegade is the old monastery and the Helligåndshus (House of the Holy Ghost) with some frescoes. The other old church, Skt Mikkels Kirke, a Gothic building dating from 1333, is in Nytorv. To the west of the church is a small tithe barn which was once used as a school. On the wall a plaque with names of famous pupils includes that of Hans Christian Andersen who lived for some years in Slagelse.

Leave the town via Sorøvej and the main Road 150 to Sorø. It is a busy road as the E66 motorway between Slagelse and Ringsted is still under construction and there is no convenient alternative route. The history of **Sorø** is bound up with that of a Cistercian monastery founded in 1161 by Bishop Absalon supported by the powerful Hvide family. The town itself only grew after the Reformation, when in 1586 Frederik II founded a grammar school which later became an academy for young noblemen. In spite of changes a school and academy have existed throughout the 400 years since then, the present main building dating from 1827. The town was granted a municipal charter in 1638 and developed around what was the highway to the old monastery. A number of fine houses in the area were built for the use of King Christian IV's sons and others who attended the academy and a walk around the town will show interesting and beautiful old buildings dating from the eighteenth century and earlier. Little remains of the original monastery other than the church, which is Denmark's biggest monastery church, looking very much as it did in Bishop Absalon's time. Many graves and memorials to royal and noble families exist, and the organ is one of the finest in the country.

The hilly and wooded country of the Suså valley around the Tystrup and Bavelse lakes is a result of glacial action and many walking routes are described in leaflets from the State Forestry Service. A pleasant drive around the area follows Road 157 along the west of Sorø lake to Lynge Eskilstrup then left through Tystrup and Vinstrup to the main Fuglebjerg-Glumsø road. Turn left and in Rejnstrup turn right to Skelby, passing a lovely little manor house and church on the left. In Skelby turn left and follow Road 239 to cross the river Sus at Næsby Bridge, then turn left to Vester Broby whose church contains some exceptionally fine Romanesque and Gothic frescoes. Past the church turn right to Løvehave then right again to the main road. Turn left and in about 1km (half a mile) right to Knudstrup. Turn right again, then follow the winding road to the railway, ignoring all turns to the right. After crossing the railway fork left to the main Road 150 at Slaglille, cross over and continue to **Bjernede**. The church, built in 1170, is the only existing round church in Sealand and is about 12m (39ft) in diameter. Four massive round pillars take up much of the space and the large granite font is probably as old as the church. A fine view can be obtained from the octagonal tower. Return to the main road, turn left and continue through **Fjenneslev** to Fjenneslev Kirke on the right. Built in the eleventh century with the two towers added around 1200, the church has well preserved frescoes dating from 1150-1200 and outside the church is an unusual rune stone. Return to the main road and continue into **Ringsted**.

With its central position in Sealand, close to the E66 motorway and with good rail connections to Copenhagen and to south and west Sealand, Ringsted makes a good centre for exploring Sealand. It is a fine shopping centre and has good hotel accommodation and an excellent Youth Hostel. During its long history the town suffered a number of disastrous fires which destroyed many of the older buildings. A number of interesting and elegant houses and other premises from the late eighteenth century include Postgården, built in 1794 as the royal post office and bearing the monogram of Christian VIII. The most impressive building in the town is Skt Bendts

Korsør Museum and old fortress tower

Kirke. Around 1080 a stone church stood here, and in 1160 King Valdemar the Great started building Denmark's first brick church, consecrated in 1170. Fire damage and the addition of the tower in 1550 resulted in what is seen today. A number of interesting features include the twelfth-century font and the monks' seats dating from the thirteenth century, but the most interesting fact must be that between 1131 and 1341 a total of fifteen royal burials took place here, including those of Valdemar the Great, Eric Menved and Queen Dagmar.

In 1806 the Benedictine monastery attached to the church was destroyed by fire and little remains except the monastery garden in Klosterhaven and some foundations to the south of the church. In Klostergården is the Agricultural Museum with collections of farm equipment, textiles, household utensils and hand tools from the past 150 years and a permanent exhibition called 'From Scythe To Combine'. At the opposite end of the town in Køgevej stands the old windmill, restored to working order in 1985 and now a museum and working cornmill.

From Ringsted take Road 269 to **Haslev**, situated in pleasant open hilly country. Until 1870 the town did not exist but the coming of the railway changed all that. Today Haslev is a thriving town with a number of technical, grammar and high schools and medium sized

PLACES TO VISIT IN SOUTH SEALAND

Vordingborg
Castle ruins. Goose Tower viewpoint. Historical museum. Botanic Garden. Fifteenth-century church.

Knudshoved Odde
Woodland and nature reserve.

Kastrup
Twelfth-century church.

Udby
Church with frescoes and memorial to poet Grundtvig.

Gavnø Manor
Fine gardens and park. Art collection. Falck Museum.

Næstved
Medieval churches of Skt Morten and Skt Peder with frescoes and metal fonts, Kompagnihus, Stenboderne, Helligåndshus with museum. Cavalry barracks. Herlufsholm.

Fensmark
Holmegårds Glass Factory and Museum.

Karrebæksminde
Old fishing harbour.

Holsteinborg Manor
Park and concerts in chapel.

Ørslev
Church with unique fourteenth-century *Dansefrise* painting.

Børreby Manor
Sixteenth-century manor house.

Skælskør
Harbour, thirteenth-century church with tithe barn, Møllebakken Bronze Age mound.

Korsør-Halsskov
Major ferry port, fortress. Town and Ferry Museum. Klarskovgård Savings Bank Museum. Tårnborg ruins.

Trelleborg
Viking circular fortified camp.

Slagelse
Skt Peders Kirke, Slagelse Museum, old monastery, Helligåndshus, Skt Mikkels Kirke, tithe barn.

Sorø
Historic academy with royal

industries. In addition, a major book publishing firm and the South Sealand Electricity Company are based here. The present church has been built around the original medieval village church from which the early Renaissance pulpit from 1579 has been retained. A museum tells the history of the village and its subsequent development and another in the electricity company premises covers electricity supply and apparatus from the end of the last century.

Follow Bregentvedvej, cross the main road and after leaving the outskirts of the town continue through woods for about 2km (a mile). Turn left at the T-junction to a car park on the left to visit the landscaped park of Bregentved, Sealand's largest estate whose mansion dates from 1891. Return to the T-junction, continue ahead to the major road, turn left then right to go around Torup Sø. Turn left at the next junction for about 1km (half a mile) to the Gisselfeld car connections. Denmark's biggest monastery church. Suså valley forest walks.

Bjernede
Only round church in Sealand.

Fjenneslev
Twin-towered church with twelfth-century frescoes. Rune stone.

Ringsted
Skt Bendts Kirke first brick-built church. Fine eighteenth-century buildings. Agricultural museum and working windmill.

Haslev
Railway town. Centre for schools. Local history museum. Electricity Museum.

Bregentved
Landscaped park.

Gisselfeld
English style park and gardens with small museum.

Store Heddinge
Medieval church.

Højerup
Stevns Klint chalk cliffs, church falling into sea, museum.

Rødvig
Marine Engine Museum. Flint Oven Museum.

Vemmetofte Kloster
Former nunnery. Estate with facilities for holiday-makers.

Fakse Ladeplads
Harbour, church.

Blåbæks Møller
Old restored wind and watermills.

Fakse
Unusual church. Faxe Brewery. Chalk quarries. Geological and Cultural History Museum.

Sparresholm Manor
Horse Carriage Museum.

Præstø
Nysø Mansion with Thorvaldsen sculpture collection. Cobbled streets and fishing harbour. Fire Service Museum. Museum of dolls and dollshouses.

Jungshoved Church
Moated castle ruins.

park on the right. The Renaissance castle built in 1554 but with later alterations stands in the most beautiful and extensive English style park in Denmark. There is a small museum in the grounds.

From Gisselfeld car park continue past the main entrance to the house, turn left then left again towards Ulse. Turn right at the main road, cross the motorway and continue to main Road 151 at Olstrup. Turn left towards Dalby then right through Rode and Frenderup, passing Øster Egede Church and the convent Jomfruens Egede. Continue on the Fakse road and turn left at the main Road 154 to **Store Heddinge**, a town with a number of interesting buildings, notably north Europe's only medieval church with an octagonal nave. It dates from about 1200 and was modelled on the cathedral in Aachen. A number of rooms entered through hidden doors arouse speculation and the design seems to have been dictated as much by

Gisselfeld Manor house and garden

defence needs as by the requirements of a church.

From the town centre rejoin the main road and go left to **Højerup**. At the end of the road is a car park. A short walk leads to the edge of the 40m (131ft) high Stevns Klint, white chalk cliffs with layers of flint. Højerup Church was built in about 1250, but since then erosion of the cliff has resulted in the collapse of part of the building and churchyard. A new church was built a little way inland in 1913 and bells from the old church transferred. Nearby is a very interesting museum dealing with the history, crafts and culture of the area including shipping and chalk quarrying.

From Højerup go through the very attractive village of Lille Heddinge and turn left to **Rødvig**, a fishing harbour now very popular

Stevns old church and cliffs

as a holiday and yachting centre. The Marine Engine Museum is a recent attraction and the restored flint oven houses a museum and viewing platform by the harbour. Leaving the harbour, take the road to Havnelev and go through Lyderslev to Store Spjellerup where the church was built of local Fakse chalk in the thirteenth century. Turn left to pass Vemmetofte Kloster, a fourteenth-century fortified manor which was a nunnery from 1735 to 1976. The estate in beautiful surroundings includes a beach, camp site and other amenities for visitors.

Continue through Strandskov to **Fakse Ladeplads**, built in the nineteenth century as a harbour to serve the local chalk quarries but now a popular holiday resort with marina and fishing harbour. The church was built in 1875 financed by the huge profits from local chalk quarrying. Follow the main road towards Fakse but at the junction into the town take a small turning on the left to Blåbæks Møller. A watermill with two overshot wheels dates from about 1472, and the windmill above was built in 1828. Both mills have been restored and are protected buildings. Continue into **Fakse**, where the church has an unusually large nave and interesting frescoes. Brewing of beer in 1879 in a small thatched cottage has grown into the famous Faxe Brewery supplied by pure water from a well bored 80m (262ft) into the underlying chalk. Chalk quarrying is the other major local industry, first started in the thirteenth century, so the local Geological and Cultural History Museum is of particular interest. A Viking leader from Fakse named Rollo led raids on England and France in the tenth century, and after embracing Christianity became Robert Duke of Normandy in 911. He died in 927 and his descendant, William the Conqueror, founded a line of English kings.

Follow Road 154 to Rønnede and continue on Road 54 past the motorway junction. Turn left at Vester Egede to Sparresholm Manor where the Horse Carriage Museum houses a collection of over 150 horse-drawn vehicles ranging from farm carts to royal coaches, together with harnesses and equipment and a carriage builders' workshop. Continue through Everdrup and Brøderup to the main road and into Tappernøje. Turn left into the town towards the coast, turning right along the coast Road 209. In about 3km (2 miles) turn left to Nysø, a seventeenth-century Dutch baroque mansion which has a small museum containing a collection of works by the Danish sculptor Bertel Thorvaldsen. The road leads on into the charming little town of **Præstø** with cobbled streets leading to the small fishing harbour on the almost land-locked fjord. There is a Fire Service Museum and a museum of dolls and dollshouses which displays the way of life during the last century. Around the shore of the fjord and in the neighbouring woods there are many paths for walking and cycling.

Road 265 leads south from Præstø, and at Tjørnehoved turn left across the marshy valley then right to Jungshoved Church in a beautiful position near the ruins of the moated castle with views across to Møn and Nyord. Return to the main road and follow signs through Mern and Ørslev back to the starting point at Vordingborg.

NORTH SEALAND
AND COPENHAGEN

North Sealand includes the most heavily populated area of Denmark and one quarter of the country's total population lives in Greater Copenhagen. The metropolitan region of Copenhagen is the subject of three of the routes in this chapter, and includes the city and the whole of north-east Sealand including Roskilde and Køge. The purchase of a 'Copenhagen Card' at any tourist office or railway station entitles the holder to unlimited free rail and bus travel throughout the region, free admission to over fifty museums and other sights and other discounts during its period of validity of 1 to 3 days and represents extremely good value, particularly for those wishing to avoid traffic and parking problems within the city. A useful guide booklet is given with the card.

ROUTE 27 • IN AND AROUND COPENHAGEN

The name Copenhagen, or København, is derived from 'Merchants' Harbour', first mentioned in 1043 as a small fishing and trading port on the Øresund, the strategically important stretch of water between Sweden and Denmark which is the main entrance to the Baltic. Bishop Absalon built a castle at Copenhagen in 1167, the foundations of which may still be seen. In 1417 in order to curb the power of the Hanseatic League and return trade to Denmark more fortresses were built on both sides of the sound and the capital was moved from Roskilde to Copenhagen where it has remained ever since.

Copenhagen is a busy and lively city with many attractions and entertainments of all kinds. The city centre can be explored on foot and the suburbs are easily reached by frequent bus or 'S-train' (suburban) services, free with the Copenhagen Card. A quick city tour by bus starting from the city hall or a boat tour of the canals and harbour are good ways of getting a general impression of the city.

A walk around the city can be combined with a special sightseeing bus, free to Copenhagen Card holders, which follows a set route and

Strøget, the busy pedestrian street in Copenhagen

allows passengers to get on and off at any of the stops. A route map with English notes is available.

In Vester Brogade near Central Station is the main entrance to Tivoli Gardens, a surprising mixture of fairground, amusement arcades, a variety of eating places from snack bars to good restaurants, entertainments and beautiful peaceful gardens and lakes. Without spending an øre one can walk (with the card!) through to the exit on H.C. Andersens Boulevard opposite the city hall with Jens Olsens Astronomical Clock and a 106m (348ft) high tower with a viewing point. Guided walking tours start from the fountain in the square and bus tours from stands by the Lur Blowers' Column. Beyond the bus stand, a traffic-free shopping route begins, comprising five consecu-

The Bobble Fountain in the Tivoli Gardens, Copenhagen

tive streets running from Rådhuspladsen to Kongens Nytorv and known as Strøget. This word does not appear as a street name. There is a fine selection of shops, boutiques and cafés to suit all tastes and pockets.

Nytorv at the end of Frederiksberggade has some street lamps outside the old town hall presented to the city in 1858 by Messrs Cochrane & Co (contractors for gas and waterworks, Woodside Ironworks, Dudley, England). Follow Nørregade to Vor Frue Kirke, with many statues by Denmark's famous sculptor, Bertil Thorvaldsen.

Behind the cathedral is Store Kannikestræde, the Latin Quarter, and a turning on the right leads through Lille Kannikestræde to the cobbled square of Gråbrødretorv and along Klosterstræde to Helligånds Kirke, one wing of which is over 500 years old. Turn left along Amager Torv, part of Strøget, to Kongens Nytorv with the Royal Theatre, home of the Royal Danish Ballet and Opera to the right. Beyond the square is Nyhavn, built about 300 years ago and often visited by old restored sailing vessels, a splendid sight among the old houses. Sightseeing boat tours leave from the harbour, and from nearby Havnegade ferries leave for Bornholm, Oslo and Malmö.

From the harbour bridge turn left along Toldbodgade to Amalienborg Plads, an elegant square surrounded by four rococo mansions built in 1750-60 which became royal palaces in 1794 after a disastrous fire in Christiansborg Palace. Changing of the Guard can be seen every day at noon. The magnificent equestrian statue of King Frederik V in the square was completed in 1768 and nearby is the baroque marble Frederiks Kirke or Marmorkirken, completed in 1894.

Go through the Amalie Garden and promenade, past old warehouses which have been beautifully converted to hotels and apartments and continue along the waterside past the Langelinie Pavilion to the *Little Mermaid* statue which appears much smaller than may be expected from photographs. The view over the water of the inner harbour to the warehouses of Christianshavn is impressive. Walk back through the star-shaped fortifications of the 325-year-old Copenhagen citadel, now converted to a park. Old citadel buildings and the citadel church can still be seen. To the south in Churchill Park, opposite the English church of St Alban, is the Frihedsmuseum (Danish Resistance Museum) illustrating Denmark's fight for freedom in 1940-5.

From the museum walk along Esplanaden and turn right into Grønningen where a sightseeing bus can be taken to the State Museum of Fine Arts, Denmark's largest art museum. Nearby is the Botanical Garden laid out in 1874 on part of the old city ramparts and including a large palm house and botanic and geological museums. The same bus stop is near the Kongens Have or King's Garden and Rosenborg Castle, the exterior of which has remained unchanged since its completion in 1633. The interior is a museum but the main interest lies in the priceless collection of Crown jewels, regalia and treasures of the royal family displayed in the special vault beneath the castle.

From the King's Garden walk along Nørre Voldgade, turn left into Kultorvet and along Købmagergade to the Round Tower built in 1642 as an observatory for Christian IV. A spiral ramp leads to the top from which a fine view over the old town can be obtained. Along Købmagergade to the right is an unusual museum of toy theatres (Dukketeatremuseum) and in Valkendorfsgade there is a Toy Museum and Post and Telegraph Museum. At the end of Købmagergade, cross Strøget, go through Højbro Plads and across the bridge into Christiansborg Slotsplads. Over the canal opposite the palace is Holmens Kirke, the former anchor forge building dedicated in 1619 as a naval church and containing a number of interesting memorials to naval heroes. On the palace side of the canal is Børsen, the 1624 Stock Exchange building with its curious twisted spire.

The site of Christiansborg Palace, the seat of the Danish parliament since 1417, was first occupied by Bishop Absalon's castle of 1167. Subsequent structures were mostly destroyed by fires and the

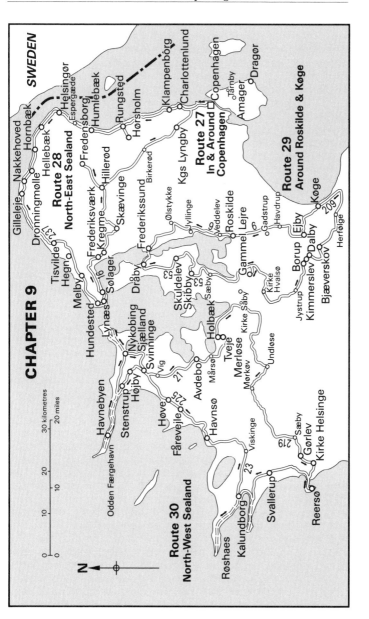

present palace dates from 1916. The royal stables which survived the fire of 1794, the royal reception rooms and other rooms may be visited, and in the cellars below, the foundations and other remains of Absalon's and subsequent castles are visible.

 The old Royal Arsenal Museum in Tøjhusgade built in 1598-1604 contains one of the world's finest collections of weapons. Along Porthusgade is Thorvaldsens Museum, specially designed to display the sculptor Bertel Thorvaldsen's collections of paintings and antique art. Cross the canal to the National Museum with extensive collections covering Danish history and culture from the early Stone Age to the present time, then cross H.C. Andersens Boulevard to the Ny Carlsberg Glyptotek containing large and important collections of classical art and nineteenth-century French and Danish paintings and sculpture. From here it is a short distance back to Central Station.

 The sightseeing bus goes from the station past the Copenhagen City Museum where the history of the town and city is presented with a reconstruction of an old street, then on to the Frederiksberg Gardens, a fine English style park which is open to the public. The castle was formerly the royal summer residence. Reached either through the extensive park or from the next bus stop, Copenhagen Zoo is a major establishment with one of the most up to date Children's Zoos in Europe.

 Within walking distance of the zoo is the Carlsberg Brewery and museum with its striking architecture including the 'Elephant Gate', a cooling tower supported on four massive granite statues of elephants, and the Empress Hall of the reception rooms of the museum. From the zoo, the sightseeing bus passes the Royal Copenhagen Porcelain Factory, which is open to visitors, before returning to the station.

 In contrast to the older churches and buildings, Grundtvig's Church in the district of Bispebjerg was erected entirely of yellow bricks between 1921-40 and is big enough to be a cathedral. It contains the largest organ in Denmark and is a monument to the Danish hymn writer and educationalist N.F.S. Grundtvig.

 Local city buses go to Christianshavn, an interesting area of old streets with warehouses, canals and picturesque houses within the old ramparts and bastions on the other side of the inner harbour. It is overlooked by the tall spire of Vor Frelsers Kirke which has an external spiral staircase giving marvellous views over the city and surroundings.

 To the south of the city the island of **Amager** is well served by buses from. Much of the island was settled by Dutch market gardeners in 1521. They brought their own costumes and customs, contributing to a unique atmosphere portrayed by the museum at Store Magleby just south of Copenhagen airport. The old medieval fishing

PLACES TO VISIT IN AND AROUND COPENHAGEN

Tivoli Gardens
Amusement park.

City Hall
Astronomical Clock. Viewing tower.

Vor Frue Kirke
Cathedral with statues by Thorvaldsen.

Nyhavn
Old restored houses and old sailing vessels.

Amalienborg
Royal palace.

Frederiks Kirke
Marmorkirken marble baroque church.

Langelinie
Promenade with *Little Mermaid* statue.

Frihedsmuseum
Danish Resistance Museum 1940-5.

State Museum of Fine Arts
Denmark's largest art museum.

Rosenborg Palace
Museum of royal collections and Crown jewels. King's Garden.

Round Tower
Observatory with superb views.

Holmens Kirke
Naval church in former anchor forge. Memorials to naval heroes.

Christiansborg Palace
Parliament. Royal reception rooms. Royal stables. Ruins of earliest castles in cellars.

Thorvaldsen Museum
Works by Danish sculptor and his own art collection.

National Museum
Danish life and culture from the Stone Age.

Copenhagen City Museum
History of the city and recon-structed street.

Royal Copenhagen Porcelain Factory
Factory and museum.

Christianshavn
Old streets, houses and canals. Old fortifications. Vor Frelsers Kirke with outside spiral stairs.

Store Magleby
Amager Museum.

Dragør
Museum of seafaring town. Ferry terminal for Sweden.

village of **Dragør** on the east coast has remained unchanged with narrow cobbled streets and picturesque cottages clearly showing the Dutch influence. The historical and cultural museum is near the busy ferry terminal with frequent sailings to Limhamn in Sweden.

ROUTE 28 • NORTH-EAST SEALAND
North-east Sealand certainly lives up to its description as the Kings' Pleasure Garden.

From the eastern end of the 02 Copenhagen ring road near the Tuborg breweries go through Hellerup to **Charlottenlund**, a former royal country seat last occupied by dowager Queen Louise and now used by the Danish Fisheries and Marine Research Institution. In the park is an arboretum and the Danish Aquarium.

Continue along the coast road with an almost unbroken view across the sound, and at **Klampenborg** is Dyrehavsbakken, or simply 'Bakken', claimed to be the world's oldest amusement park. It is situated in a deer park known as Jægersborg Dyrehave, a state forest. A State Forestry Service leaflet in English, describes an 11km (7 mile) waymarked walk which may be broken into shorter sections, and it is possible to walk much further within the confines of the park. Bakken is very popular with the Danes and is within the Copenhagen S-train area. A short way from the amusement park, in Ordrupgård, is an outstanding collection of Danish and French nineteenth- and twentieth-century paintings, originally a private collection now state owned.

The coast road continues through Skodsborg and the former fishing hamlets of Vedbæk and **Rungsted**, now popular yachting harbours with views over the Øresund to the Swedish island of Ven. The Danish author Karen Blixen lived near here as a child and is buried at Rungstedlund. Rungstedvej leads to **Hørsholm** and the Slotshaven, the gardens of the now demolished Hirschholm Castle, and the site of the parish church built in 1822. The stables and farm buildings house the National Hunting and Forestry Museum and a small district museum. Further north along the coast road beyond Nivå at **Humlebæk** is Louisiana, a fine museum of modern art and sculpture in a lovely park on the edge of the sound.

The road continues to **Helsingør**, entering the town near the railway station and busy ferry port with frequent sailings of train and car ferries to and from the Swedish port of Helsingborg, only 5km (3 miles) away. Helsingør's situation is the clue to its existence as Krogen Castle was built here in 1420 to defend the way to the Baltic and enforce the collection of tolls from shipping using the narrow sound. The sound toll financed the rebuilding and enlarging of the original castle to the great fortified palace of Kronborg, setting for Shakespeare's *Hamlet*, which appears today much as it did in the sixteenth century. The casemates contain the statue of the legendary Holger Danske who is supposed to awake if ever Denmark needs defending. The whole castle including the ramparts and coast batteries may be visited. The Danish Maritime Museum is within the castle.

The town (Shakespeare's Elsinore) contains many houses and other buildings from around the sixteenth century and later, with charming cobbled streets. The convent church of Skt Mariæ has a magnificent organ which was played by the famous composer Buxtehude when he was organist here from 1660-8. The church together with the fifteenth-century Carmelite convent form one of the best preserved groups of Gothic buildings in the world. Helsingør Town Museum in the Carmelite house contains a permanent exhibition covering the town's history throughout the time of the imposition of the sound tolls. The cathedral church of Skt Olai completed in 1559 has a notable baptistry and other interesting features. On Strandpromenaden near the north harbour the Øresund Aquarium is run in conjunction with the Copenhagen University marine biology laboratory.

North of the town is the beautiful Marienlyst Palace and pleasure gardens, originally laid out in the sixteenth century for the queen who thought Kronborg Castle too severe. The palace with its exquisite Louis Seize interiors and a collection of paintings relating to the town and its surroundings is now part of Helsingør Museum. Further along the coast road is a section of the Danish Technical Museum. A railway runs all along the north coast from Helsingør as far as Gilleleje and carries a steam service on Sundays during the summer.

At **Hellebæk** turn left through the attractive village street and across the railway to a small car park near Hellebæk Hammermølle, an interesting water-powered 'Hammer Mill' in a thatched building which was in use from 1600 to 1864 and was used to forge weapons since 1764. The mill has been restored to working condition and there are numerous walks in the nearby woods, described in a State Forestry Service leaflet with map.

Continue along the coast road to **Hornbæk**, the oldest fishing hamlet on the north coast of Sealand with tax records going back to 1497, when the village paid its taxes with fish products. Many of the old fishermens' cottages are well kept with thatched roofs and neat gardens and the church built in 1737 to replace two which were blown down contains an extremely fine collection of ship models. The town is now a fashionable and expensive holiday residential area with a fine beach and the area has extensive tree plantations established to give shelter from the frequent gales.

In the next village along the coast, **Dronningmølle**, a turning on the left past the station leads to the Rudolph Tegners Museum, where sculptures by the artist Rudolph Tegner are positioned in the park. More of his works, including sketches, paintings, water colours and drawings are displayed indoors.

Back on the coast road continue to **Nakkehoved** and turn right along Fyrvejen to the old lighthouse, built in 1772. The lighthouse, fired by coal, was the first of its type in the world. A modern lighthouse stands along the coast to the west towards **Gilleleje**, the most northerly town in Sealand. A fishing hamlet existed from about 1500, surviving a number of massive sand drifts and storms during the following centuries. Its present harbour dates from 1962 and the town

Kronborg Castle

centre to the east of the canal dug in the late nineteenth century to drain Søborg lake remains a very attractive fishing village with thatched half-timbered whitewashed houses, one of which is furnished as a seventeenth-century fisherman's home and contains Gilleleje Museum. The beautiful white church with its metal spire overlooks the town and forms a prominent landmark.

The coast road continues through lovely scenery past Gilbjerg Hoved, the most northerly point of Sealand. The coast path and headland, from which the cliffs of Sweden are visible, was a favourite haunt of the Danish philosopher Søren Kierkegaard to whom a memorial was erected in 1935. The whole of the coast through

Smidstrup and Rågeleje is a popular holiday area and at Tisvildeleje the coast road finally turns inland through Tisvilde village.

South of the village is an area of forest known as **Tisvilde Hegn** planted originally to stabilise the shifting sand which on a number of occasions had overwhelmed villages and farms in the coastal area. Bear right along Road 237 to a small car park and walk through the woods to Tibirke Church, built around 1230.

Continue and turn right on Road 205 towards Frederiksværk. On the right a small nature museum covers the natural history of north Sealand and in about 2 km (a mile) follow a sign 'Slotsruin' on the right to the ruins of Asserbo Castle which in the twelfth century was made a monastery by Bishop Absalon. Nearby is the so-called Troldeskov or Magic Wood where pine trees planted around 1800 have grown into weird twisted shapes under the influence of the sea wind and poor soil.

Road 205 continues for about 1km (half a mile) then just past the Kro turn right towards Liseleje. Go ahead at the crossroads to **Melby** where the twelfth-century church has frescoes on the arches including a picture of a fool painted around one of the ventilators. The restored windmill at Melby dates from 1878. Turn right at the church through Tollerup and Nødebo to Hundested at the end of the Halsnæs peninsula.

Hundested or 'place of seals' came into being about 1800 as a fishing village and trade grew after the coming of the railway in 1916. Ferry services connect to Grenå in Jutland and a local service to Rørvig across the entrance to the Isefjord. The coastal scenery is magnificent with fine views from the cliffs near the lighthouse north of the town near the former home of the Greenland explorer Knud Rasmussen. After his death a small museum was set up here covering his travels and discoveries. To the south of the town is **Lynæs**, the oldest fishing village in the area with attractive fishermens' houses, a marina and holiday facilities. Follow the road past Lynæs harbour to **Sølager** on the north of the entrance to Roskilde Fjord. A small ferry crosses the fjord to Kulhuse but the route continues left to Amager Huse. Turn right and follow Road 16 along the north shore of Roskilde Fjord to **Frederiksværk**, unique in being Denmark's only steel town.

Today the old forges and ironworks have gone, and the small buildings along Krudtværksalleen where gunpowder was made are now used for workshops and cultural activities. The Powder Mill Museum occupies a working watermill and other buildings. A modern steel rolling mill and iron foundry still operate on the outskirts but the centre does not resemble that of an industrial town at all, with the canal crossed by numerous bridges set among gardens and trees. The town museum details the development of the town and its industry and the church situated between the canal and the main shopping street is early twentieth century with a mosaic and altarpiece by Niels Skovgaard.

Leave the town along Hillerødvej (Road 16) which passes the twelfth-century church at **Kregme**. It has a rare thirteenth-century round window and interesting frescoes, and from its position on a hill a fine view over the Arresø, Denmark's largest lake. Just after the church is the Birkely Museum Farm. The grounds provide a good picnic site with views over the lake.

At Store Lyngby turn right to **Skævinge** and stop in the car park by the thirteenth-century church containing a sixteenth-century painting of Holger Danske defeating the giant Burnamund.

Follow the road through Meløse back to the main road and on the left just after the major road junction are the ruins of the twelfth-century Æbelholt Kloster, one of Denmark's largest medieval abbeys with a museum and herb garden.

Follow signs into **Hillerød** where the major attraction must be the magnificent Frederiksborg Castle. Built in 1600-20 for Christian IV on the site of an earlier manor, it is in Dutch Renaissance style and during the years 1671 to 1840 all Danish monarchs were crowned in the chapel here. From 1812 the National Historical Portrait Collection was housed in the castle, but a fire in 1859 caused so much damage that it was nearly abandoned. However, due largely to financial support and encouragement the damaged buildings were restored and established as the Museum of National History, which is the situation today. The castle chapel has been the ceremonial chapel of the Danish orders of chivalry, the Order of the Elephant and the Order of Dannebrog, since 1693, and the names and heraldic plaques of members of these orders make an interesting study, including as they do many familiar English and American names.

The town of Hillerød tends to be overlooked because of the castle, but there is much of interest, including old buildings, often hidden behind modern shops, and the North Sealand Folk Museum. An unusual museum is the monetary history collection of Danish and foreign coins and bank notes with related objects, housed in the Provinsbank building. A pleasant boat tour can be made from Torvet around the lake to the castle and back.

Many waymarked and other walking and cycle routes traverse the castle park, the extensive Gribskov forest to the north and the Store Dyrehave (Great Deer Park) south of the town. Details of these and of a waymarked walking or cycle route north to Gilleleje along paths and minor roads may be obtained from the local tourist office.

Leave the town by the road past the castle, through the park, then under the railway. Continue ahead at the major road junction, going towards **Fredensborg** where the elegant Fredensborg Palace occu-

PLACES TO VISIT IN NORTH-EAST SEALAND

Klampenborg
'Bakken' Amusement Park. Deer Park with walks. Ordrupgård collection.

Rungsted
Rungstedlund home and burial place of Karen Blixen.

Hørsholm Slotshaven
National Hunting and Forestry Museum.

Humlebæk
Louisiana Museum of modern art and sculpture.

Helsingør
Ferry terminal. Kronborg Castle (Elsinore). Maritime Museum. Carmelite convent and Skt Mariæ Church. Museum in Carmelite house. Cathedral Church of Skt Olai. Øresund Aquarium. Marienlyst Palace. Danish Technical and Transport Museums. Steam railway.

Hellebæk
Water-powered hammer mill and forge. Forest walks.

Hornbæk
Oldest north Sealand fishing village.

Dronningmølle
Rudolph Tegners Museum of Sculpture.

Nakkehoved
Old coal-fired lighthouse.

Gilleleje
Fishing village with museum in fisherman's house.

Tisvilde Hegn
Forest planted to prevent sand drift. Tibirke Church, now restored. North Sealand Nature Museum. Asserbo Castle and monastery ruins. Troldeskov twisted pine trees.

Melby
Twelfth-century church with frescoes. Restored windmill.

Hundested
Fishing harbour. Ferry to Grenå in Jutland. Rasmussen Museum. Lynæs fishing village. Sølager ferry across Roskilde Fjord.

Frederiksværk
Site of ironworks and gunpowder factory. Museum in water-powered powder mill. Town museum. Modern church.

Kregme
Church with rare window and frescoes. Views over Arresø. Birkely Museum Farm.

Skævinge
Unusual sixteenth-century church.

Æbelholt Kloster
Abbey ruins and museum.

Hillerød
Frederiksborg Castle with museum
Castle chapel. North Sealand Folk Museum. Monetary history collection. Boat trips on lake.

Fredensborg
Eighteenth-century royal palace.

Kongens Lyngby
Frilandsmuseum (Open-Air Museum), Brede Cloth Mill Museum. Sorgenfri Palace park.

pies a superb site overlooking the beautiful surroundings of Denmark's second largest lake, Esrum Sø. The whole complex repre-

Hellebæk Hammermølle

sents a fine example of eighteenth-century Danish architecture and is in regular use as the royal family's summer residence. Fredensborg can easily be reached from Helsingør, visited earlier on this route.

Return towards Hillerød and after passing under the railway fork left along Holmgårdsvej onto Københavnsvej, Road 201. Follow this road through Store Dyrehave towards Birkerød and Kongens Lyngby, and at the junction where the motorway begins, take the slip road on the right, signed **Kgs Lyngby** (Kongens Lyngby) and turn left at the end of the slip road to follow signs to museums and the car park on the right for the Frilandsmuseum. The Open-Air Museum is part of the National Museum and is a collection of old farmsteads, cottages, mills and other buildings brought from their original sites and re-erected and furnished ín a natural environment. An excellent guide to the exhibits in English is available. This is one of the best such museums in Europe and warrants more than a brief visit. Just outside the northern entrance is the old Brede Cloth Mill which is part of the National Museum used for special exhibitions.

From the Frilandsmuseum continue along Kongevejen past Sorgenfri Palace, an eighteenth-century royal residence. The town of Lyngby has many fine town houses from the eighteenth century and later, and the church, originally from the twelfth century but mainly

Gilleleje Church

fourteenth-century, has some interesting frescoes. The old village centre has beautiful old cottages and farmhouses, and with its situation on a river — the Mølleå connecting three lakes and flowing past several old mills to the sea — the area provides many pleasant walks and boat trips along the river and lakes.

The return to Copenhagen can be via the main road or motorway.

ROUTE 29 • AROUND ROSKILDE AND KØGE

This route takes in the ancient city of Roskilde on one of the loveliest fjords in Denmark and the old market town of Køge on the Baltic coast south of Copenhagen. With one small exception all the route lies within the Copenhagen area in which public transport and many admission charges are free with a Copenhagen Card. Alternatively, **Roskilde** has its own local 'Roskilde Card' giving unlimited free admission to the main sights in the city and substantial discounts at others during its 2 day validity. The cards are available from the tourist office, Youth Hostel and most hotels.

By the year 1000 Roskilde had become an important trading centre and royal cathedral town. A rampart and moat were built in the twelfth century by which time it was one of the largest towns in northern Europe. The coming of the railway to Roskilde in 1847 led to its expansion into the busy commercial, industrial, educational and research centre of today.

The impressive *domkirke* (cathedral) stands on the site of a stone church built in the early eleventh century. The cathedral is the burial place of all the Danish monarchs from Margarethe I who died in 1412 to Frederik IX who died in 1972. Among the interesting features must be counted the chapel of Christian I built around 1460. Much more can be seen in and around this outstanding building and there is an excellent guide in English.

In Stændertorvet markets are held every Wednesday and Friday and the town hall built in 1884 has a 500-year-old tower from the medieval church of St Lawrence. The palace built in 1733 on the site of the medieval Bishop's palace as residence for visiting royalty now houses the Palace Collections. Across Skt Olsgade is Liebes Gård, one of the oldest preserved houses in Roskilde. Built in 1804, it contains the Roskilde Museum with collections of peasant culture, folk costumes, Hedebo embroidery and toys, together with a comprehensive archaeological collection and an exhibition on the geology of the fjord. Associated with the museum is Brødrene Lützhøfts Efterfølger (grocer's shop), in Ringstedgade, which is restored to its 1910 condition and displaying and selling goods typical of that period.

From the cathedral walk past the site of Skt Hans Kirke, one of the churches demolished in 1536, and through the public park. Cross the busy ring road Skt Clara Vej and go along Skt Ibs Vej and Havnevej, then up Kirke Bakken to Skt Jørgensbjerg, originally a tiny fishing hamlet with the church dating from about 1080. North of the church is the site of the former leper hospital, with wonderful views over the harbour and fjord. Walk down the steps to Strandgade and the busy harbour from where there are steamer trips on the fjord.

Along the waterfront is the Viking Ship Museum which was built as a research centre for the preservation and study of the five Viking ships recovered from the fjord in 1957-9.

Follow Frederiksborgvej from the ring road to join main Road 6 along the east side of Roskilde Fjord to Ølstykke, and at the major junction take Road 211 to **Frederikssund**, an industrial town situated at the narrowest and most picturesque part of the fjord. A museum here is devoted to the works of J.F. Willumsen, a prolific Expressionist painter and sculptor who on his death in 1958 bequeathed his large collection of older foreign paintings, sculpture, drawings and ceramics together with some of his own works, letters and notes.

Cross the bridge to the peninsula of Hornsherred and turn right through Neder Dråby to the late seventeenth-century mansion of Jægerspris which was the country home of Countess Danner, the commoner wife of Frederik VII. She founded a school for deprived children on the estate and on her death in 1874 bequeathed the mansion and estate to an institution to continue this work. She decreed that most of the rooms should remain untouched as a memorial to Frederik, so they contain furniture and personal effects from the time when the couple lived there during the nineteenth century. Some of the early furnishings and equipment of the charity are also on display.

Go back through the town and turn right towards Lyngerup and Holbæk, passing near a Dutch type windmill in working order and **Dråby** Church which has some interesting Gothic frescoes and a very fine altarpiece from 1630 decorated with noblemen's coats of arms. Continue to Lyngerup and turn right along the main Road 53, then left at the crossroads to **Skuldelev**. It was off Skuldelev Strand that the Viking ships in Roskilde Viking Ship Museum were sunk in AD1080. From Skuldelev continue through Østby to Selsø Manor, built in 1576 but mainly unchanged since renovations in about 1800. In the basement dating from 1560 the manor kitchen is the oldest in Denmark. Selsø Church with an interesting interior overlooks Selsø lake which is a noted bird reserve.

Follow the road across the lake to **Skibby**, the main town on the peninsula. The church was built in 1175 and has central pillars and an interesting chancel with frescoes dating from 1348, the first to be uncovered in Denmark in 1855. A very old monstrance is displayed behind a grille. Leave the town going south onto Road 53 then turn left to Gershøj, one of the attractive old Hornsherred villages. Follow the road past holiday sites to Sæby then left onto the road along the side of the fjord through Lyndby to the motorway junction. Do not go onto the motorway but continue ahead under the bridge to join the old main Road 155, turning left to Gevninge and there turn right following signs to **Gammel Lejre**. In the village is a small local museum, Kongsgården, in an eighteenth-century farmhouse. Just beyond it is a handmade sign saying 'Skibssætningen' pointing up a rough track for about 300m (330yd) to a small car park on the left. To the right is a Viking ship burial site, one of the most important in the country, with standing stones in the shape of a ship some 80m (262ft) long with numerous graves in and around it. Many other burial mounds can be seen in the neighbourhood.

Return down the track to the road, turn left then right at the T-junction, following signs for 'Forsøgscentret' and 'Oldtidsbyen'. The long avenue leads towards Ledreborg, an outstanding example of a beautiful baroque mansion whose interior and exterior have remained unchanged since the eighteenth century. The terraced park is open daily and the main buildings including the chapel are open for limited periods.

Before reaching the house, signs point the way around the estate to the Historical-Archaeological Research Centre. Films, demonstrations and opportunities for visitors to try old crafts and methods are

Frederiksborg Slot

all provided on the extensive site. The centre is on the Ledreborg estate in beautiful country which holds a number of genuine prehistoric sites.

Return along the avenue, turn right into Lejre village, cross the railway and turn right again towards Særløse. Turn right onto Road 255 and follow it to the left through Kirke Hvalsø then watch for signs on the left for Jystrup. Follow the winding road to Skjoldenæsholm, where many waymarked paths run through the estate grounds. From the first car park a path leads to Gyldenløveshøj, the highest hill in Sealand and the site of many RAF. 'drops' during World War II. Just south of the park entrance on the right is the Sporvejsmuseum, a collection of old trams from Copenhagen, Århus and Odense. It is a working museum, and some trams are licensed to carry passengers. Note that this museum is outside Greater Copenhagen so the Copenhagen Card cannot be used to gain admission.

Continue through Jystrup and cross the main Road 14, passing the eighteenth-century Svenstrup Manor and under the railway into **Borup** where the church has some fine sixteenth- and seventeenth-century furnishings. From the railway bridge keep ahead to **Kimmerslev** where the twelfth-century church in a beautiful position beside Kimmerslev Sø contains some fine Renaissance furnishings and a rare Gothic crucifix dating from 1250. Passing the church and lake on the left, the road leads on to **Dalby** with another thirteenth-century church which, although not very impressive from the outside, is well worth a visit.

Turn back towards Kimmerslev and take the road to the left, going south across the motorway to the main Road 150, then turn left to **Bjæverskov** where the appearance of the church has not changed since about 1300. Its interior is also interesting with a high Renaissance altarpiece from about 1600. Past the church turn right through Lidemark and Tågerød Skov then turn right towards Ringsbjerg. Take the next turning left over the motorway to Herfølge. After crossing the railway turn left along main Road 151 then right towards Herfølge Church. Opposite the church turn right to Vedskølle and on to Vallø Slot, originally built in 1580 and restored virtually to its original appearance after a fire in 1893. The idyllic park and gardens are open to the public and together with the adjoining Vallø deer park provide a delightful recreation area with waymarked paths and walks. Continue to Valløby and turn left along Road 209 into Køge.

Køge has a history going back to the Iron Age, and developed into a wealthy trading centre in the Middle Ages. A walk around the town will reveal many buildings from the sixteenth and seventeenth centuries and a circular route can start at the tourist office in Torvet, the largest market square in the provinces. Go to the right and along Brogade as far as the bridge, looking particularly at the upper stories

PLACES TO VISIT AROUND ROSKILDE AND KØGE

Roskilde
Cathedral, palace collections, Roskilde Museum, St Jørgensbjerg village and church. Steamer trips on fjord. Viking Ship Museum.

Frederikssund
J.F. Willumsen Art Museum.

Jægerspris Mansion
Memorial rooms to Frederik VII and Countess Danner.

Dråby
Church with frescoes and seventeenth-century altarpiece. Working Dutch style windmill.

Selsø Manor
Eighteenth-century great hall and rooms. Old manor kitchen.

Gammel Lejre
Kongsgården, eighteenth-century farmhouse museum. Skibssætningen Viking ship

burial site.
Ledreborg eighteenth-century baroque manor and park. Historical-Archaeological Experimental Centre.

Skjoldenæsholm
Walks to highest point in Sealand. Sporvejsmuseum (Tramway Museum).

Kimmerslev
Twelfth-century church by lake.

Vallø Slot
Park, gardens and deer park.

Køge
Medieval market town, church, Køge Museum, classical town hall, Art Museum, Gammel Køgegård Mansion.

Ejby
Twelfth-century green sandstone church.

of the buildings. Return to the square and go down Vestergade, noting the iron foundry building at number 29 with its courtyard over the gateway of which is the seventeenth-century town clock, still in working order. Across the square Kirkestræde has several houses from the sixteenth and seventeenth centuries including number 20, Denmark's oldest dated half-timbered building, erected in 1527.

Between Kirkestræde and Nørregade is Skt Nikolai Kirke, built in its present form around 1450. The tower forms a prominent landmark and on the east side is a bay in which a light was placed to guide ships. The interior is impressive and is furnished with many interesting features and under the tower is a clock mechanism from 1568 which shows the phases of the moon. Return along Nørregade to number 4 where two seventeenth-century buildings house the Køge Museum. Nearly thirty display rooms show how the town and its surroundings have developed from prehistoric times to the present day. In the garden behind the museum building stands one of Denmark's oldest houses, moved here from the square in 1914. The building next to the museum is part of the town hall complex, and

Fredensborg Palace chapel

beyond that, overlooking Torvet, is the very dignified classical façade of the town hall, the oldest still in use as such in the country.

Just by the church in Nørregade the recently opened Art Museum shows sketches, models and other work involved in the preparation of an artist's finished product, both graphic art and sculpture. In the town there are a number of craft workshops where visitors may watch work in progress.

Where the Køge river flowed into Køge Bugt a harbour existed almost 1,000 years ago. Traces of fourteenth-century wharfs have been found, and today there are three busy harbours.

Leave the town along Vestergade and Ølbyvej to Gammel Køgegård, a mansion set in a beautiful park at the foot of the tree-clad Køge Ås or ridge on which a waymarked walk leads through pine and mixed forest for 6¹/₂km (4 miles). Return to Ølbyvej and continue to Ølby then turn left to **Ejby** where the church on a hill was built in 1150 from unusual green sandstone. Only the nave remains of the original church which was extended using bricks in the fourteenth century. The fourteenth-century font is one of the largest in the country and other features of the church are of interest. From the church take the road north to Store Ladager then right to a T-junction. Turn left through Kirke Skensved through Havdrup and Salløv to join the main Road 6 back to Roskilde.

Jægerspris Slot

ROUTE 30 • NORTH-WEST SEALAND

This route starts from **Kalundborg**, ferry port for services to Århus in Jutland and Kolby Kås on the island of Samsø. The principal town of the region it is famous for its magnificent twelfth-century church with five towers, each capped with a copper-clad spire, standing high above the fjord. Built in 1170 in the shape of a Greek cross it was quite unique because of its daring construction, and it stands in the centre of one of the best preserved medieval quarters in Denmark. In nearby Præstegade is the old tithe barn and Latin School, while to the west of the church in Adelgade is Lindegården, a lovely six-winged half-timbered sixteenth-century manor house now housing the district museum. The banqueting hall with stucco decorated walls and ceiling is quite exceptional. The collections include regional costumes, relics from medieval Kalundborg and a model of the old town, together with old workshops and interiors from town houses and peasant homes. Also in Adelgade is Bispegården, the old town hall, and numerous other well preserved houses are to be seen in the vicinity.

The old treasury tower 'Folen' near the tourist office marks the site of the twelfth-century Kalundborg Castle, destroyed in the Swedish war of 1659. The nearby Kaalund Kloster, originally the castle barn, has been restored and is used by the local administration. Before leaving the town, walk up to Møllebakken for a fine view over the harbours and fjord. If there is time to spare it is worth driving along Esben Snares Vej to Kongstrup cliffs where there are good walks and views, then continue to **Røsnæs**, where there are plenty of opportunities for walking in an area rich in prehistoric monuments and considered one of the most beautiful places in Denmark.

Leave Kalundborg via Klosterparkvej and Nørre Alle, passing the very modern Nyvangskirke, built in 1974. Follow Road 23 towards Jyderup and at the major junction beyond Viskinge take Road 155 in the direction of Svinninge. In Bregninge follow signs left to Eskebjerg and **Havnsø**, a traditional fishing village and popular holiday resort. Ferries go to the island of Sejerø, and there is a mail boat service to the protected island of Nekselø. Follow the coast road to Starreklinte and turn left on Road 225 to Dragsholm, the manor house where the Earl of Bothwell, husband of Mary Queen of Scots, was kept prisoner in the dungeons. The house is now a hotel and restaurant. Continue to **Fårevejle**, passing Vejrhøj, the highest hill in the area. The Romanesque church at Fårevejle, built about 1600, has an impressive altarpiece and pews for the squire and parish clerk, and Lord Bothwell is buried here. The museum in the village includes exhibits describing the reclamation of the nearby Lammefjord, second largest reclaimed area in Europe, (5,000 hectares) and a small exhibit concerning Earl Bothwell.

The next village, **Høve**, has a museum dealing with the history of the Odsherred region through the ages. Continue on Road 225 with a superb view from Høve Stræde across the bay to Sjællands Odde, and turn left in **Svinninge** towards Højby, passing Sommerland Sjælland, with plenty of activities for the family. **Højby** Church has some good frescoes from the early fifteenth-century including a painting of St George slaying the dragon, and a beautiful medieval triptych.

From Højby continue to **Stenstrup** where the museum places special emphasis on agriculture in the area from prehistoric times. The road to Lumsås passes Troldstuerne, a double-chambered passage grave. Join Road 21 at Lumsås and continue to Sjællands Odde, driving along the top of the ridge with views over the sea on each side. Go down the hill into **Havnebyen** to see the old fishing harbour, fish auction and fish smoking houses. The main road continues to Odden ferry harbour, terminus of the ferry service to Ebeltoft in Jutland.

Return along the main road and turn left at Lumsås to **Nykøbing Sjælland**, the 'S' distinguishing it from the other towns of the same name in other provinces. This Nykøbing is the major town in a popular holiday area, with a good marina and a museum including a bakery, old grocer's shop and exhibitions on local history, industrial art and old trades, together with an interesting herb garden. Beyond the town the road leads to **Rørvig** and the ferry across the Isefjord to Hundested. There are some attractive beaches along the north shore and good walks, especially around Dybesø. Return to Nykøbing and follow the road past the harbour and along the coast to Annebjerg where an exceptionally fine collection of antique glass, the largest in northern Europe, is to be found in the Annebjerg Mansion. Continue along the coast to Kildehuse then turn right to Svinninge. Join the main Road 225 south and turn left onto Road 21 through Vig and in the direction of Holbæk. Beyond Gundestrup the road runs alongside the **Avdebo** dam across the head of Lammefjord. Stop in the parking place and climb the steps to the top of the dam for a marvellous view. The water in the fjord is higher than the land which was drained in 1873 to reclaim land for agriculture.

Keep on Road 21 through Mårsø and where the major road bears right as a dual carriageway keep straight ahead on Road 155 and immediately turn left at the crossroads to **Tveje Merløse** and follow signs to the church whose distinctive twin towers will be seen on the left. Built between 1100 and 1125, the church has been restored to something approaching its original appearance and the frescoes of varying age have been restored. It has been described as one of the most beautiful village churches and is the oldest twin-towered church in Denmark.

From the church continue into **Holbæk**, which grew up around a castle founded in the early thirteenth century. A Dominican monastery was founded about 1270 but the town was devastated by fire in 1513 and by Swedish soldiers in 1658-60. The main street, Ahlgade, was constructed in the thirteenth century and the only really old building remaining is the Elefantapotek dating from about 1600, becoming the *apotek* in 1705. The church was built in 1872 to replace an earlier building demolished in 1869. Some of the furnishings and fixtures including chandeliers from 1661 and some epitaphs, the oldest of which dates from 1594, together with the clock and church bells, the oldest cast in 1450, came from the old church but the carillon is modern.

Opposite the church the District Museum in a group of half- timbered houses dating from 1660 to about 1867 displays material relating to culture from prehistoric times through the Middle Ages and later and to the German occupation and Resistance movement in 1940-5. A number of interiors portray various shops and workshops. Nearby two wings from the old fifteenth-century Blackfriars monastery survive, one becoming the grammar school in 1535 and now used as parish offices. The other surviving wing became the town hall after the Reformation and is now used as an assembly hall.

From Holbæk go via Munkholmvej past Eriksholm estate where

Courtyard in Køge

walks are possible in the woods and on to Munkholm Bridge, at the end of which is Langtved Færgekro, an inn which is a reminder of the ferry which plied here before the building of the bridge. From the bridge there are fine views of fjord scenery. At the crossroads turn right along Road 53 and under the major trunk road to Tølløse. Bear right past the Romanesque church, cross the railway and go ahead at the crossroads towards Ugerløse. Take the next turning on the right opposite Tølløsegård and past the church fork left to Tjørnede. Turn right at the T-junction towards Algestrup then take the next turning on the left signed to Igelsø and Maglesø. After passing the gravel works there is a lay-by at the top of the hill with a view of Maglesø, a lake 55m (180ft) above sea level and completely hidden in the fold of the hills. The hills are known as the Sealand Alps and the roads are narrow, twisting and steep.

Continue towards Igelsø and at the main road go right then left towards Mogenstrup. Continue to Søndersted then go left to Undløse. Turn right along Road 231 towards Mørkøv, passing the old brick manor of Kongsdal on the left then after some sharp bends the manor and church of Torbenfeld, again on the left. The manor church has very ornate gables and the manor itself, founded in the fifteenth century, was once owned by Frederik III and his youngest son Prince

Old warehouse in Køge, now an art centre

George who married the English Queen Anne Stuart in 1708. Although private the manor may be seen from the road.

At the next junction turn left then right into Bennebo. Turn left for about 2km (a mile) and turn right at a T-junction. After about 1km (half a mile) turn left for about 2km (a mile) then right at the first T-junction and left at the next to reach main Road 225. Turn left past the inn, Bromølle Kro dating from 1198 and said to be the oldest in Denmark. Immediately turn right, following the road towards Buerup, then fork right then left past Hallebygård to the road beside Tissø, one of Denmark's largest lakes. Turn left along the shore Road 219 into Sæby then right to **Gørlev** where the church contains one of Denmark's oldest rune stones.

Leave Gørlev along Helsingevej (Road 277) to **Kirke Helsinge** with one of west Sealand's largest village churches, then turn right to **Dalby**. Keep to the right along Dalbyvej to Rævehøj, site of a 4,500-year-old burial chamber which is 2½m (8ft) high inside, being one of the highest known. Turn left along Reersøvej to the village of **Reersø** on a peninsula which is virtually an island. The lovely village with thatched cottages retains much of its nineteenth-century atmosphere, and a house dating from the late eighteenth century has been furnished and equipped as a typical farm labourer's cottage from about 1800. A small marina and fishing harbour are located to the

PLACES TO VISIT IN NORTH-WEST SEALAND

Kalundborg
Outstanding church, medieval town, museum, castle ruins.

Dragsholm
Manor prison of Earl of Bothwell.

Fårevejle
Interesting church, museum.

Høve
Museum dealing with Odsherred development.

Svinninge
Sommerland Sjælland recreation and amusement park.

Højby
Church with notable frescoes.

Stenstrup
Museum on agriculture from prehistoric times. Troldstuerne burial chamber.

Sjællands Odde
Narrow peninsula with Havnebyen fishing harbour. Odden ferry terminal for Ebeltoft.

Nykøbing-Sjælland
Interesting museum. Annebjerg antique glass collection.

Tveje Merløse
Beautiful twin towered church.

Holbæk
Thirteenth-century main street. Museum in group of old houses.

Maglesø
Superb views and walks in Sealand Alps.

Gørlev
Rune stone in church.

Dalby
Rævehøj burial chamber.

Reersø
Thatched cottages. Museum in farm cottage. Fishing harbour.

Lerchenborg
Manor with H.C. Andersen memorial rooms and archaeological museum.

south of the village.

Return along Reersøvej and keep straight on past the bird reserve, a very important breeding ground for waders. Turn left along main Road 22 to **Svallerup**, with an old tithe barn beside the church, and on to Ugerløse. Beyond the village turn left through Årby and Melby to the lovely baroque manor of Lerchenborg which contains memorial rooms to Hans Andersen who visited the manor in 1862. There is also an archaeological museum, and part of the house is open as well as the superb gardens. Concerts are held in the hall and a road through the estate leads to the Asnæs peninsula with wonderful views across Kalundborg Fjord. Unfortunately the surroundings have been spoiled by a large power station and oil refinery. From the manor return to Kalundborg via the main road past the refineries.

────────10────────
SOME SPECIAL ISLANDS

D enmark has 500 islands but those looked at in this chapter are rather special, each requiring a journey of at least an hour to be reached. Because of their relative isolation each has its own distinctive character, the largest and most isolated being Bornholm, some 150km (90 miles) east of Copenhagen in the middle of the Baltic. Ærø, part of the Funen Archipelago, is the least isolated but the journey to it is quite beautiful, especially from Svendborg and Fåborg. The Kattegat islands of Samsø, Læsø and Anholt also have their own special attractions.

ROUTE 31 • BORNHOLM
Bornholm is a rocky granite island about 19km (12 miles) wide and 48km (30 miles) long and quite unlike the rest of Denmark, its geology resembling that of the Norwegian mountains. It was first mentioned about AD890 by the Anglo-Saxon writer Wulfstan but evidence of early Stone Age man is shown by relics in the museum at Rønne. Unique to Bornholm are the old rock carvings depicting ships, spoked wheels and footprints. Believed to be from the Bronze Age, together with small saucer-shaped depressions, they are thought to be connected with agricultural rites. Iron Age relics prove without doubt that Bornholm even then was a maritime base in the Baltic and there are some 250 Bronze and Iron Age monoliths and about forty rune stones on the island. Unlike those in the rest of Denmark, these latter carry Christian inscriptions and the earliest is believed to date from about AD1050. Most of them are situated in or near churches, sometimes being built into the masonry. Bornholm's four fortified round churches are unique and there are three other fortified churches of more traditional pattern.

 The island is believed to have become part of Denmark during the Viking period and in medieval times it was the centre of a power struggle between the crown and the church. Later, Bornholm's position in the Baltic on the routes taken by the Hanseatic merchants led to its becoming an important trading centre but it suffered badly during the Swedish wars. Eventually an uprising led by Jens Kofoed, a native of the island, resulted in Bornholm being handed back to the Danish crown. In more recent times Bornholm was occupied by the Germans during World War II. At the end of the war the German commander refused to surrender to the Russians, resulting in the bombardment of two main towns, Rønne and Neksø, followed by Russian occupation for a year before the island was handed back to Denmark.

The most popular route to Bornholm is by overnight ferry from Copenhagen, a 7 to 8 hour journey. Alternatively, go from Copenhagen, Dragør or Helsingør to Sweden and drive to Ystad for the ferry to Bornholm, a crossing of $2^1/_2$ hours. Both routes go to Rønne which is also served by a ferry from Sassnitz in East Germany. For travellers without cars there is an express bus service from Copenhagen to Bornholm via Sweden. It is recommended to book in advance and it is essential if taking a car. A variety of accommodation is available on the boats and should be booked ahead, but expect the boats to be very crowded in school holiday periods. The quickest way is by air from Copenhagen Kastrup airport to Rønne airport.

Bornholm has an excellent bus service described in a very useful booklet giving details and times of all services including special tickets and tour packages offering bus travel and free admission to a number of places of interest. The booklet has an English explanation. The bus company also publishes a *Tourguide* leaflet written in Danish, German and English with five suggested tours using buses and walking. There are many opportunities for walking, particularly in the state forests and along the coast, and a good way of exploring is to use the buses, possibly with a 1-day or 7-day ticket.

Another excellent way of seeing the island is by bicycle, which may be taken on the ferry or hired on Bornholm. A number of cycle routes marked with green signs saying 'Cykelvej' follow special cycle tracks, forest roads, old railway lines or quiet country roads.

The route starts from **Rønne** whose most attractive medieval quarter with narrow cobbled streets surrounding the harbour was fortunate in avoiding destruction during the bombardment of 1945. The old 'main streets' are Grønnegade, Storegade and Østergade, the latter two meeting by the church in Kirkepladsen. From the tourist office near the ferry port walk up Havnebakken to Skt Nicolai Kirke whose distinctive spire-topped half-timbered tower stands as a landmark overlooking the harbour. Rebuilt in 1915-18, it still contains the old Romanesque font and some of the original stonework can be seen in the north-east corner. Walk up Østergade to Lille Torv and Søndergade where the old guardhouse built in 1744 with stone brought from Hammershus can be seen. In the same street number 11 is a typical timber-framed skipper's house with a small observation

Erichsens Gård, Rønne

tower looking out over the harbour. Back through Lille Torv is Store Torv, formerly the parade ground for the local militia but now the main town square with most of the larger shops.

In Skt Mortensgade the Bornholm Museum has an excellent local history collection from prehistoric times to the present day, and some original furnished rooms and workshops including a doctor's surgery and grocer's shop. There is also a fine collection of Bornholm clocks, a good navigation department and an art gallery.

Walk back through Store Torv into Store Torvegade and down Smallegade to Laksegade, one of the loveliest parts of the old town, where Erichsens Gård is a small museum furnished as a market town home of the late nineteenth century. Down in Storegade and Grønnegade are many other fine old houses, including the oldest house in the town at number 4 Grønnegade, parts of which date from the sixteenth century. Return to the harbour through Snellemark.

Along Søndergade and Søndre Alle near the Youth Hostel the defence tower Kastellet now houses the Defence Museum recording the resistance of Bornholm through the ages up to 1945. Near the tower is an old coastal redoubt with cannons still on their carriages.

Leave Rønne via Nordre Kystvej and Haslevej. Cyclists can use a superb cycle path through the woods on the left of the road. Turn right in the direction of Klemensker, and at **Nyker** is the Ny Kirke or

New Church, so-called since the Middle Ages and possibly the earliest of the four round churches of Bornholm. At the end of the main street the massive bell tower stands in the churchyard, its oldest bell dated 1639. The church itself, built around the eleventh century, has a huge central pillar with frescoes around the top from about 1250-1300. The old hour glasses by the pulpit date from 1690. The rune stone in the porch was found in two pieces, one built into the fabric of the church and the other in the kitchen floor of a local farm. The pieces were matched together in 1853 and restored. Two royal seals, one from Eric Menved (1286) and one from Frederik VI (1815) are on display in the church.

From the church take the road to Hasle, turning right along the main road. In about 3km (2 miles) the island's largest rune stone, the twelfth-century Brogårdsstenen discovered in 1868 acting as a bridge over a nearby stream, stands at the corner of the road to Klemensker. Continue into **Hasle** with its lovely stone church built in the fifteenth century with later additions, and containing a beautifully carved and gilded altarpiece and oak pulpit. Attractive old houses and steep streets lead to the harbour and the town makes a good centre for walking to the south through pine woods with lakes and sand dunes and north along the coast path through several fishing hamlets to where a steep flight of 108 steps leads down through a narrow gully in the steep cliffs along a fault-line in the underlying granite rock. Cars can park at the end of a short road leading from the main Hasle to Allinge road, while cyclists can use the coast path. The steps lead to Jons Kapel where legend has it that a monk called Jon lived in a nearby cave and preached to local peasants.

Continue along the main road and turn left down steep roads to **Vang**, once a port for the nearby granite quarries and now a small resort with a memorial to Vang's stonemasons by the harbour. Return to the top of the hill, turn left and in about 3km (2 miles) turn left just past the entrance to the Bornholm Zoo and nature park. The turn is signed to Hammeren and is winding, steep and used by buses and coaches so care is needed. The marked cycle path from Rønne via Hasle continues along past Vang to this area, avoiding the busy roads.

Several parking and picnic places give access to many fine footpaths in this area known as **Slotslyngen** and preserved as an area of natural beauty by the Forestry Service. Further along the road is the main car park for Hammershus, the impressive ruins of Scandinavia's largest fortress. The walk to the ruins is across a bridge over a deep ravine, and the castle on its isolated rocky knoll must have been virtually impregnable. The oldest parts date from about 1255 and ownership during the Middle Ages passed back and forth between the archbishop and the king. Continuous alteration and

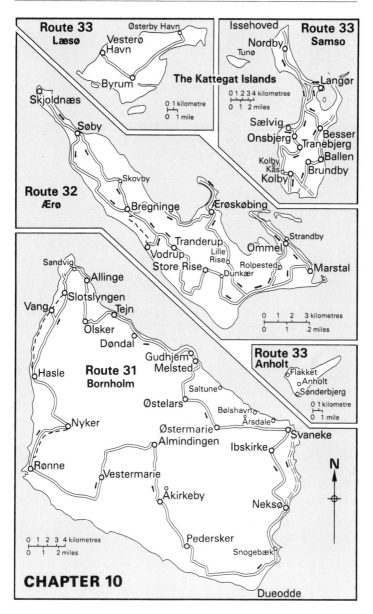

Route 33
Læsø

Østerby Havn

Vesterø
Havn

Byrum

The Kattegat Islands

0 1 kilometre
0 1 mile

Route 33
Samso

Issehoved

Nordby

Tunø

Langør

0 1 2 3 4 kilometres
0 1 2 miles

Sælvig

Onsbjerg

Besser

Tranebjerg

Ballen

Kolby
Kås

Kolby

Brundby

Skjoldnæs

Søby

Skovby

Bregninge

Ærøskøbing

Route 32
Ærø

Tranderup

Vodrup

Store Rise

Lille
Rise

Strandby

Ommel

Rolpested

Dunkær

Marstal

0 1 2 3 kilometres
0 1 2 miles

Sandvig

Allinge

Slotslyngen

Vang

Tejn

Olsker

Døndal

Route 33
Anholt

Gudhjem
Melsted

Flakket

Anholt

Sønderbjerg

0 1 kilometre
0 1 mile

Hasle

Route 31
Bornholm

Saltune

Østelars

Bølshavn

Årsdale

Nyker

Østermarie

Almindingen

Ibskirke

Svaneke

N

Rønne

Vestermarie

Åkirkeby

Neksø

0 1 2 3 4 kilometres
0 1 2 miles

Pedersker

Snogebæk

CHAPTER 10

Dueodde

enlargement took place up to the seventeenth century when the stronghold was in Swedish hands. Finally abandoned in 1743, the ruins became a source of building material until the site was declared an ancient monument in the nineteenth century.

From the car park a marked path goes through woods to the granite quarry at Moseløkken which is still in operation but can be visited during working hours. The return path passes a lovely woodland lake and a length of medieval paved road, and affords impressive views of the castle ruins. Take the road to the left to Hammer Sø car park from where there is easy access to the steep granite headland known as Hammeren, separated from the rest of the island by a wide rift valley containing the lake. There are good walks to the lighthouse and the ruins of Salomons Kapel.

Continue to the twin resorts of **Sandvig** and **Allinge**, once medieval fishing villages which still have some attractive old houses. Between the two, close to the cycle path and near the school is Bornholm's largest collection of old rock carvings, including eleven ships, one with a sun-wheel. They are signed Madsebakke from the road. Allinge Church has a rune stone nearby and a memorial to a number of Russian soldiers who died here during 1945-6 and are buried in the churchyard. From Allinge harbour a catamaran service goes to Sweden, also boat tours to **Christiansø** and **Frederiksø**, the islands fortified in 1684 after Denmark lost its provinces in south Sweden. These are worth visiting to see the two defence towers, one of which is now a museum.

From Allinge take the road towards Klemensker, to the round church at **Olsker**. Ols Kirke is the highest of the round churches, dedicated to the Norwegian Olav and dating from around 1150. It stands on a hilltop 112m (367ft) above sea level. From the church return to the coast road at **Tejn**, one of the principal fishing ports on the island, and follow the road towards Gudhjem. Between the road and the coast is Stammershalde, site of a number of Iron Age burial grounds. Further along, the road passes the beautiful valley of **Døndal**, a preserved area open to the public with a picturesque waterfall in rainy periods. A path leads from here along the coast to Helligdomsklipperne, a spectacular coastal rock formation. One can follow the 7km (4 mile) long 'life-savers path' from here into Gudhjem.

The coast road is quite beautiful, going to the left down hairpin bends to **Gudhjem** harbour, from where the main boat service to Christiansø departs. The settlement here is very old, being a trading and fishing centre. The houses are mostly built on the very steep rocky hillside and some of the old fish smoking houses remain, distinguished by their chimneys. However, today's health requirements confine the trade to more modern installations. The church was built in 1893 alongside the remains of a thirteenth-century

Looking down on Gudhjem

chapel, and coming up the hill out of the town the fine white windmill
is on the left. Turn onto Melstedvej then across to the old railway
station, closed in 1952 and now the home of Gudhjem Museum with
local historical collections and an exhibition of Bornholm textiles.

Return to the main road and cross back to the old coast road,
Melsted Langgade, and at the fishing hamlet of **Melsted** bear right
towards the main road and the yellow painted Melstedgård, an old
farmhouse dating from 1796. It is now a scheduled building housing
the Bornholm Agricultural Museum. Follow the main road in the
direction of Svaneke for about 1km (half a mile) then turn right along
a minor road for about 3km (2 miles), to the main Rønne road. Turn
left to **Østerlars** Kirke, largest of Bornholm's round churches. The
main structure is from around 1150, with the addition of buttresses in
the late middle ages to support the wall, and the whole three storey
building is of great interest, especially in its context as a former
defence work. The cylindrical central pillar decorated with restored
fourteenth-century frescoes is unique. The late sixteenth-century
altarpiece and pulpit have been restored. There is a rune stone in the
porch and the usual Bornholm style free-standing bell tower with two
interesting seventeenth-century bells.

Continue into Østerlars and turn left at the main road towards
Svaneke. The road comes to **Østermarie**, where the present church

Østelars Kirke, the largest of Bornholm's round churches

stands near the ruins of a medieval church partly demolished in 1885. The work was stopped when it was realised that it was of important architectural significance. The stone gable-roof construction is similar to that found in Knuds Kirke on Bornholm and in churches in Sweden, France and Ireland but the connection between them is unclear. Continue along the Svaneke road for about 3km (2 miles) then turn right on Louisenlundvej towards Neksø. In about 500m (547yd) is a sign to 'Louisenlund' and a parking place by a small copse containing the largest collection of Bronze and Iron Age monoliths on the island. This particular group was studied and preserved by King Frederik VII in 1850 who then gave the site to his wife Louise, hence the name.

Return to the main road and continue towards Svaneke. A fine view of the coast ahead can be seen from the crest of the hill past the windmill Kuremøllen, and further along on the right a turning leads to Brændesgårdshaven amusement park. As the main road enters the town a Dutch style windmill stands on the left. Beyond is a post mill and between them a strange triangular water tower which looks as if it was designed as a navigation mark for boats at sea.

Svaneke, a well kept market town dating from the Middle Ages is Denmark's most easterly town. Ship building and trading brought prosperity in the eighteenth and nineteenth centuries which is reflected in many of the buildings seen today, and a horse-drawn bus makes trips around the town for sightseers. There are busy sailing and fishing harbours with a boat service to Christiansø.

From Svaneke either follow the coast road past the white windmill at Årsdale and Gulhalds Batteri, now a picnic site, to Neksø, or go inland to **Ibskirke**, whose church has a fortified tower for defence purposes. The separate bell tower stands in the churchyard. Continue in the direction of Neksø for about 4km (2 miles) then turn right then right again at a T-junction for about 500m (547yd) to a car park by Lisegård at the entrance to Paradisbakkerne, the 'Paradise Hills'. This is a privately owned area of fragmented granite covered with heather and mixed woodland with scattered lakes. There are numerous paths and tracks among which it is easy to get lost. However, several waymarked routes give opportunities for some good walking, starting from Lisegård. One route leads to the famous Rokkestenen, a large erratic boulder weighing an estimated 35 tons.

From Lisegård take the road back to **Neksø**, the island's second largest town. It was a trading centre in the Middle Ages, and during the Russian bombing of May 1945 virtually the entire centre of the town was destroyed or damaged, although some old houses survived on the outskirts. The timber-framed church has an attractive appearance with its square tower topped by a spire. Near the large modern fishing port and harbour stands one of the oldest buildings which has been restored to contain the museum dealing with fishery and local history.

Continue south from Neksø via the small fishing hamlet of Snogebæk and along the coast road, then near some aerials and a large tower turn left to **Dueodde**, the island's southernmost point with high dunes and a superb beach with fine white sand, once exported as 'writers sand' before blotting paper was invented . Walk through the dunes to the lighthouse, one of the highest in Scandinavia which may be visited and climbed for the view — there are 196 stairs!

Return to the main road and turn left towards Rønne. In about 5km (3 miles) watch for signs to Slusegård Vandmøllen, a watermill in a little thatched building by a stream with a path to the beach. About 1km (half a mile) further along the main road keep straight ahead following signs to Pederskirke (*not* Pedersker). The church has an attractive painted wood ceiling and interesting relief work on the east end arch. Continue on the road towards Rønne then turn right to **Åkirkeby**, the oldest market town on the island with a charter dating from 1346. Its main attraction is the island's largest medieval church, for many years Bornholm's principal church. Around the year 1200 the tower was altered and the building reinforced for defence. The furnishings are some of the most impressive on the island, the font being an outstanding example of Romanesque carving. Almost as

Street in Ærøskøbing

old as the church, it is in sandstone and carries eleven carved panels and a long runic inscription. The altarpiece, communion table and pulpit are all fine examples of early seventeenth-century work.

Take the road north to **Almindingen** and turn left at the Østermarie road then left again after about 500m (547yd) onto the main Rønne road, to a car park on the left. Not far from the car park are the remains of the ramparts of Gamleborg, probably dating from Viking times and used as a refuge against attack, and Lilleborg, ruins of the earliest medieval fort on Bornholm dating from about 1150 when the round churches were built.

Almindingen is an extensive rocky area with many small lakes, once covered with scrub and heather and providing common grazing for cattle. During the nineteenth century the area was enclosed by a long stone dike to exclude cattle and the natural forest of oak and hornbeam was supplemented by extensive planting of beech, spruce

222

The square and the town pumps, Ærøskøbing

and Douglas fir. The area now forms Denmark's third largest forest and provides great scope for walking in some really outstanding scenery and for studying wildlife, including deer. Not to be missed is Ekkodal, part of Bornholm's longest rift valley, with oak woods along the rocks of the valley. Continue further along the road and turn left to Rytterknægten where another parking place lies by a high lookout tower giving fine views over most of the island in clear weather. More walks are possible from here and maps of the area showing way-marked routes are available from tourist offices.

Back on the main road turn left towards Rønne and in 4km (2 miles) turn left to **Vestermarie** Kirke, built in the nineteenth century to replace the older one. Much of the property from the old church is in Bornholm Museum. Six rune stones found in the neighbourhood are now in the churchyard. Continue south to **Nylars** Kirke, last of the four round churches, built around 1150 in the familiar pattern. Originally there were many frescoes, the oldest on Bornholm and possibly dating back to 1250, but only some of those on the central pillar have been restored. The unusual bell tower stands in the churchyard.

From the church go ahead to the main road, turn right and continue back to Rønne and the end of this route.

PLACES TO VISIT ON BORNHOLM

Rønne
Major ferry port. Skt Nicolai Kirke, Bornholm Museum, Erichsens Gård. Defence Museum.

Nyker
Eleventh-century round Ny Kirke with frescoes.

Brogårdsstenen
Largest rune stone on island.

Hasle
Fifteenth-century church with fine interior. Cliff steps to Jons Kapel.

Slotslyngen
Wooded area with walks.

Hammershus
Ruins of Scandinavia's largest fortress.

Moseløkken
Working granite quarries.

Allinge-Sandvig
Madsebakke rock carvings. Russian war memorial by church. Catamaran service to Sweden. Boats to Christiansø and Frederiksø.

Olsker
Ols Kirke, highest round fortified church on island.

Gudhjem
Ferry terminal for Christiansø. Museum. Attractive harbour.

Melsted
Melstedgård housing the Bornholm Agricultural Museum.

Østerlars
Østerlars Kirke
Large fortified round church.

Østermarie
Remains of medieval church.

Louisenlund
Bronze and Iron Age monoliths.

Svaneke
Most easterly town in Denmark. Horse-drawn bus service.

Ibskirke
Interesting fortified church.

Paradisbakkerne
Rough heath and woodland. Rokkestenen erratic boulder.

Neksø
Interesting church and museum.

Slusegård Vandmølle
Thatched watermill.

Pederskirke
Church with decorated interior.

Åkirkeby
Largest church on Bornholm with outstanding carved font.

Almindingen
Large forest area with walks. Ekkodalen rift valley. Gamleborg and Lilleborg ruins. Rytterknægten lookout tower.

Vestermarie
Church with six rune stones.

Nylars
Fortified round church with oldest frescoes on island.

ROUTE 32 • ÆRØ

With good reason the island of Ærø is known as the 'pearl of the south Funen sea'. Ferry services from Fåborg to Søby in the west, from Rudkøbing to Marstal in the east and from Svendborg to Ærøskøbing, 'capital' of the island, make it easy to plan a visit, especially as tickets are interchangeable. An additional summer service goes from Mommark on Als to Søby. With a car it is advisable to book especially in the holiday season but by far the best way of exploring the island is by bicycle. Cycles can be hired on arrival or the tourist office can arrange a 'package' to include the cycle. Being a popular holiday resort the island has a good selection of hotel and guest house accommodation as well as holiday chalets, three good camp sites and two Youth Hostels.

The most scenic ferry route is from Svendborg. The boat makes its way down Svendborg sound with breathtaking views of the high bridge and the coasts of Funen and Tåsinge, past the small islands of Skarø, Hjortø and Drejø to **Ærøskøbing**. Stepping off the ferry is rather like stepping back in time. The town is the only one in Denmark to be protected as an entity and it still looks much the same as it must have done in the seventeenth century, with a few eighteenth-century additions! The main street in the old town is Vestergade, with many eighteenth-century houses once owned by the sea captains who brought much prosperity to the town, and smaller half-timbered houses with elaborately carved and painted front doors which are also found in the adjoining streets of Smedegade and Gyden. In Vestergade is Denmark's oldest post office dating from 1749 and still open for the sale of stamps . At the top of the street Søndergade leads left to Torvet, with the town's twin pumps, in use up to 1952, and the former grammar school fronted with lime trees, behind which is the beautifully simple eighteenth-century church. The altarpiece, font and pulpit are from an earlier building. In Søndergade is Kjøbinghus, the oldest house in the town, built in 1645 and having the oldest front door in the country still in use. At the end of the street Østergade and Nørregade both have lovely old houses with roses and hollyhocks around the doors.

Nørregade leads down to Brogade with the Ærø Museum on the corner, illustrating the history of the town and island. A short way down Smedegade is Museumsgården with the unique 'Bottle Peter's' collection of some 400 model ships in bottles and other models made by the sea captain Peter Jacobsen, providing a fascinating survey of shipping types in miniature. The same museum contains an equally fascinating collection of wood carvings and sculptures, furniture and clocks collected by Hans Christian Pedersen, a local antique collector whose father and brother made many of the carvings which include both religious and secular pieces. A third museum, Hammer- ichs Hus, is a beautifully furnished house on the corner of Brogade and Gyden dating from 1700 and containing fine collections of faience and tiles.

Leave the town via Vesterbro in the direction of Søby, passing the unusual town windmill on the right, and take the next turning on the

One of the many dolmens on Ærø

 left to join Smedevejen then turn right and continue to Lille Rise where there is a picnic place with fine views over the island from the hilltop near the road. Continue in the direction of Marstal and turn left along the sea dyke Drejet which protects the reclaimed land of Gråsten Nor where there is a small airfield. A plantation beside the road gives some protection from on-shore winds. Continue towards Marstal and in 2km (a mile) turn left through the little village of Græsvænge with its flower-lined street to **Ommel** with its lovely thatched cottages and tiny harbour. It is said that one of the elderly residents of Ommel has never left the village, even to visit Marstal 3km (2 miles) away, and there are still people living on Ærø who have never left the island. Continue to Ommelshoved to enjoy the beautiful landscape and views towards the nearby islands and across the bay to Ærøskøbing.

Return through Ommel to **Marstal**, the largest town on the island, partly due to the fact that Ærøskøbing itself is a conservation area with limited possibilities for expansion. Marstal grew rapidly during the nineteenth century although there are a number of older captains' houses in the old town near the harbour. It is an old maritime town with many proud traditions from the days of sail. The harbour once sheltered 300 wooden schooners, cutters and other vessels, many of them built in the local shipyards, and wooden ships are still built here. A busy repair yard, the working harbour, ferry terminal and one

Bregninge Church

of the biggest yacht harbours in the country are all protected by a breakwater built by local sailors and farmers about 150 years ago using granite erratic boulders. At the end of it stands an old lime kiln, now a protected building. In Prinsengade overlooking the harbour is Jens Hansens Søfartsmuseum, a maritime museum with a splendid collection of ship models, maritime and navigation equipment and local archaeological and other collections. Near the ferry terminal in Teglgade is Minors Hjem, an old sailor's home open as a small museum. In the town the beautiful seamens' church dating from 1737 has a twelfth-century font and a fine altarpiece showing Christ stilling the waves, and the apostles' faces are modelled on old Marstal sea captains of the period.

Leave the town along Møllevejen towards Ærøskøbing to the parking place at the end of the dyke with superb views along the coast westwards to Vejnæs Nakke and eastwards to Ærøshale. Continue ahead past the turning to Ærøskøbing along a minor road which bends right past Lindsbjerg, where three fine dolmens can be seen. Turn right to Dunkær then turn left to **Store Rise** Church which is the oldest on the island, dating back to the twelfth century. Its size, position on rising ground and copper-clad spire make an impressive sight and the carved wooden altarpiece is from about 1450. After visiting the church go through the village and turn right at the T-

PLACES TO VISIT ON ÆRØ

Æeroskøbing
Protected seventeenth- to eighteenth-century town, Ærø Museum, Hammerichs Hus.

Marstal
Søfartsmuseum, seamen's church.

Lindsbjerg and Rise Mark
Good examples of dolmens.

Store Rise
Oldest church on the island.

Tranderup
Thirteenth-century church.

Bregninge
Thirteenth-century church.

Søbygård
Medieval castle mound and ramparts.

Søby
Thatched windmill.

junction. Continue in the direction of Rise Mark then turn right and in about 1km (half a mile) turn right again. At the next bend in the road another dolmen is seen on the left. At the next junction turn left and follow the very narrow winding road to the tiny hamlet of Olde with attractive thatched cottages. Continue through Olde in the direction of **Tranderup**, keeping left through the village after the junction with the Ærøskøbing road. The thirteenth-century church originally had a spire which was replaced in 1832 by a tower designed by C.F. Hansen who designed the cathedral in Copenhagen. The interior has a carved altarpiece and frescoes from the early sixteenth century.

Tranderup is almost continuous with Vindeballe, which still has its old smithy. Turn left towards **Vodrup** and the car park at Vodrup Klint with fine views along the coast. A path leads to the beach below the curious terraced coastline formed after the last Ice Age and cyclists can follow farm tracks through the fields to Bregninge. Motorists should return to Vindeballe and turn left to **Bregninge**, a village with a main street more than 2km (a mile) long. Its early thirteenth-century church is the most beautiful one on Ærø. The oak-shingled spire is typical Slesvig pattern and was added to the tower in about 1500. The magnificent altarpiece was carved in Odense by Claus Berg about 1530 and there is an early twelfth-century font and a Renaissance carved pulpit dated 1612 with an interesting hour glass. The remarkable frescoes above the altar were uncovered in 1915-22 by the National Museum. The bell rope used to hang through the open mouth of a figure of a joker in the roof of the nave. An interesting record of the old 'Kirkestierne' or Church Paths on the island may be seen in the porch.

Take the road on the right past the mill to Skovby then bear left back to the main road at Leby, both villages with attractive cottages and farms. Turn right on the main road to **Søbygård** where high earth ramparts form one of the best medieval castle mounds in the country, built in the early twelfth century probably as defence works for the natural harbour which existed before the navigable Vitsø was dammed and drained. Nearby is a preserved windmill, Vester Mølle.

The road leads into the fishing town of **Søby**, with a busy harbour and shipyard, and narrow winding streets overlooking the sea. Ferries sail to Fåborg and in the summer months to Mommark. A prominent landmark is the well preserved Dutch style thatched windmill from where the road runs north-west to Haven and **Skjol-dnæs**, the northern tip of the island. There are fine views across the water to Als from the beach near the lighthouse.

Return to Søby and turn right along Buevej and Skovvejen to the dyke across the Vitsø Nor, an idyllic spot for bird watchers, with Vitsø Mølle overlooking the marshy area. Continue along the lanes through Leby Kobbel and Tværby to Bregninge, turn right then left at Bregninge Kro to Borgnæs. Follow the coast road into Ærøskøbing, turn left down Vestre Alle and left again along Sygehusvejen past the camp site to the beach road to Urehoved, with good views north to Drejø and across the bay towards Søby. Return by the same road to the town and ferry back to Svendborg, but before leaving notice the curious white building on the harbour quay. Originally the cookhouse used by ships' crews forbidden to cook on board in port because of fire risk, it later became a lighthouse and is now a public toilet!

ROUTE 33 • THE KATTEGAT ISLANDS

The Kattegat is the stretch of sea bounded on the west by Jutland, on the south by Funen and by Sealand and Sweden to the east. Six islands in the Kattegat are reached by ferry journeys of an hour or more, but only three will be considered in detail. Of the others, Sejerø is just over 60 minutes journey by car ferry from Havnsø in north-west Sealand and is a popular holiday resort with a camp site, hotel and summer Youth Hostel. Endelave is about the same journey time from Snaptun on Horsens Fjord, again on a car ferry, and is popular with yachtsmen and as a holiday resort. There are good beaches, one small hotel and a camp site and opportunities for walking. The third and smallest of these islands is Tunø, about an hour's trip from Hov, north of Horsens Fjord, but cars are not allowed. There are good facilities for yachtsmen and a small camp site. The tower of the fourteenth-century church has been used as a lighthouse since 1801.

It is strongly advised to book in advance if taking a car to any of the islands, particularly in the summer months.

Samsø

The island is 116sq km (45sq miles) in area with a wide variety of scenery and good beaches on both east and west coasts. It is the geographic centre of Denmark, equidistant from the coasts of Jutland, Funen and Sealand. In addition to beaches it has cliffs, forests and marshland, farms and moorland, and in the north an impressive area of moraine left after the Ice Age.

The shortest ferry route takes 80 minutes from Hov in Jutland to Sælvig at the centre of the west coast and from which this tour begins. Another service with a 2 hour sailing time is from Kalundborg in west Sealand to Kolby Kås in the south.

As on Ærø, the best way to explore is by cycle, but a good bus service reaches most parts. With a car it is essential to book both outward and return journeys because the ferries also carry goods and supplies to and from the island.

A carefully planned day trip can give $6^{1}/_{2}$ hours or more with a chance to see most of the interesting places, but for longer stays there are hotels and guest houses, a Youth Hostel and four camp sites.

From Sælvig ferry follow the road through the dunes and turn right towards Tranebjerg. At **Onsbjerg**, once the island's main town, the fifteenth-century church has a gold crucifix dating from around 1200, so giving it the name of Holy Cross Church. Shortly after leaving Onsbjerg, an old 'Ting Hill' known as Kongehøjen (The King's Hill) on the right with a memorial to King Frederik VII provides good views over the island.

Continue into **Tranebjerg**, 'capital' of the island. Samsø Museumsgård is an old farm with furniture and interiors from the seventeenth century and a good prehistoric collection. Everything, including the linen, is in immaculate condition and well displayed, although unfortunately there are no brochures in English. Møllebakken opposite the tourist office has a viewpoint on the base of the old mill. The fourteenth-century church with a huge tower built in about 1500 for defence purposes has a late sixteenth-century pulpit and other furnishings, also frescoes on the north wall of the nave depicting St Christopher, patron saint of travellers. In the churchyard is one of the country's best maintained late medieval tithe barns.

Leave via Marsk Stigsvej, opposite the church, to Pillemark then continue along Tranemosevej in the direction of Vesterløkken, passing Tranemose, the island's largest lake, rich in bird life. Continue in the direction of Kolby Kås, Samsø's major ferry harbour, passing the sand and gravel hills on the left which are characteristic of the island. Take the road to **Kolby** village, passing Kolby mill on the left, then turn right opposite the church along the village street past a number of old half-timbered houses and continue to **Vesborg**. The lighthouse was

Ballen harbour, Samsø

built on the site of a medieval castle some of whose ruins can still be
seen, and from the car park a beautiful path goes around the southern
tip of the island.

Return to Kolby, take the small street on the right, and at the end
turn right to Brattingsborg, a nineteenth-century manor house on an
estate which has existed since 1695. The grounds contain remains
of castle mounds whose history is completely unknown. The road
leads past the house through woods to the coast where there are
many attractive paths and a number of burial mounds, passage
graves and dolmens.

Return to the manor and keep right to Ørby and Brundby, passing
typical Samsø farms. Ahead through **Brundby** is the island's best
known landmark, Kolhøj Mølle, a post mill built in 1650 and newly
restored. Follow the road to **Ballen**, a fishing hamlet and holiday
resort with a good bathing beach and from the harbour take the
unsigned coast road between the craft shop and restaurant and
continue through Langemark to **Besser** Church. In the churchyard
are some very old headstones, situated to the right of the building
near the road. Besser village has some very pretty thatched houses.

A diversion may be made to the car park at the beginning of
Besser Rev, a narrow spit of land a few metres wide and about 5km
(3 miles) long, with the remains of a battery built during the war with

231

England in 1807-14 at the northern tip. There is a fine view of Stavns Fjord and its islands, a beautiful area of great biological, archaeological and historical importance which is now a nature reserve.

From Besser village continue through Alstrup and Toftebjerg to the main road, turn right towards Nordby then right again towards Stavns. Just by the junction can be seen the line of the old Kanhave Kanal built around AD800 by the Vikings to link the fjord and fortified settlement on Hjørtholm with the Kattegat. Turn left in Stavns and follow the road round the fjord to **Langør**, a busy marina and fishing hamlet with good views over the fjord.

Return along the edge of the fjord, bearing right to the main road and follow it across Nordby Hede to Mårup, past an antique showroom in a lovely old farm. Continue to **Nordby** in the centre of which is a tower which looks like a lighthouse but is a belfry built to call the villagers to church, since the church is too far away for its bell to be heard. The village is very attractive with a large pond overlooked by some beautiful half-timbered thatched houses. Many cottages have roses and hollyhocks growing by the front doors.

Take the road signed to **Issehoved**. It gets very narrow as it reaches the moraine area, becoming a steep gravel road and eventually a rough track. There are several car parks but it is worth driving to the end if your car will take it! The area is known as Nordby Bakker, a nature reserve with woodland and grass covered hills with a profusion of wild flowers, covered with a network of waymarked paths. One path leads down to Issehoved, the northern tip of the island. An alternative to the rough track is to drive from Nordby village to Ballebjerg, highest point in the north of Samsø, with a car park, toilets and a lookout tower giving superb views across the hills of Nordby Bakker and over the sea to Tunø Island. Waymarked paths lead from here over the *bakker* and south along the coast, shown on a leaflet with Danish text produced by the State Forestry Service.

Return to Nordby and follow the main road south past the church set back on the right of the road between Nordby and Mårup. Its lonely position is due to the fact that it originally served two medieval villages, long since disappeared. One of them, Glistrup, was close to the church. Follow the road along the coast back to Sælvig and the ferry harbour.

Læsø

The ferry service from Frederikshavn takes about $1\frac{1}{2}$ hours and docks at Vesterø Havn on the north-west coast of the island, about 8km (5 miles) from the principal town of Byrum. A bicycle is an ideal means of exploring and there are a number of hotels and guest houses, two camp sites and a Youth Hostel on the island.

Læsø is slightly larger than Samsø but has only half its population. Two thirds of the island is uncultivated offering large areas of

PLACES TO VISIT ON THE KATTEGAT ISLANDS

Samsø

Onsbjerg
Fifteenth-century church with gold crucifix. Old 'Ting Hill'.

Tranebjerg
Museum with interiors and prehistoric collections. Church with frescoes and tithe barn.

Vesborg
Lighthouse built on old fort.

Brundby
Kolhøj Mølle post mill.

Ballen
Fishing hamlet and holiday resort.

Besser Rev
Narrow spit overlooking Stavns Fjord, a nature reserve.

Langør
Fishing and yacht harbour.

Nordby
Attractive village with pond and belfry in village centre.

Nordby Bakker
Nature reserve with fine walks and views.

Ballebjerg
Viewpoint from tower and good walks.

Læsø

Vesterø Havn
Fishing and Maritime Museum. Vesterø Søndre Kirke.

Byrum
Church. Tractor bus tour. Hjemstavnsgård Museum.

Højsande
Dune reserve.

Anholt
Bird sanctuary. Lighthouse.

unspoiled landscape with pools, heath and scrub and a broad foreshore along most of the coast. Tree felling for fuel to feed the boilers used for salt production in the Middle Ages and heavy sand drifts in the seventeenth century resulted in the inland dunes of the north-east known as Højsande, rising to about 30m (98ft) above sea level. The Knotten peninsula is a bird sanctuary and the group of low flat off-shore islands in the south includes salt marsh and meadow offering ideal conditions for wading birds

The oldest house in **Vesterø Havn** dated 1872 is now the Fishing and Maritime Museum. The thatched half-timbered building contains an interesting collection of old fishing and marine equipment, navigation instruments and life saving apparatus. South of the ferry harbour the attractive thirteenth-century Vesterø Søndre Kirke has furnishings and frescoes from the fifteenth century.

The church in **Byrum** is of the same age and in the town is a viewing tower from which the whole island can be seen. A daily tractor bus tour and a horse-drawn bus service from Krogbækgård provide an opportunity to view the wildlife on the southern off-shore islands.

Seaweed-thatched houses are a feature of the island, a good example being the 250-year-old Hjemstavnsgård, a local history museum just north of Byrum. Continuing north, the Klitplantage or forest provides plenty of opportunities for walking and nature study. A state forestry leaflet is available showing the waymarked paths. There are strict rules restricting smoking and use of matches in the whole area because of fire risk. Along the northern shore are superb sandy bathing beaches and from the village of Østerby Havn, where the lifeboat is stationed, there is a path through the dunes to the Knotten peninsula.

Anholt

This tiny island of 22sq km (8sq miles) and 160 inhabitants lies about 45km (28 miles) off the Jutland coast and has an interesting history. During the Napoleonic Wars the British Navy occupied the island from 1809 to 1814 and since all naval shore bases are by custom named as ships the Danish island of Anholt became known as 'H.M.S. Anholt'.

A ferry from Grenå takes about $2\frac{1}{2}$ hours. It does not run every day and since much of the island is closed to motor vehicles it is best to walk or cycle. Accommodation is available in Anholt Kro or private houses and there is one camp site.

Originally covered with pine forest, the trees were felled in the early nineteenth century resulting in large stretches of drifting sand dunes and stony plains. This area known as Ørkenen (Desert) can be viewed from Nordbjerg, a 48m (157ft) high ridge near the ferry landing. North of the ridge is a bird sanctuary for waders and it is possible to walk or cycle along the beach round the island. The lighthouse built in 1780 is under a preservation order but is still in use.

USEFUL INFORMATION FOR VISITORS

ANCIENT MONUMENTS AND CASTLE RUINS

Most ancient monuments such as dolmens, passage graves, castle ruins, etc are freely accessible at all times in daylight hours. If on private land the owner may make a small charge for access but some of the finest are close to a public road. Those with restricted access are listed here.

Emborg
Øm Kloster
Open: May to August daily except Monday 9am-6pm. April and September daily except Monday 9am-5pm.

Hillerød
Æbelholt Kloster
Æbelholtvang
Meløse
Open: May to August daily except Monday 10am-4pm. Limited opening at other times.

Hobro
Fyrkat Viking Fort
Fyrkatvejen 45
Open: all year daily 9am-7pm.

Kerteminde
Ladby Skibet
Vikingvej 123
Viking chieftans grave.
Open: May to October daily except Monday 10am-6pm. October to May daily except Monday 10am-3pm.

Slagelse
Trelleborg Viking Fortress
Hejninge
Open: April to September daily 10am-6pm.

AREAS OF OUTSTANDING NATURAL BEAUTY

There are many beautiful areas in Denmark, but those outstanding are:

Dollerup Bakker
Near Viborg
National Trust area of glacier-formed landscapes.

Mols Bjerge
Near Ebeltoft
Beautiful area of glacial 'mountains' with superb coastal views.

Rebild Bakker National Park
Skørping
Area of juniper-covered hills and deep valleys.

Råbjerg Mile
Desert area of drifting sand dunes near Skagen.

CASTLES AND COUNTRY HOUSES

This list includes a selection of the many manor houses open to the public but does not include those where only the grounds are open to the public.

Auning
Gammel Estrup
Open: May to October daily 10am-5pm, November to April daily 11am-3pm.

Copenhagen
Christiansborg Royal Reception Rooms
Prins Jørgensgård 1
Open: May to September. Guided tours in English daily except Monday at 11am, 1pm and 3pm. Limited opening at other times.

Christiansborg Ruins
Open: May to September daily 9.30am-4pm. October to April daily except Saturday 9.30am-4pm.

Rosenborg Slot
Øster Voldgade 4a
Open: May to September daily 10am-4pm. Limited opening at other times.

Dronninglund
Voergård
Voergårdvej
Open: May to August, Saturdays 2-5pm, Sundays and public holidays 10am-5pm, season weekdays 2-5pm.

Hadsten
Clausholm
Clausholmvej
Open: Easter to May, mid-August to mid-October Saturdays 2-5pm, Sundays and public holidays 10am-12noon and 2-5pm. June to mid-August daily 10am-12noon and 2-5.30pm.

Helsingør
Kronborg Slot
Open: May to September daily 10am-5pm. April and October daily 11am-4pm.

Hillerød
Frederiksborg Slot
Open: May to September daily 10am-5pm. April daily 11am-4pm.

Kolding
Koldinghus
Open: May to September 10am-5pm daily. Limited opening at other times.

Kværndrup
Egeskov
Open: May to September daily 10am-5pm.

Nysted
Ålholm Slot
Open: June to August daily 11am-6pm.

Næstved
Gavnø Slot
Open: May daily 10am-5pm, June to August daily 10am-4pm.

Salling

Spøttrup Castle
Spøttrup
Open: April, Sundays and public
holidays 11am-5pm, May to
August daily 10am-6pm, September daily 11am-6pm.

Skibby

Selsø Manor House
Selsøvej
Open: mid-June to early August
daily 11am-5pm. May to mid-June
and mid-August to September
Saturday and Sunday only 1-4pm.

Sæby

Sæbygård
Sæbygårdvej 60
Open: July daily 2-5pm.

Troense

Valdemars Slot
Slotsalleen 100
Open: May to September daily
10am-5pm.

CHURCHES AND CATHEDRALS

Most Danish village churches are
open during the daytime, but
occasionally they may be locked
and the key held by the *graver* or
verger. The address of the key
holder is given on the notice board.
Larger cathedrals and parish
churches have set opening times
which may be obtained from the
tourist office. Many churches have
information leaflets available,
sometimes in English. Visitors are
asked not to enter churches when
services of a private nature are in
progress.

GARDENS

Assens

The Seven Gardens
Å Strandvej 62
Å Strand
Open: May to October daily 10am-
5pm.

Astrup

Villestrup Baroque Garden
Open: mid-May to September daily
10am-5pm.

Copenhagen

Botanical Gardens
Gothersgade 128
Open: May to August daily
8.30am-6pm, September to
December daily 8.30am-4pm.
Palm House open all year daily
10am-3pm.

Haslev

Gisselfeld Manor
Open: May, Monday to Friday
10am-5pm. Saturday and Sunday
10am-6.30pm. June to mid-August
daily 10am-7pm. Mid-August to
end August daily 10am-5.30pm.
September to October daily 10am-
4pm.

Kolding

Geographical Gardens
Christian IV Vej
Open: April and May daily 10am-
6pm, June and July daily 9am-
8pm, August daily 10am-8pm and
September daily 9am-6pm.

Nykøbing-Mors

Jesperhus Blomsterpark
Legindvej 13
Open: mid-May to mid-September
daily 9am-6pm. In season 9am-
9pm.

Ranum
Vitskøl Monastery Garden
Viborgvej 474
Open: end May to early September
daily 10am-7pm.

Varde
Tambours Have
Bredmosevej
Nordenskov
Open: May and September daily
10am-6pm. June to August daily
10am-9pm.

Ålestrup
Jutland Rose Garden
Open: end June to end of summer
daily until sunset.

LEISURE AND RECREATION PARKS

Billund
Legoland
Open: May to September daily
10am-8pm. Rides and traffic
school daily 10am-5.30pm, 7.30pm
in peak season.

Bornholm
Brændesgårdshaven
Svaneke
Open: May to September daily
10am-6pm. In season daily 9am-
9pm.

Copenhagen
Tivoli Gardens
H.C. Andersens Boulevard 22
Open: end May to early September
daily 10am-midnight.

Bakken Klampenborg
Open: April to August daily 2pm-
midnight.

Hobro
Klejtrup Sø World Map

Søren Poulsensvej 5
Klejtrup
Open: May to August daily 9am-
8pm, September daily 9am-6pm.

Marielyst
Sommerland Falster
Godthåbs Alle 7
Open: early June to mid-August
daily 10am-6pm.

Nimtofte
Djurs Sommerland
Randersvej 17
Open: end May to end August
daily 10am-6pm, July daily 10am-
8pm.

Nykøbing-Sjælland
Sommerland Sjælland
Gammel Nykøbingvej 169
Open: mid-May to August daily
10am-6pm. In season daily 10am-
8pm.

Odense
Fyns Tivoli
Søndre Boulevard 304
Open: April to August daily
2-10pm.

Ringkøbing
Sommerland West
Hovervej 56-8
Hee
Open: third weekend May to third
weekend August daily 10am-5pm,
July daily 10am-6pm.

Saltum
Fårup Sommerland
Pirupvejen
Open: mid-May to June and
August daily 10am-6pm, July daily
10am-8pm.

Tinglev
Sommerland Syd

Open: mid-May to end August
daily 10am-6pm, July daily 10am-
7pm.

Varde
Fårup Sommerland
Gellerupvej
Open: June to August daily 10am-
6pm.

Ålborg
Tivoliland Ålborg
Karolinelundsvej
Open: end March to mid-Septem-
ber daily 2-9pm.

MUSEUMS

Entry fees for museums vary;
some are free. About 240 museums are mentioned in this guide
and only a selection can be listed
here. Details of other museums
and opening hours may be
obtained, in English, through the
tourist information offices via the
Dandata system.

Auning
Danish Agricultural Museum
Gammel Estrup
Open: May to October daily 10am-
5pm. Limited opening other times.

Bjerringbro
Museum of Electricity
Bjerringbrovej 44
Tange
Open: June to August, Monday to
Friday 10am-6pm. Saturdays,
Sundays and public holidays
10am-5pm.

Bornholm
Bornholm Museum
Skt Mortensgade 29

Rønne
Open: May to September weekdays 10am-4pm. Limited opening
at other times.

Gudhjem Museum
Stationsvej 1
Gudhjem
Open: June to mid-September
daily 10am-12noon and 2-5pm.

Copenhagen
Nationalmuseet
Frederiksholmskanal 12/Ny
Vestergade 10
Open: mid-June to mid-September
daily except Monday 10am-4pm.
Limited opening at other times.

Thorvaldsens Museum
Porthusgade 2
Open: all year daily except
Monday 10am-5pm.

Ny Carlsberg Glyptotek
Dantes Plads 7
Open: May to August daily except
Monday 10am-4pm. Limited
opening at other times.

Dragør Museum
Havnepladsen
Dragør
Open: May to September Tuesday
to Friday 2-5pm, Saturdays and
Sundays 12noon-6pm.

Ebeltoft
Missers Doll Museum
Grønningen 15
Open: June to September 10am-
5pm, May and October 10am-
12noon and 2-4pm.

Frigate *Jylland*
Strandvejen
Open: Easter and May to Septem-
ber daily 10am-5pm.

Esbjerg
Esbjerg Museum
Nørregade 25
Open: all year daily except
Monday 10am-4pm.

Fisheries Museum and Aquarium
Tarphagevej
Open: all year weekdays 10am-
5pm (4pm in winter), Saturdays
and Sundays 10am-6pm (5pm in
winter) and mid-June to mid-
August daily 10am-8pm.
Seals fed daily at 11am and
2.30pm.

Fanø
Fanø Maritime and Costume
Collection
Hovedgaden 28
Nordby
Open: May to September daily
10am-12noon and 2-5pm.

Fredericia
Fredericia Museum
Jernbanegade 10
Open: all year weekdays except
Monday 1-5pm, Sundays and
public holidays 10am-5pm and
mid-June to mid-August daily
10am-5pm.

Frederikshavn
Bangsbo Museum
Dr Margrethesvej 1
Open: April-Oct daily 10am-5pm.

Frederiksværk
Powder Mill Museum
Open: April to October daily 11am-
4.30pm.

Fåborg
Den Gamle Gaard
Holkegade
Open: mid-May to mid-September
daily 10.30am-4.30pm.

Gjern
Jyske Automobile Museum
Open: May to mid-September daily
10am-6pm. Limited opening at
other times.

Glamsbjerg
Hjemstavnsgården
Klaregade 23
Gummerup
Open: April to October daily except
Monday 10am-5pm.

Gram
Midtsønderjyllands Museum
Gram Slot
Open: April to October, Tuesday to
Friday 10am-12noon and 1-5pm.
Saturdays and Sundays 10am-
5pm.

Grenå
Djursland Museum
Søndergade 1
Open: late June to late August,
Tuesday, Thursday and Friday
10am-5pm. Wednesday 10am-
7pm, Saturdays and Sundays
2-5pm. Closed Monday. Limited
opening at other times.

Haderslev
Haderslev Museum
Dalgade 7
Open: May to September Tuesday
to Friday 10am-5pm, Saturdays
and Sundays 12noon-5pm.

Slesvig Carriage Collection
Sejlstensgyde
Open: mid-June to mid-August
daily 2-5pm.

Hantsholm
Lighthouse Museum and Gun
Emplacement Museum
Open: April to mid-June and
September to November, week-

days 8am-3pm. Saturdays and
Sundays 11am-4pm. Mid-June to
August daily 10am-5pm.

Helsingør
Maritime Museum
Kronborg Slot
Open: May to September 10am-
5pm, April and October 11am-
4pm.

Danish Technical Museum
Main Building
Nordre Strandvej 23
Open: all year daily 10am-5pm.

Traffic Department
Ole Rømers Vej
Open: all year Monday to Friday
10am-4pm, Saturdays and
Sundays 10am-5pm.

Herning
Herning Art Museums
Birk
Open: May to October daily except
Monday 10am-5pm. Limited
opening at other times.

Herning Museum
Museumsgade 1
Open: all year weekdays except
Mondays 10am-5pm. Saturdays
and Sundays 11am-5pm.

Danmarks Photomuseum
Museumsgade 3
Open: all year daily except
Monday 1-5pm.

Hillerød
North Sealand Folk Museum
Jægebakken
Helsingørsgade 65
Open: mid-June to mid-September
daily except Monday 2-5pm.
Limited opening at other times.

Hirtshals
Hirtshals Museum
Vanggårdsgade 10
Open: June to August daily 10am-
5pm. Limited opening at other
times.

Hjørring
Vendsyssel Historical
Museum
Museumgade 2
Open: June to mid-September
daily 10am-5pm, mid-September
to May weekdays 1-4pm. Sundays
and public holidays 10am-4pm.

Holbæk
Holbæk Museum
Klosterstræde 14-16
Open: May to October daily except
Monday 10am-4pm, November to
April daily except Monday 1-4pm.

Holstebro
Holstebro Art Museum
Sønderbrogade 2
Open: mid-June to mid-August
daily except Mondays 11am-5pm.
Other times daily except Mondays
12noon-4pm.

Horsens
Museum of Industry
Gasvej 17-19
Open: July and August daily
except Monday 10am-5pm,
September to June daily except
Monday 1-5pm.

Open-Air Museum
Glud
Open: April to October daily 10am-
5pm.

Humlebæk
Louisiana Museum of Modern Art

Gammel Strandvej 13
Open: all year daily 10am-5pm.

Hundested
Knud Rasmussen's Museum
Knud Rasmussen's Vej 9
Open: mid-April to mid-October
daily 11am-4pm. Limited opening
at other times.

Hvalpsund
Hessel Agricultural Museum
Hesselvej 40
Open: April to October daily 10am-
5.30pm.

Kalundborg
Kalundborg Museum
Adelgade 23
Open: May to August daily except
Monday 11am-4pm. Limited
opening at other times.

Kalvø
Kalvø Mini-Museum
Open: mid-April to mid-October
Tuesday to Sunday 2-6pm. June,
Tuesday to Friday 9am-12noon
and 2-6pm.

Kerteminde
Johannes Larsen Museet
Møllebakken
Open: April to October daily except
Monday 10am-4pm.

Kongens
Frilandsmuseet
Kongevejen 100
Open: mid-April to September daily
10am-5pm. Limited opening at
other times.

Korsør
Town and Ferry Museum
Fæstningen
Open: mid-June to August

daily 10am-4pm. Limited opening
at other times.

Kværndrup
Veteran Transport Museum
Egeskov Castle
Open: June to August daily 9am-
6pm, May and September daily
10am-5pm.

Køge
Køge Museum
Nørregade 4
Open: June to August daily 10am-
5pm. Limited opening other times.

Lejre
Historical-Archaeological Research
Centre
Slang Alle 2
Open: May to September daily
10am-5pm.

Læsø
Museumsgården
Museumsvej
Byrum
Open: June to August daily
12noon-4pm. In season daily
10am-4.30pm. Limited opening at
other times.

Museum of Fishing and Shipping
Vesterø Havnegade
Vesterø
Open: mid-June to mid-August
daily 12noon-4pm.

Løgstør
Lim Fjord Museum
Kanalvejen 40
Open: mid-June to August 10am-
5pm. May to mid-June Saturdays
2-5pm. Sundays 10am-5pm.

Mariager
Mariager Museum
Kirkegade 4B
Open: all year daily 10am-4pm.

Maribo

Frilandsmuseum
Meinkesvej
Open: May to September daily
10am-5pm.

Middelfart

Henner Frisers House
Brogade 8
Open: June to August daily 10am-
12.30pm and 1.30-5pm, May and
September daily 1.30-5pm.

Nyborg

Nyborg Museum
Mads Lerkes Gård
Kongegade
Open: May to October daily
10am-4pm.

Nykøbing-Falster

Czarens Hus
Færgestræde
Open: May to mid-September
weekdays except Monday 10am-
4pm, Sundays 2-4pm.

Nykøbing-Mors

Morslands Historical Museum
Dueholm Kloster
Open: all year daily 10am-4pm.

Nykøbing-Sjælland

Odsherreds Museum
Kirkestræde 12
Open: mid-June to October daily
except Monday and Saturday
10am-4pm.

Nysted

Ålholm Automobile Museum
Ålholm Parkvej 7
Open: June to August daily 10am-
6pm. April, May, September and
October, Saturdays and Sundays
10am-6pm.

Næstved

Næstved Museum
Helligåndshuset
Ringstedgade
Open: daily except Monday
9am-5pm.

Odense

Carl Nielsen Museum
Claus Bergsgade 11
Open: June to August daily 10am-
4pm, September to May weekdays
2-8pm. Saturdays and Sundays
10am-4pm.

Falck Museum
Klostervej 28
Open: May to October weekdays
10am-4pm. Sundays and public
holidays 1-5pm.

H.C. Andersen Museum
Hans Jensens Stræde 39-43
Open: June to August 9am-6pm.
April, May and September daily
10am-5pm.

DSB Jernbanemuseum
Dannebrogsgade 24
Open: May to September daily
10am-4pm.

Funen Village
Sejerskovvej
Open: June to August daily 9am-
6.30pm. April, May, September
and October daily 9am-4pm.

Præsto

Præsto Dukkehussamlingen
Grønnegade 14
Open: June to August daily except
Monday 11am-4pm.

Ribe

Quedens Gård
Overdammen 10-12
Open: March to May and October
daily 10am-12noon and 2-4pm,
June to September daily 10am-
5pm.

Ringkøbing
Ringkøbing Museum
Kongevejen 1
Open: June to October Monday to
Friday 10am-5pm. Saturdays
10am-2pm, Sundays 2-5pm.
Limited opening at other times.

Strandgården
Husby Klitvej
Open: June to mid-September
daily 10am-5pm.

Roskilde
Roskilde Museum
Skt Ols Gade 18
Open: June to August daily 11am-
5pm. Limited opening other times.

Viking Ships Museum
Strandengen
Open: April to October daily 9am-
5pm, October to March daily
10am-4pm.

Rudkøbing
Langelands Museum
Jens Winthersvej 12
Open: June to August Monday to
Friday 10am-4pm, Saturdays
2-4pm. Sundays and public
holidays 10am-4pm, September to
May, Monday to Friday 10am-4pm.
Saturdays, Sundays and public
holidays 2-4pm.

Ryomgård
Djursland Railway Museum
Ryomgård Station
Open: mid-June to mid-September, Wednesday to Saturday 2.30-
6pm, Sunday 3.30-6pm. Limited
opening at other times.

Rømø
National Museet Kommandørgård
Juvrevej
Kongsmark

Open: May to September daily
except Monday 10am-6pm.

Samsø
Samsø Museumgård
Tranebjerg
Open: May to mid-October daily
except Monday 10am-4pm.

Silkeborg
Silkeborg Cultural Museum
Hovedgården
Open: April to October daily 10am-
5pm. Limited opening at other
times.

Silkeborg Art Museum
Gudenåvej 9
Open: all year daily except
Monday 10am-5pm.

Skagen
Skagens Museum
Brøndumvej 4
Open: April and October daily
11am-5pm, May and September
daily 10am-5pm and June to
August daily 10am-6pm.

Michael and Anna Ancher's House
Markvej 2
Open: May to September daily
10am-5pm. In season daily 10am-
6pm.

Skjern
Danish Veteran Aircraft Museum
Stauning Lufthavn
Open: May to October Monday to
Friday 11am-5pm, Saturdays and
Sundays 1-5pm. Limited opening
at other times.

Stege
Møns Museum
Storegade 75
Open: daily except Monday
10am-4pm.

Store Heddinge
Stevns Museum
Højerup Klint
Open: May to September daily
except Monday 1-5pm, July daily
1-5pm.

Stubbekøbing
Motorcycle and Radio Museum
Nykøbingvej 54
Open: June to August daily 10am-
5pm, May and September,
Saturdays and Sundays 10am-
5pm.

Svendborg
District Museum
Anne Hvides Gård
Fruestræde 3
Open: May to October daily 10am-
4pm. Limited opening at other
times.

Sæby
Sæby Museum
Søndergade 1B
Open: mid-May to mid-September
daily 10am-5pm. Limited opening
at other times.

Sønderborg
Sønderborg Castle Museum
Sønderbro
Open: May to September daily
10am-5pm, April daily 10am-4pm.

Thisted
Museum for Thy and Han Herred
Jernbanegade 4
Open: June to August daily 10am-
5pm, September to May, Monday
to Friday 9am-3pm and Sundays
2-5pm.

Troense
Søfartssamlingerne
Strandgade 1
Open: May to October daily 9am-
5pm.

Tønder
Tønder Museum and Art Museum
Kongevejen 55
Open: May to October daily except
Monday 10am-5pm.

Vejle
Vejle Museum of History
Flegborg 18
Open: all year daily except
Monday 11am-4pm.

Viborg
Skovgaard Museum
Domkirkestræde 4
Open: May to September 10am-
12.30pm, 1.30-5pm. October to
April 1.30-5pm. October to April
1.30-5pm.

Viborg Stiftsmuseum
Hjultorvet 9-11
Open: June to August daily 11am-
5pm, September to May, Tuesday
to Friday 2-5pm and Saturday and
Sunday 11am-5pm.

Vinderup
Hjerl Hede Open-Air Museum
Open: April to October daily 9am-
5pm, July daily 9am-7pm.

Ærø
Bottle Peter's House
Smedegade 22
Ærøskøbing
Open: June to August daily 9am-
5pm, September to May daily
10am-4pm.

Jens Hansens Søfartsmuseum
Prinsengade 1
Marstal
Open: April to October daily 10am-
4pm. Mid-June to mid-August daily
9am-5pm.

Åbenrå
Åbenrå Museum
H.P. Hanssensgade 33B

Open: mid-May to mid-September daily except Monday 10am-4pm.

Ålborg
Ålborg Historical Museum
Algade 48
Open: all year daily 10am-5pm.

North Jutland Art Museum
Kong Christians Alle
Open: all year daily except Monday 10am-5pm, mid-June to mid-September daily 10am-5pm.

Ålestrup
Danish Bicycle Museum
Borgergade 10
Open: May to October daily except Monday and Friday 10am-6pm, Friday 12noon-6pm.

Århus
Den Gamle By
Viborgvej
Open: May and September daily 10am-5pm, June to August daily 9am-5pm.

Museum of Prehistory
Moesgård Alle
Oddervej
Open: March to mid-September 10am-5pm daily. Closed Mondays at other times.

Års
West Himmerland Museum and Art Museum
Søndergade 44
Open: daily except Monday 2-4pm.

PUBLIC HOLIDAYS

Banks and shops are closed on public holidays, and the visitor is advised to be aware of them, particularly those which are unique to Denmark. Maundy Thursday, Good Friday, Easter Sunday and Easter Monday are all public holidays. So too are Great Prayer Day (the fourth Friday after Easter), Ascension Day, Whit Sunday, Whit Monday (which is also a religious festival) Constitution Day, (5 June), Christmas Eve, Christmas Day, Boxing Day, New Year's Eve and New Year's Day. Shops and banks are open until 12noon on Constitiution Day, Christmas Eve and New Years Eve.
Shops are generally closed on Saturday afternoons.

SAFARI PARKS, BIRD GARDENS AND AQUARIA

Bandholm
Knuthenborg Safari Park
Open: May to mid-September daily 9am-6pm.

Bindslev
Tuen Eagle Sanctuary
Skagensvёj
Open: late June to mid-September. Limited opening hours. Enquire locally.

Copenhagen
Denmark's Aquarium
Kavalergården 1
Charlottenlund
Open: March to October daily 10am-6pm, November to March weekdays 10am-4pm. Saturdays and Sundays 10am-5pm.

Givskud
Lion Park
Open: mid-July to mid-August daily 10am-6pm. Spring and autumn daily 10am-4.30pm.

Rødby
Lungholm Wolf Park
Rødbyvej 20
Open: June to October daily 10am-6pm.

Vissenbjerg
Terrariet
Open: May to September daily 9am-6pm, October to April daily 10am-4pm.

Funen Aquarium
Roldvej 53
Open: all year daily 10am-8pm.

TIPPING

Tipping in Denmark is almost non-existent. The bill, when presented, is inclusive of service charge and VAT. Taxi fares include the service charge. However, in washrooms and toilets it is usual to give the attendant 1 or 2 Kroner.

TOURIST INFORMATION OFFICES

All major tourist information offices can obtain detailed information in English about specific attractions in any part of Denmark, through their computerised 'Dandata' service. Some attractions are only open 'in season', generally meaning the Danish school holidays, from the last week of June to the first week of August inclusive.

Canada
PO Box 115, Station 'N', Toronto, Ontario M8V3S4, Canada
☎ (416) 8239620

Denmark
Touristinformationen
H.C. Andersens Boulevard 22
DK 1553 Copenhagen V
☎ 01 11 13 25

A full list of tourist offices is obtainable from the Danish Tourist Board. For local information it is only necessary to write to Turistbureauet, followed by the post code and the name of the town. In major towns, offices which bear a green 'i' sign can give information on any region in Denmark.

United Kingdom
Sceptre House
169/173 Regent Street
London W1R 8PY
☎ 01 734 2637 or 2638

USA
655 Third Avenue, 18th floor
New York
NY 10017
USA
☎ (212) 9492333

Scandinavian National Tourist Offices
8929 Wilshire Boulevard
Beverly Hills
Los Angeles
California CA 90211
USA
☎ (213) 8541549

TRANSPORT

Air Services (Internal)
Discounts are available on certain departures if the tickets are purchased in Denmark, and there are special reductions for families, groups, children and young people.

Reservations and tickets for
domestic flights:
SAS
1 Hammerichsgade
Copenhagen
☎ 01 15 52 66
☎ 01 54 17 01 (traffic enquiries)

Air taxi services to Samsø, Ærø,
Læsø and Anholt: Copenhagen Air
Taxi
København Lufthavn Roskilde
☎ 02 39 11 14

Boat Trips
Boat trips are a good way of
exploring some of the lakes and
other waterways in Denmark. Full
details are available from local
tourist offices and a selection is
given here.

Copenhagen
Havens Motorfærge
Information Office
Gammel Strand
Copenhagen
☎ 01 13 31 05
Tours with and without a commen-
tary daily from June to August.

Odense
Odense River Cruises
Munke Mose
Filosofgangen
Odense
June to mid-August, daily.

Silkeborg
Hjejlen Ap S
Havnen
Silkeborg
Veteran steamer service twice
daily in July. Other services from
end May to end August daily.

Svendborg
Sundfarten 'Helge'

Svendborg Tourist Office
Møllergade 20
Svendborg
Cruises in veteran steamer on
Svendborg sound, June to mid-
August daily.

Bus and Coach Services
Long-distance bus services in
Denmark.

Copenhagen to Bornholm
Bornholmerbussen
Yderholmen 18
2750 Ballerup
☎ 02 68 44 00

Hantsholm to Copenhagen
Søndergårds Rutebiler
Fa Niels Søndergård
Industrivej 6
Fjerritslev
☎ 08 21 12 75
(Facilities for passengers in
wheelchairs).

Ålborg to Copenhagen
Thinggård Ekspresbusser
Rutebilstationen
Postbox 116
9100 Ålborg
☎ 08 11 66 00

Århus to Copenhagen
Abildskaus Rutebiler
Graham Bellsvej 40
8200 Århus N
☎ 06 23 08 88

Ferry Services (Internal)

A leaflet on ferry services is
available from the Danish Tourist
Board. Timetables are contained in
the DSB timetable and are also
available from a number of private
shipping companies.

Details of the major services are as follows:

FERRIES ACROSS THE GREAT BELT

Halsskov-Knudshoved
15-28 sailings daily. Journey time 1 hour. Reservations strongly advised.
☎ 01 14 88 80

Hundested-Grenå
6 sailings daily. Journey time 2 hours 40 minutes.
Reservations ☎ Hundested 02 33 82 33 or Grenå 06 32 16 00

Kalundborg-Århus
5 sailings daily. Journey time 3 hours.
Reservations ☎ Kalundborg 03 51 19 11 or Århus 06 12 02 77

Korsør-Nyborg
12 sailings daily. Journey time 1 hour 15 minutes.
Reservations ☎ 03 57 02 04

Sjællands Odde-Ebeltoft
6-10 sailings daily. Journey time 1 hour 40 minutes.
Reservations ☎ Sjællands Odde 03 42 63 00 or Ebeltoft 06 34 16 00

Tårs-Spodsbjerg
16-18 sailings daily. Journey time 45 minutes.
Reservations ☎ 09 50 10 22

FERRIES TO THE ISLANDS

Copenhagen-Rønne (Bornholm)
1-2 sailings daily. Journey time 7-8 hours.
Reservations ☎ Copenhagen 01 13 18 66 or Rønne 03 95 18 66

Esbjerg-Nordby (Fanø)
30-34 sailings daily. Journey time

20 minutes.
No reservations possible on this service. General enquiries ☎ 05 12 33 77

Frederikshavn-Vesterø Havn (Læsø)
2-4 sailings daily. Journey time 1 hour 30 minutes.
Reservations ☎ 08 49 90 22

Fåborg-Søby (Ærø)
5 sailings daily. Journey time 1 hour.
Reservations ☎ 09 61 14 88

Grenå-Anholt
Limited service. Enquire locally for details.
☎ 06 32 36 00

Hov-Sælvig (Samsø)
10-12 sailings daily. Journey time 1 hour 20 minutes.
Reservations ☎ 06 59 17 44

Kalundborg-Kolby Kås (Samsø)
5-6 sailings daily. Journey time 2 hours.
Reservations ☎ 03 51 19 11

Rudkøbing-Marstal (Ærø)
5 sailings daily. Journey time 1 hour.
Reservations ☎ 09 51 10 27

Svendborg-Ærøskøbing (Ærø)
5 sailings daily. Journey time 1 hour 15 minutes.
Reservations ☎ 09 21 02 62

Train Services

Modern inter-city express trains connect the main towns of Jutland and Funen with Copenhagen and Sealand every hour, supplemented by express diesels (*lyntog*) on the most important stretches. Children under the age of 4 years travel free, and those between 4 and 12 at half price. Discounts are available for groups of three or more persons, and for those over the age of 65. The DSB *køreplan* (timetable) gives full details of all buses and trains in Denmark, including private railways. Most internal and international ferry timetables are also included. It may be obtained from any railway station in Denmark.

Steam Train Lines

Full details of the following steam train services are contained in the leaflet *Veteraner på Skinner* published by:
Mariager-Handest Veter-
anjernbane
Ny Havnevej 2
9550 Mariager
☎ 08 54 18 64

Bryrup-Vrads Veteran Railway
Saturday, Sunday and public holidays, May to October.

Helsingør-Gilleleje Steam Excursions
Sundays in June, July and August.

Limfjord Railway
Ålborg to Grønlandshavnen
Sundays, mid-June to end August.

Mariager-Handest Veteran Railway
Sundays and public holidays in June, July and August. Also Tuesday, Thursday and Friday in July.

Maribo-Bandholm Veteran Railway
Sundays in June, July and August.
Thursdays and Saturdays in July.

USEFUL ADDRESSES

Camp Sites
A list of sites is available from tourist offices. A valid International Carnet, obtainable from motoring organisations or camping clubs, is required for stays on all camp sites in Denmark.

Cyclists and Walkers
Information booklet and map available in English from:
Dansk Cyklist Forbund
Kjeld Langes Gade 14
1367 Copenhagen K
☎ 01 14 42 12

Information on cycling and walking tours from:
Dansk Vandrelaug
Kultorvet 7
DK1175 Copenhagen K

Information on cycle hire is contained in the leaflet *Take the Train, Rent a Bike* available from DSB railway stations. Tourist offices and Youth Hostels will also advise on cycle and canoe hire.

Disabled Visitors
Practical information is obtainable from:
Bolig- Motor- og Hjælpemiddeludvalget
Hans Knudsens Plads 1A
DK 2100 Copenhagen Ø

Ferry Services to Denmark
Scandinavian Seaways
Scandinavia House
Parkeston Quay
Harwich
Essex CO12 4QG
Reservations ☎ 0255 240240

Fred Olsen Lines
Crown House

Crown Street
Ipswich
Suffolk IP1 3HB
☎ 0473 233044

London Office
Scandinavian Seaways
DFDS Travel Centre
15 Hanover Street
London W1R 9HG
Open: Monday to Friday 9am-5pm,
Saturday 9am-2pm.
☎ 01 493 6676

*Hotel Accommodation Booking
Service*
Hotel Booking Copenhagen
Hovedbanegården
DK 1570 Copenhagen
☎ 01 12 28 80 Monday to Friday
9am-5pm.

Easy-Book International Booking
Service
Nordre Frihavnsgade 23
DK 2100 Copenhagen Ø
☎ 01 38 00 37 (7am-11pm
weekdays).

A list of hotels throughout Denmark is available from the tourist
office, free of charge.

Motorists
FDM Forenede Danske Motorejere
Blegdamsvej 124
DK 2100 Copenhagen
☎ 01 38 21 12

Motorists who are involved in an
accident in Denmark should
contact:
Dansk Forening for International
Motorkøretøjsforsikring
Amaliegade 10
DK1256 Copenhagen K
☎ 01 13 75 55

Motorists should note that there
are no filling stations on motor-
ways. A parking disk (*parker-
ingsskive*) is compulsory in most
town centres and is obtainable free
from tourist offices.

Youth Hostels
Youth and Family Hostels in
Denmark are under the control of
Danmarks Vandrerhjem, whose
central office is at:
Vesterbrogade 9
DK1620 Copenhagen V
☎ 01 31 36 12

A list of Youth Hostels throughout
Denmark is available from the
tourist office free of charge.

VIEWING TOWERS

Copenhagen
Round Tower
Købmagergade
Open: June to August weekdays
10am-8pm, Sundays 12noon-8pm.
April, May, September and
October weekdays 10am-5pm,
Sundays 12noon-4pm.

Frederikshavn
Cloostårnet
Brønderslevvej
Open: mid-June to mid-August
daily 10am-8pm. Limited opening
at other times.

Gedser
Gedser Lighthouse
Gedser Odde
Open: April to September daily
9am-sunset.

Hvide Sande
Nørre Lyngvig Lighthouse
Fyrvej
Open: in season daily during
daylight hours.

Nykøbing-Falster
Water Tower
Hollandsgård
Open: mid-June to mid-September
weekdays 11am-4pm, Sundays
10am-12noon.

Ry
Himmelbjerget Tower
Open: in season. Enquire locally
for opening times.

Vordingborg
Goose Tower
Open: mid-May to mid-September
daily 1-5pm. Mid-June to mid-
August daily 10am-5pm.

Ålborg
Ålborg Tower
Søndre Skovvej
Open: April to September daily
10am-5pm.

WINDMILLS AND WATERMILLS OPEN TO VIEW

Fakse
Blåbæks Møller
Open: apply to the farmhouse
during the daytime.

Fåborg
Kaleko Mølle
Prices Havevej
Open: mid-May to mid-September
daily 10.30am-4.30pm.

Hellebæk
Hellebæk Hammermølle
Open: April to October daily except
Monday 10am-5pm.

Højer
Højer Mill
Open: April to October daily except
Friday 10am-4pm.

Skjern
Bundsbæk Mølle
Bundsbækvej 27
Open: in season Monday to
Thursday 11am-5pm, Saturdays
and Sundays 1-5pm.

Sønderborg
Dybbøl Mill
Dybbøl Banke
Open: April to September 1-4pm,
mid-June to mid-August 10am-
5pm.

Tranekær
Tranekær Slotsmølle
Lejbøllevej 3
Open: mid-May to August, Monday
to Friday 10am-5pm. Sundays and
public holidays 1-5pm.

OTHER PLACES OF INTEREST

Copenhagen
Carlsberg Brewery
Ny Carlsberg Vej 140
Elefantporten
Open: all year.
Conducted tours Monday to Friday
at 11am and 2.30pm.

Royal Copenhagen Porcelain
Factory
Smallegade 45
Open: all year except mid-July to
end August.
Conducted tours on Tuesday and
Thursday only at 9.45am.

Næstved
Holmegårds Glassworks
Fensmark
Open: all year Monday to Thursday
9am-12noon and 12.30-1.30pm,
Friday 9am-12noon. Saturdays,
Sundays and public holidays during
summer 11am-3pm.

INDEX